Life As We Know It

Life As We Know It

Extraordinary Stories
From Ordinary People

THE BEST OF BULLETIN BOARD, VOL. 2

Edited by Daniel Kelly

PIONEER BOOKS

Andrews and McMeel
A Universal Press Syndicate Company
Kansas City

Additional copies of this book may be ordered by calling (800) 642-6480.

Library of Congress Cataloging-in-Publication Data

Life As We Know It: extraordinary stories from ordinary people / edited by Daniel Kelly.
p.   cm.—(The Best of Bulletin Board ; vol. 2)
ISBN 0-8362-1445-5
1. Anecdotes 2. Bulletin boards. I. Kelly, Daniel. II. Series.
PN62671.L54 1996
081—dc20   96-5582
CIP

Contents

Foreword

In the spring of 1995, on the occasion of Bulletin Board's fifth birthday, **Bob Woolley** of St. Paul—one of the column's original contributors, and surely its most prolific—left this message on the Bulletin Board Hot Line:

"What an amazing variety of topics we've covered! We've wagged our tongues at inappropriate verbings and at a woman who prided herself on hogging a parking spot near the mall entrance. We've read each other's most embarrassing moments. We've argued about Howard Stern, Handicapped parking spots, and gun control. We've spent precious work hours solving word puzzles and pondering 3M's toilet policies. We've been duped with April Fool's Day entries and spent Christmas Eve reading aloud **The Cowboy King**'s 'The Night Before Christmas at M' Home on the Range.' We've shared the woes of recovering alcoholics, teenagers with mono, and broken-hearted lovers. We've mourned the deaths of young **Rod Kennedy** of Luck, Wis., Bulletin Board's first two-time contributor, and of **Arling Brinck,** the murdered proprietor of the Grand Ideas T-shirt shop. We've apparently annoyed the hell out of the *Star Tribune* (though it was all meant in good fun, of course). We've helped arrange for a young fan to meet his baseball idol. We've met amazing people: **Joybubbles, Sailboat Jo, JB's Wife** (and good old **JB**, of course). We've laughed at the antics of countless small children and bumbling spouses (which describes pretty much all of us, at one time or another). We've been disgusted with each other's revelations of our private, questionably edible delicacies. We've seen ourselves in stories of Dumb Customers, bad drivers and malapropisms. We've thumbed our collective nose at bad ads, bad customer service, and bad voice-mail systems. We've immortalized both what's best and what's worst about the strangers in our midst.

"Bulletin Board has, in short, provided an indescribably welcome diversion from the sometimes tedious activities that cram our days. It has become hard to imagine life without it."

Indeed, it has—and for no one more than for me. I was touched to hear those words, as I've been touched so many, many times by Bulletin Board's readers: people who have found, in the company of people just like them and people unlike any they've ever met, a place to swap the stories of their lives—from the comic to the tragic, and all stops in between.

The readers are everything here. This is their column; without them, there is no Bulletin Board. I offer every one of them my thanks—and not just because their keenness of insight and generosity of spirit have created a job that I love. I owe them a debt of gratitude because they've shown me (and perhaps one another) that the human creature is a good deal more interesting than I would have guessed.

•

I have many people to thank at the St. Paul Pioneer Press: my editors, Dave Fryxell and Sue Campbell; copy editors Cheryl Burch-Schoff, Dana Davis, Bill Diehl, Chuck Dixon, Becky Smith-Welter and Jim Tarbox; reporters Susan Barbieri and Rick Shefchik, who (along with Dana Davis) generously offered their opinions as I took mountains of material and reduced it to chapter-size chunks; art director Marcia Wright Roepke, who inspired the book's cover design; and reporter David Hawley, who has kept the column beautifully on track whenever I've been away.

My thanks go, too, to my editor at Andrews and McMeel, Regan Brown, who has been unfailingly supportive of my efforts and of the Bulletin Board books in general.

My deepest thanks must again go to my wife, Patty, and to our daughters, Laura and Rose. Even as she kept our home together during the two months of evenings and weekends that it took me to assemble this collection, Patty read printout after printout after printout of various chapters. In the process, I rediscovered something I'd learned when we worked together, years ago: She is as fine an editor as she is a wife and mother. I am a very lucky man to have her—and to have those two wonderful girls, who never squawked as Daddy headed back to the office night after night, week after week.

And away we go!

—Daniel Kelly

CHAPTER ONE

Oh, What a World!

Maggie of the Mountains: "Something wonderful happened last night.

"I gave a gift to a very dear friend of mine, on the occasion of her fifth birthday—a very special gift. When she opened it, her face fell. I rather suspect she was hoping for Barbie paraphernalia; the book entitled *The Marvelous Land of Oz* hadn't been on the birthday wish list.

"After her parents left, I said to her: 'You didn't like your present very much, did you?'

"'No,' she said.

"I said: 'Well, when I was a little girl, about your age, my father read this story to me—and I liked it. Why don't you let me read you a chapter before you go to bed? And then decide.'

"She said: 'OK.'

"When it came to be bedtime, she went upstairs, and she lay on her bed, and I sat beside her, and I read her the first chapter. At the end of the first chapter, I said: 'Because it's your birthday, I'll read you a second chapter if you'd like.'

"She looked at me and said: 'Yes.'

"So I read her the second chapter. At the end of the second chapter, she was very still. I said to her: 'What do you think happens next?'

"'I don't know,' she said.

"'What would *you* do if you were Tip?' I asked her.

"'I'd run away!' she said.

"'Me, too. What do you think Tip will do?'

"She looked at me thoughtfully and said: 'I don't know.'

"I put the book away and gave her a kiss and walked to the door and turned the light out.

"She called my name, and she said: 'What happens next?'

"And suddenly I was 4 years old, lying in my bed, looking at my father standing silhouetted in the light from the hall: 'What happens next, Daddy?'

"He'd turn to me, and he'd say: 'I guess you'll have to wait 'til tomorrow to find out, won't you?'

"I thought I'd go mad, waiting to find out what happens next. I learned to read so I could find out all by myself. I was terrified I'd be dependent on my father for the rest of my life. I can remember taking that book down off the shelf, staring at the words as if staring at them hard enough would make me know how to read.

"And I still remember the day I took that book down off the shelf and read it all by myself, cover to cover, for the first time. I can remember the feel of the carpet, the carpet burns I got on my elbows—and it was wonderful.

"It was the greatest gift I ever received. And last night, I gave that gift to Julia.

"'What happens next?' is a very great gift, indeed."

Grandma Woo of Maplewood: "This happened to me several years ago, during the fall hunting season, when my husband left during the middle of the week to go up to the cabin in Wisconsin. I was working; I couldn't leave until Friday—and decided that rather than take our second car up there, I'd ride the Greyhound bus.

"In those days, it made a stop in downtown White Bear Lake. I got a ride to the bus stop from my son, who then went on to college.

"I sat on the steps of one of the local stores, waiting for the bus. I was joined by a very friendly lady who was pushing a small shopping cart that was partly filled with empty pop cans. She was dressed in a lot of layers of thin clothing. I still think of her as my bag lady.

"Anyway, we talked about the weather and the birds, and how she would get money from the cans that she would sell, and how the people at the Big Ben restaurant would sometimes give her a cup of coffee when she'd gathered enough money for a piece of pie.

"I was tempted to offer a couple of dollars to her—but, I don't know, somehow it didn't seem appropriate.

"When the bus came, we said goodbye—and she stood and watched as I got on and handed the driver a check for my fare. Then the driver said: 'Sorry. I can't take the check. Cash only. $8.75.' I knew I didn't have much cash with me—but, nevertheless, I dug through everything and came up with $8.55.

"He told me he was sorry, but would I please get off the bus; he needed to continue. My heart was really in my throat, because I knew my kids were gone back to college, there was nobody at home to call, and my husband would be sitting at a bus stop at the other end, waiting for me. It was about a 40-mile ride from the cabin.

"As I started to get off the bus, my bag lady came over, handed me 50 cents and told me to have a wonderful time with my husband. I wanted to refuse, but I saw absolute pure joy in her face as she was helping me.

"I hugged her, I thanked her, and I got on the bus before she could see the tears running down my face.

"Never before—and never again—have I felt as humble as I did at that moment. I've never seen my bag lady again, but maybe she will read this and know that her generosity will *never* be forgotten."

Box of St. Paul: "A wise old editor of mine had one book on his desk, *The Three Bears*—which starts out, as we all know, 'Once upon a time, there were three bears...'

"He said it was the best journalism textbook ever written.

"Asked for an explanation, he said it was to remind him, and his reporters, to get to the point. 'If you're gonna write about bears,' he'd say, 'get to the damned bears.'

"Around the table in our house, if someone's story begins to stall, a shout invariably goes up:

"Get to the bears!"

L.M. of Coon Rapids: "This was positively the most awe-inspiring encounter with nature that my family ever had.

"My children were about 3 and 5 years old when we took them on a vacation trip to the Black Hills. While in the Rapid City area, we decided to tour a place called Bear Country USA that claimed to have the largest group of black bears in captivity—about 250 of them.

"It was a drive-through, safari-type place, so you could view the animals in their natural habitat.

"It was in spring—April or May—and what we didn't know was: That is the season when bears 'do it'—and they were all, all 250 of them, 'doing it.'

"Bears on the road, bears in the ditches, bears in the fields, all of them paired off—250 copulating bears! *[BULLETIN BOARD notes: Doesn't that sound exactly like a Wall Drug–style billboard sequence? (1) Bears on the Road! (2) Bears in the Ditches! (3) Bears in the Fields! (4) All of Them Paired Off! (5) 250 Copulating Bears! Only at Bear Country USA! (We'd stop. Wouldn't you?)]*

"It was a very educational visit, but not quite what we had in mind.

"I assume that, in due time, the park had even a larger population of bears, but we never returned to find out."

Hudson Sam: "I was working in New York, in the Wall Street area; it was the first time in my life that I had had an hour for lunch, so I used to wander over to the aquarium nearby, and I became very friendly with a big Irishman who was the attendant there.

"He told me that in all of the years that he'd been there, the only amusement he had was thinking up answers to the kind of questions that people asked.

"One day, while we were talking, a middle-aged, rather matronly, dignified woman came over and said: 'The penguins all look alike. How do you tell the difference between a male penguin and a female penguin?'

"John drew himself up and said, with considerable dignity: 'Madame, that should be of interest only to another penguin'—whereupon she blushed bright red and disappeared very quickly.

"Whereupon he looked over at me and smiled and winked."

Terri J. of Wyoming: "I was watering my garden, spraying a light mist using the thumb-control method, and along came a ruby-throated hummingbird. I heard him before I saw him, and to my surprise, he was trying to shower himself in the mist as I sprayed. I couldn't believe what I was seeing.

"He played for less than a minute and proceeded to land on the ground—which I've never seen before: a hummingbird land. He landed near a puddle and bathed himself. I was as still as I could be.

"When he finished bathing, he continued to play in the mist. It was really neat.

"My thumb could no longer hold the spray in position, and when I attempted to switch thumbs, he was gone in a flash.

"I'll cherish that experience forever."

Norm of Minneapolis, remembering a visit to Sea World: "As I was wandering around the park, I came across a pool—a cement-lined pool about a hundred feet across—and in the pool were a pair of young bottle-nosed dolphins. The sign on the side of the pool said that they were too young yet to be performing in the regular shows, but that they were in training.

"A couple of volleyballs were floating in the water of the pool, and the pool was ringed with children, who would lean over and pick up the balls out of the water, throw them into the middle of the pool—and the dolphins would go out and retrieve the balls and push 'em back with their noses to the side of the pool again.

"What was really eerie, to me, about that is: I stood and watched this for about 10 minutes, and *not once* did I see a dolphin return the ball to the same child twice. I watched pretty carefully, to make sure that this wasn't just random behavior—but the more I watched, the more it became clear to me that they were actually *choosing* to bring the ball to different children each time. Not only could they differentiate between individuals around the pool, but it seemed as though they were actually trying to make sure that everyone had a chance.

"I don't blame you for being skeptical. It really was the doggonedest thing I've ever seen."

The Bonfire of Cannon Falls: "Here's a goose-bumper for ya:

"My father's death four years ago was a surprise and devastated my mother. One year later, she, too, passed away. When she'd found out she was dying from colon cancer, she'd actually seemed pleased—and remarked that she could now be with my father again.

"I'd just come home after sitting with her at the hospital all day, and with my family sleeping, the house was quiet. Alone with my thoughts, I swear I could hear my mother singing 'You Are My Sunshine'—the song she sang to me while I was young. I experienced a tingly sensation, along with an overwhelming feeling of love. Immediately afterward, the phone rang, and I received word that my mother had passed on. I now believe that the song was her way of saying goodbye.

"Some time later, I was taking a break outside at work. It was night, and the sky was a glowing gray from the full moon, with dark clouds floating by. One set of clouds caught my eye, as it appeared to drift a bit slower, and it was a familiar shape. It looked like a silhouette of my father with his arm around my mother. I smiled, thinking it was a very nice coincidence. But suddenly, I got that same tingly feeling.

"When I returned to my desk, the radio was playing the Bette Midler song 'From a Distance,' and I again passed it off as coincidence—but when I checked my calendar to jot the date down on some paperwork, the tingly sensation turned into goose bumps. It was my parents' anniversary.

"I'm convinced that my parents are together again and that they're both watching over their loved ones. It's truly a feeling of comfort."

The Finch Feeder of Menomonie, Wis.: "Last week, I heard the 'Stars and Stripes Forever' march played on the radio. In my mind, I was in my grandmother's parlor—and that's what they were called, at that time—in a small rural town in the mid-1940s.

"The parlor had a figured Persian-type carpet, a brown mohair sofa-and-chair set with crocheted arm and head pieces pinned primly in place, and a bay window filled with glass shelves of blooming plants.

"But most important was the Edison record player, which had to be wound up with a crank to play the quarter-inch-thick records. I don't know if they were even called 'records.' As a child, it was great fun to wind up the Edison to play the tunes from the previous decade, when my mother and aunts had grown up.

"My favorite, by far, was the 'Stars and Stripes Forever' march—and march I did: my personal parade, all around the parlor, until the Edison slowwwwwwwwed and . . . wound . . . down . . . and then had to be wound up again so that you could hear the tune.

"Great memories."

The Queen's Mum of Vermillion: "I was picking raspberries with an older lady the other day, and I commented that I had enjoyed the jam that she had made. She thanked me, and she said she doesn't eat jam; she enjoys making it, but she doesn't eat it.

"We kept picking for a while, and pretty soon—in a very soft voice—she said: 'I don't eat raspberries anymore.'

"I didn't have a comment.

"And then she continued: 'It was 1942, in Siberia. We had no food, and we were starving. And then I found a late raspberry bush, and we ate our fill. We ate, and we ate, and we ate . . . and I don't eat raspberries anymore.'

"There's no point to this story—except that her words just moved me, and I wanted to share 'em."

Working Mom of Vadnais Heights: "I'm a social worker, and I used to work as a psychiatric-crisis worker in an emergency room. One evening—and this was many years ago—an entire family . . . and we're talking maybe 15 or 20 people . . . brought in this sweet, older, grandmotherly-type lady and then hurried off *very* quickly.

"My job was to try to define the problem, so she and I sat down in a quiet little room. I still remember she wore a floral print dress, and she had her purse kind of neatly in her lap, and she looked just like . . . anybody's grandma. We had this fine conversation for maybe 10 minutes, and I was beginning to wonder what could have prompted an entire family to be so nervous about this lady.

"Anyway, we're talking away, and she finally looks right at me and says: 'Everything was OK until the aliens landed in my yard.' She then went on to detail the aliens' tiny spaceships—and how the aliens came into her yard, and finally they were now in her bloodstream.

"Needless to say, I called the on-call psychiatrist and we got her admitted promptly.

"Every now and then, a situation will arise at home or at work where the line

'Everything was OK until the aliens landed in my yard' seems to sum it up perfectly."

A memoir from the late '40s, when **L.A.S.** of Inver Grove Heights lived in St. Cloud and attended St. Anthony's Church: "This church was in the basement, and there was no air conditioning, no windows to open, hardly any circulation. There may have been a few fans.

"One Sunday, it was hot! hot! hot! Unbearable! Father (wish I could remember his name) came out to start Mass. After the opening prayers, he went to the pulpit to read the Epistle (today it's called the Reading) and the Gospel.

"Next was the sermon, and we were all wondering how long it would be.

"Father closed the book and stood there, and stood there, just waiting. The church was getting quieter and quieter. When he thought he had everybody's attention, he said: 'I wonder how hot it is in Hell today.'

"He turned and went back to the altar to finish Mass. You could hear a pin drop. No one moved. Everyone just sat there—stunned.

"Best sermon I ever heard. Short and to the point."

The Original Newcomer of St. Paul: "When I was a college student in Southern California, I sometimes took a small plane from our little local airport to the regional one, to connect with a commercial flight home.

"The first time I did this was also my first time on an eight-seater. No flight attendant, obviously; just the pilot—sitting close enough for me to see out the front window.

"As we took off, I said out loud: 'Gee, I wonder how this thing stays up.'

"The guy in front of me shot back: 'Faith. Shut up.'"

Doctor Friendly of St. Paul remembers a patient he saw when he was in medical school: "I was working in a rural emergency room one day when the ambulance brought in a 17-year-old who had been in a motorcycle accident. It had just started raining, and the road was slick; he'd tried to take a corner too fast and had laid the bike down and skidded quite a long way.

"Fortunately, all he had were scrapes and bruises. He had no head injury.

"Just as I was finishing up with him, a policeman came in and brought the young man his helmet, which they had taken off him at the scene. It was obviously a fancy and expensive helmet. It was a full-face unit—shiny, multicolored, metal-flake.

"One entire side of the helmet was ruined. It was deeply gouged and had obviously scraped along the asphalt with considerable impact for quite a distance. In some places, it appeared that the entire thickness of the hard shell had been penetrated, and you could see the soft inner lining.

"The young man was obviously very lucky.

"He looked at the helmet, groaned and said: 'Oh, man! I just bought that a week ago! What a waste of $150!'"

Fay's Friend: "Someone said the other day: 'Be careful what you wish for; you just might get it.'

"That's good advice.

"One of my earliest ambitions—and one that was actually realized—was to be a farmer. I try to remember that in mid-April when I'm out on some windswept, godforsaken hill a quarter-mile from the barn at 3 A.M., blinded by sleet or driving snow or drenched by an icy rain, struggling to load a flopping, slippery, icy-cold new-born calf on a toboggan, all the while fending off its irate mama, in order to take it to the barn.

"Then, it's really hard to remember just why I ever wanted to be a farmer.

"But an hour or two later, when the little bugger is dried off and warmed up and on its feet and nursing, and Mama has settled down and is talking baby talk to it, and everyone involved—human and bovine alike—agree it's the finest calf ever born, then I remember what it's all about."

Grandma Up North: "This little story comes up in my mind every Easter:

"In 1956, we had four kids, and they were under 5. We lived above a huge garage on a beautiful estate. It was a very late Easter that year, and the grounds were a brilliant green, and shrubs were bursting with color, and since the garage was below, we actually lived about three stories up.

"So, anyway, on Easter morning, about dawn, I was doing what mothers do, and I happened to look out the window. At first, I rubbed my eyes; I'm not kiddin'. I couldn't believe what I was seeing: At least a half a dozen rabbits were dancing, playing, running and doing flips in the air. And they were white.

"I want to make this clear: They were not doing . . . what rabbits do. It was as though they were full of spring and joy. It was just incredible.

"So, anyway, I hoped and prayed that they would stay, and I went and gently awakened my children and guided them to the window. And they were sleepy, but when they saw, their eyes just . . . widened. They saw those rabbits. It was like a little miracle.

"I can still see it in my mind's eye, and I think my kids do, too."

Joe of New Richmond, Wis.: "Back when my dog Omega was just a puppy, she used to just go nuts whenever the squirrels would come up to the feeder just off our deck. The squirrels would go from tree to tree to tree, out on a branch and onto the feeder. To give her some exercise, we used to open the door and let her chase the squirrels.

"Well, this went on for . . . many, many times, and she would just follow the squirrel back from the feeder to the first tree to the second tree to the third tree.

"When she was 1 year old, there was a young squirrel that probably wasn't real agile yet, and as she followed it from the feeder to the first tree to the second tree, it happened to miss its branch and fell—right down into her mouth, as she was barking at it.

"She carried it up to us—and, of course, being a black Lab, she'd been trained as a hunting dog, and she placed it in my hand and hadn't broken any skin. I care-fully released it back into the wild—but she was *so* proud of herself.

"From then on, whenever we'd let her out to chase the squirrels back out of the bird feeder, she would go to the exact-same spot and wait for that squirrel to fall out of the sky into her mouth.

"At 15 years old, she finally got too sick and too tired for us to let her go on anymore, and we were afraid that she was going to get hurt trying to climb the stairs, so we decided to put her to sleep. And when we got her body back, we decided that the best place to bury her was that miraculous spot where the squirrel fell out of the sky right into her mouth.

"I like to think that she's resting happy nowadays in that spot."

Kelly of St. Paul: "I'm a professional dog groomer. A few years ago, I had a woman bring me a very geriatric poodle. She told me that the dog was due to be put to sleep that afternoon, since she had a severe heart problem. But she wanted me to groom the dog first so that she would look good for her funeral.

"So when the woman left, I started to work on the poodle, and I had her almost finished when the dog started to shake all over. And then she just fell over dead.

"Now I'm in the situation where I don't know what to do with the dog. Do I finish grooming a dead dog, or do I let the owner pick up a very wet, very bad-looking dog? Well, I decided to finish grooming the dog, dead.

"And when I came upstairs and told my husband about it, he just couldn't stop laughing. We both got a severe case of the giggles.

"And when the woman came to pick up her dog, I had to pinch my thigh to keep from laughing when I handed her her dead, groomed dog."

Beautiful Dreamer of St. Paul: "I first saw it in a going-out-of-business import shop in Har Mar Mall, just hanging there—a bit too gaudy for my taste—as I passed it by . . . only to be drawn back again for a closer look.

"I wrapped it around my shoulders. This rainbow-colored chiffon shawl had, on the reverse side, a solid carpet of shimmering sequins—the background being silver ones and the design (is it a pear, or a bell?) being all in gold.

"On occasion, whether appropriate or not, I have worn this sparkly thing. One time, while crossing the street to the depot, a driver hollered out of his car: 'Fresh!' I took that as a compliment.

"Alas, sequins are not tightly sewed, and I would notice them on a carpet or I would see holes where the glimmer used to be. Today I went to Jolly's to buy some sequins. The sign said: 'Closed at this location.'

"On to Minnesota Fabrics. Who would have thought they came in different sizes? Five millimeters was too small.

"Over to Frank's. Found an assortment bag with myriad sizes, shapes and colors: lavender, turquoise, violet discs; copper flowers; red snowflakes.

"I am falling in love with sequins.

"On and on I sewed, wherever a bare spot needed light. I feel as though I am entering a long-term relationship with this garment.

"I feel a connection to pioneer women and their quilts, sewing in quiet contemplation while the chilly rain drizzles down. No radio noise and no TV. Quietly sewing, quietly sewing, conjuring up all kinds of possibilities where this garment can be worn.

"And to think I almost passed it by."

The Proverbial Octogenarian: "I want to tell you about a sign I saw more than 50 years ago. I was pheasant hunting in the northwestern part of our state, riding in my car, and I pointed out a sign that said: 'No Hunting Aloud.'

"Laughingly, I said: 'Look at what that dumb farmer said! He didn't even know how to spell.'

"My cousin, who was sitting next to me, said: 'That's *my* sign!'

"Boy, I wished I could have crawled under the floorboards."

Burt of West St. Paul: "I'm an old man—crowding 79 years. I've been a deer hunter for 65 years—from Colorado to Wyoming to Montana to Minnesota.

"A few years back, I switched from the modern big-game rifles and ammo to a Kentucky flintlock—black-powder, muzzle-loading rifle, caliber .45. In 12 years, 12 deer. Along the line, I had trouble during wet weather: Light rain and/or wet snow would dampen the priming powder in the pan and dampen the flint. Result: no ignition from the flint to the priming powder to the main charge in the barrel behind the bullet.

"The problem: how to protect the lock, hammer and flint and priming powder from rain or snow. The question: what sort of an appliance to address that problem.

"Then the light dawned, bright and clear: a condom! So I procured one and unrolled about 4 inches of it, and then I stretched the open end over the entire lock area; the elasticity of the condom enabled me to pull the hammer back into the full cocked position and fire the rifle. The firing destroyed the condom, but the procedure worked.

"I went to a drugstore pharmacy counter, and there was a young man and his female coworker. She was counting out a large number of pills, filling a prescription, and the young man asked if he could help me. I said yes—that I wanted three dozen condoms. He said: 'What?' I repeated: 'Three dozen condoms—and if they come in sizes, I prefer the large.'

"His female coworker, overhearing my request, reacted by dropping all her pills on the floor.

"The young man did a double-take at this old gaffer, who had to be about 80, and then went to the shelf and obtained three dozen condoms. He had a sort of a bemused smirk on his face, and as he handed 'em to me, he said: 'I hope you get a lot of action out of these.'

"I said: 'Thank you. Just so they keep my powder dry.'

"He said: 'Powder dry?'

"And I said: 'Yes, I get better ignition that way.' And I left.

"I often wonder how long he stood there, mouth open, wondering just what that old gaffer was up to—and how long it took for his female co-worker to regain her composure."

R.J. of Hammond, Wis.: "After college, one of my first jobs was as a state livestock inspector, charged with enforcing animal-health regulations at the stockyards in Indianapolis.

"I was the first woman in that job and the only woman actually working out in the stockyards, and the men had all placed bets on how long I'd last. They were sure that the cold weather, or the bad odor, or the bad language, or the big, bad animals were going to drive me out—which is kind of silly to think about. If a 2,500-pound bull wants to knock someone down, does your gender really matter? Or if you weigh 120 or 220?

"I started in December, and no one had predicted that I would last the winter—so I really felt a lot of pressure to prove myself. One of those first weeks, I was walking through the hog yards, and a great big barrow—that's a castrated male hog—didn't want to walk across the scales, and he ran back and came barreling down the alley right toward me.

"I was gonna be the hero and turn the sucker back, so I was standing with my feet apart and my arms flapping out at my sides, yelling at him.

"At that time in my life, I hadn't been around hogs very much, and I certainly didn't know about their propensity to hurl their bodies through the smallest possible openings. So, of course, he ran right between my legs. One minute, I'm standing there trying to look cool and like an authority figure of some sort—which was hard enough to begin with, because I didn't begin to look my age (at that time)—and the next moment, I'm whizzing backward at warp-swine speed through the stockyards, feet not touching the ground and everybody watching, with their mouths hanging open. Not a soul missed the performance.

"Every gate was wide open, and I thought we were gonna go clear to Kansas, but finally he turned a corner and ejected me face-down in a pile of pig oompah. Let me reassure you: There is no way to preserve one's dignity while arising from a pile of pig poop.

"I can still see the horrified expressions on the faces of the men. Nobody dared move or say a word. Finally, I snapped: 'Well, dammit, *laugh!* I sure would if it was one of you!' I guess they were too astonished to laugh. I'm sure they'd never seen a government official flying backward on a pig before—or a woman, either, flying backward on a pig.

"Some of the bets were canceled that day, and I lasted seven years on that job. It was a real humbling experience—and in typical pig fashion, that big dude put things in perspective for me that day."

Hondo of D.C.: "A number of years back, when I was still young and very impressionable, I was summoned to the corner office of our chief executive officer—the chairman of the board of a very large company in Minneapolis.

"I wasn't quite sure what to think of that—particularly when I sat down, and immediately the chairman of the board, sitting across from me, pulled out some dental floss. He proceeded to clean his teeth, slowly but surely, as he questioned me about some of the goings-on at the company.

"I tried not to pay *too* much attention to the little bits of things flying here and there and gathering up on the floss. I was feelin' pretty good about things, and not payin' too much attention to that floss thing—until right as the conversation was coming to an end, he summarized a point by holding the floss between his lips and giving it a quick yank to clean it off—leaving the floss totally bare.

"You never know."

K.K. of Maplewood: "This occurred at a 'fine' (read that, 'incredibly, unbelievably expensive') restaurant in Amsterdam. An appetizer of oysters on the half shell arrived, and one of the shells contained a worm, swimming energetically around the oyster.

"Innocents abroad, we assumed this discovery would mean a free appetizer—if not a free meal—and we called the waiter over to the table.

"Without a word, he picked up the shell, tipped the entire contents into his mouth, smiled, and walked away. The rest of the meal was uneventful."

Princess Grace of Mahtomedi: "In the very early '70s, some of my friends and I were lucky enough to be in Paris on a one-week trip sponsored by our school.

"The waiters and concierge at the old hotel where we stayed were so supercilious and condescending to us that we mercilessly decided to mispronounce some basic French words.

"Every time the waiters would bring us our food, each of us would murmur *merci BOE-cup*—or *merci BOO-COO*. Then we would try to keep very serious faces while they flinched and cringed throughout the meal.

"One even tried to correct us, and my friend butchered the French phrase for 'I'm sorry; I don't understand'—and the waiter gave up.

"I'm sure it drove them insane. Every time we politely asked the concierge for information—mispronouncing chosen words, of course—he would grit his teeth and respond in English . . . in an attempt, I'm sure, to avoid that assault on his mother tongue.

"Anyway, it was a blast—and it *was* fun to see their faces on the last day, when we pronounced all of those words so perfectly.

"I believe, as we left, one waiter even muttered a choice phrase of his own—but I didn't catch it. That was too bad."

The Blue Ribbon of St. Paul: "When I was about 18, some friends of mine and I decided to take a trip to Florida. My friend Lori was extremely fair-skinned—green-eyed, blonde hair, *really* white skin. She was also very pretty—and basically knew it.

"We were lying in the sun trying to get a tan, and Lori had slathered on this product called For Faces Only with a Sun Protection Factor of 40. After lying there soaking up the sun for about two hours, I looked over at her and began to laugh, and she said: 'What?'—you know, kind of angrily.

"Evidently this product worked beautifully—except that she had sweated, and she had inadvertently wiped the sweat off her upper lip and left behind this bright-red mustache—as though she had been drinking cherry Kool-Aid.

"She was pretty vain, and she stayed inside for two days."

Jim of Woodbury: "The year is 1965. The place: Daytona Beach, Florida.

"My buddy and I take off in our $200 1958 Dodge station wagon—bright red and white, with the big fins—and we head for the great spring fling in Fort Lauderdale. We've got a mattress in the back end, and we eat fast food the whole way.

"I think our budget for the whole trip was perhaps $300 between us. Every time we stopped for gas, we also stopped for a quart of oil.

"A couple of times, we're woken up in the early hours of the morning—with the police wondering why in the heck we were sleeping overnight on a residential street . . . in Indianapolis . . . and Nashville. But that's a different story.

"Anyway, after a day or two on the beach in Daytona Beach—and I might mention that this was just plain old fun and alcohol-free—we looked at each other and said: 'Well, you know, we kinda look like beach bums. We'll let our beards grow. And what about some blonde hair?'

"I'm kind of a dark person, by nature; went into the pharmacy and asked for some blonde dye. They said: 'Oh, we use hydrogen peroxide.' So we bought a bottle of that stuff and went out to the car; I guess it was about 10 o'clock in the morning.

"Put a little of that stuff in our hair, kinda combed it through, worked it in real good. Looked at each other five or 10 minutes later, and there wasn't any change. So we went out on the beach for a while. Took the bottle with us. Looked at each other; still no change. So we put a little bit more in. Went and had a little bit of lunch, and it looked like it was getting a little bit lighter—but it just didn't seem to be doin' the job, so we put a little bit more in. Along about dinnertime, we had probably given ourselves about five doses of hydrogen peroxide and had spent probably six or eight hours in the sun.

"Went to bed that night—bed being the back of the car—and woke up the next morning to the knock-knock-knock on the window, and here's another cop sayin': 'Hey, guys! You can't park on Daytona Beach, because the tide's comin' in'—and sure enough, the beach was deserted and there was the tide lappin' at the wheels.

"Well, we pulled the car out—and as we glanced at each other, we kinda screamed a little bit, because our hair was pure white. We're not talking blonde here; we're talking clean, clear white—white as the driven snow in Minnesota.

"Jaunted on back to Minnesota a week later. I was livin' at home. Walked into my home, and my mom screamed. It's Saturday evening, and she says: 'That beard! That hair! What have you done? Your court appearance on that car accident is on Monday!'

"So my two older sisters—wonderfully creative, energetic as they are—hurried over on Sunday afternoon and brought two or three different kinds of dye.

"Well, they got my hair turned kinda black again, and I shaved. Lost the court case; cost my insurance company $125 for a little bit of damage. But the dye started kinda not working right—and to cut a long story short:

"Somethin' happened to the roots, and for the next three or four years—after tryin' to wash that stuff out, let it grow out, cut it off—every time I went out in the sun, my head had kind of an interesting orange glow.

"I guess my recommendation is: Don't combine hydrogen peroxide with hair dye.

"Good evening."

Linda of St. Paul: "In the mid-'70s, my husband and I had a '54 pickup truck—Chev—that we used to drive down to southeastern Minnesota to visit friends, frequently. One cold fall Saturday afternoon, we were coming along the big curve going into Zumbro Falls when we saw this animal wandering back and forth across the road, trying to get hit by cars.

"We stopped and looked at it; it was a skunk, with his head wedged up to his ears in an orange-juice can. He was obviously getting goofy inside his can, because every time we'd try to shoo him off by pegging a rock at him or something—thinking he'd find a way to go off and loosen this can—he'd go right back up to the road.

"So we watched, and we couldn't stand it; we knew he'd be hit. A farmer had stopped on the other side, and *he* wasn't gonna touch this thing. So the skunk wandered toward the ditch, and I said to my husband that if he would hold my hand on the high side of the road, I would go down and try to yank this thing off the skunk's head—because the skunk was getting kind of lifeless. So I went in the ditch, grabbed the can, and shook—all I did was lift the skunk in the air; he sort of sprayed a little, and I went screeching up to the road again.

"So then my husband said that, well, he'd try. So he went down there, and he talked to the skunk—and this is being observed by the farmer—and said: 'Now, you pull on your end, and I'll pull on my end, and you'll get out of this thing.' He wiggled a little, and the skunk wiggled a little—and danged if the can didn't come off. The skunk wiggled his way up the hill into some field, and the farmer gave us a look like we were entirely crazy.

"Just one of those things you have to do. Anyway, it's been a good story for years."

Mikey of Rochester: "I was coming back to Rochester from a business trip, and I thought I'd unwind a bit before I stopped home. Bought a newspaper and was gonna stop in the park, sit on a bench and read it.

"It rained, so I went into a little gazebo—and it was strewn with store-bought roses: long-stemmed yellow and red roses. I thought that was a little odd.

"I sat down there to read my paper, sort of thinking ill of the younger generation—who had gone and had a wedding and left all of these roses around to rot.

"A couple minutes later, a thin young man came and tapped on my shoulder, in earnest—sort of frightening and nervous. Said: 'Excuse me, sir.' Stammered, mumbled a lot. 'I need to talk to my girlfriend,' he said. I'm wondering what he's talking about, and he blurted out: 'Can you *leave?*'

"And so I did. About that time, I tumbled to what all the roses were about.

"As I walked away and got in my car, I could see this young Lochinvar on his knees, hands clasped, proposing in the truly, truly formal style—in a gazebo bedecked with roses.

"It's just nice to know that such romanticism still lives."

Red of Hastings: "About 10 years ago, I was managing a convenience store in Arizona. It was Christmas morning, about 8 o'clock in the morning; I'd worked there for two hours already and hadn't seen a customer. Hadn't seen a car go by in front. The only car in the parking lot was mine.

"Finally, a car went by and kinda slowed down after it went by the store; turned around and came back.

"I thought: 'Uh-oh.'

"Cars pulls up. Young girl about 20 years old got out of the car, came in, looked around the store a little bit. Went over to the rack where we were selling roses. Picked out a nice rose. Came up to the counter. Paid for it. I gave her her change, and she stepped back a minute—and then stepped back up to the counter, and she said 'Merry Christmas' and handed me the rose and turned around and walked away.

"Nicest Christmas present I ever had. Nicest thing ever said to me."

Short Timer of Barron, Wis.: "The nicest thing ever said to me was only two words—but they washed straight through me, brought tears to my eyes and re-connected me, in a way.

"It was about a year after a nasty divorce, and my 6-year-old and I were taking in the Fort Snelling Memorial Day ceremonies. Out of nowhere, it seemed, a stranger was suddenly engaging the two of us in fairly personal conversation. She was easy to talk to, despite my air of caution, and soon I found myself telling her and my son about my return from Vietnam, 16 years before.

"Her only response was a full-eye-contact 'Welcome home.' No one had told me that before, and I was stunned. I can't explain it, except that I suddenly felt ... accepted.

"The lady melted into the crowd, as they say, but I still think of her often and wonder who else out there she has brought home. God bless you, lady."

Pa Pong of the Rat's Nest: "Five or six years ago, when I had only one artificial leg, I was playing croquet with some friends in the back yard. In the course of the game, I hit one of my friends' croquet ball with my ball. This entitled me to place my ball next to hers and knock her ball out of play. So I put my artificial foot on the ball and wound up for a mighty swing.

"I missed the ball completely and hit my artificial leg right at the ankle. Her croquet ball rolled about three inches, but my leg sailed right over the next-door neighbor's fence, and I went ass over teakettle.

"When I looked around, everyone else was on the ground, too. At first, I thought it was out of sympathy—or, more likely, self-preservation. Then I realized they were rolling around on the ground in hysterics. It took a lot of coercing to get someone to jump the fence and retrieve my leg."

A.J. of God's Country, a young addict who asked Bulletin Boarders for support—which they gave her in abundance—as she sought to kick her drug habits: "It is August 19th, 1994. It is Friday.

"You know, a year and a half ago on a Friday night, I would have been gettin' ready to go out and whoop it up—whoop it up with my bottle in hand and anyone who wanted to whoop with me. But right now, I have plans to go out with my little brother tonight. He's comin' over right now to look at my kittens.

"I'm standin' here lookin' at this cloud that's passin' in the northeastern sky, and it is the biggest, puffiest, whitest cloud I have ever seen—and in about an hour and a half, the sunset will turn it this fiery pink-red color. I know this because I've spent a lot of time lookin' at the sky, the clouds, the stars, the trees, the flowers, the snow in the wintertime, the rain in the summer over the past year.

"I have one year of sobriety underneath my belt—one year of being dry, clean from drugs, clean from tobacco. And I am proud of myself.

"I have more to say—I really do—but my little brother just showed up, and I will call you guys back because I have somethin' sittin' on my heart, and I've gotta share it with someone. So I will call you back later on tonight. But *whoooo!* I have made it—one year!"

A.J., later: "It's many hours later. The cloud *did* turn a really cool fiery orange and pink and red, and it was great.

"I'm starting to see clouds and life and everything differently, and I'm starting to realize that being dry is one thing and being sober is another. I spent the last year doin' it alone, doin' it by myself—not drinkin', not smokin', not usin' drugs. And just recently, I finally found the courage to start attending A.A. meetings—and it's looking good. You know, I'm trying to be as optimistic as I can.

"I'm starting to remember things. I'm starting to *feel* again; this, like, *haze* is being lifted off of my mind, and I'm starting to realize that I don't have to do this alone. There are people out there who not only are there to help me, they *want* to help me. They want to help me build my life again.

"It feels good. . . . It looks like a good road ahead. You know, I see that light, and I feel that light.

"My cat Gabriel is callin'. She's cryin'; she wants food and water and love. You know what? I've got love to give, and it makes me feel good."

Jade & Buttercup's Mom of South Minneapolis: "Working at a chain discount department store, like I do, I thought I'd seen and heard absolutely everything—but I've found out that that wasn't true.

"Yesterday, a coworker of mine came to me and said that a gentleman had called the lingerie department asking for assistance on the telephone. He started telling what he wanted: some lacy silk items that he was interested in.

"In the middle of this, he stopped—and all of a sudden said: 'Look, these things are for me. I'm a cross-dresser. Do you have a problem with that?'

"Well, my friend was only a little bit surprised—because, I mean, cross-dressers are people like everybody else *[BULLETIN BOARD NOTES: or much like everybody else];* they shop at our stores as well as other people *[BULLETIN BOARD GUESSES: perhaps better—albeit in different departments].*

"He then proceeded to ask her to stash some of the items in the men's fitting rooms so he could come in and try 'em on when no one was around to see him.

"My coworker was very willing to comply, as our first job is to 'Serve the customer.' She had to put her foot down, though, when he asked her to tell him what he looked like in 'em—if it was good, if it wasn't. Her only reply was: 'Sir, I would have no way of knowing what looks good and what doesn't. I've never seen anything like it before.'

"Well, I've never *heard* anything like this story before. This guy—he expected her to come into the men's fitting room while he modeled women's underwear? I don't think so. Serving the customer has its limits, let me tell you."

Curious of Eagan: "When I was about 11 or 12, I was up at my cousins' in northern Wisconsin over Christmas vacation. We were out snowmobiling on the lake, and we decided to stop at a resort to get some hot chocolate and warm up.

"After we got done with our hot chocolate, I decided I was gonna go use the bathroom before we headed back out on our snowmobiles. When I sat down in the one-seater toilet at this resort, there was a *Playgirl* centerfold on the wall, behind some plexiglass, and on the plexiglass was a fake rubber-plant leaf connected on exactly where an 11- or 12-year-old little girl would like to see. So I sat forward and pulled up the leaf—and I couldn't see much, because of the way the leaf was attached. So I sat back and went to the bathroom and thought about it a minute—and decided I'd try it one more time. So I lifted up the leaf again and took a good long time at trying to figure out how I could see what was underneath there. Couldn't really see anything, so I left the bathroom and started walking back out. I had to walk through the bar area and a video-game area—and I walked out, and suddenly all of these people were laughing at me!

"Little did I know: When you would pull the leaf up on the plexiglass, there was a wire, and it was hooked up out into the bar area, and they had a rotating red light out there. So you'd pull up the leaf, and the light would go around—and everybody in the bar would know what you were doing in the bathroom.

"I think my face is still red. That was the most embarrassing thing that's ever happened to me. And my cousin just sat and laughed. She thought it was the greatest thing that could happen to me."

Dan of Arden Hills: "I was in Wisconsin a couple years ago, visiting a client who owned a large print shop.

"I had to use the facilities, and upon walking into the men's room, there was this big circular trough. I remember walking up to it, thinking: 'This is the weirdest urinal I've ever seen in my life.' I was about to use it when I noticed a normal-looking urinal around the corner, so I went to use that.

"This was fortunate, because immediately afterwards, the client walked in, went to the circular trough and washed his hands in it.

"I could only think: Can you imagine what would have happened if my client had walked in and caught me peeing in his sink?"

Ellen of Columbia Heights—who is, by the way, a rather delicate-sounding woman of . . . a certain age: "My friend Willa's brother was sitting in a closed stall in a men's restroom in New York City.

"A voice from the next stall said: '*Corn?* When did I have *corn?*'"

CHAPTER TWO

Unclear on the Concept

Not ... quite ... with ... the program:

Paula of Cumberland, Wis.: "My brother John lives in Catlin, Illinois, and he has a big corn feed/wiener roast/hayride/beer bash thing every year, to help finish off his sweet-corn crop. Oh, you know, a hundred or so of his closest friends show up.

"One young couple from Chicago drove down, and these kids hadn't left the city much. They were just totally enthralled with this farm; they wandered around, named the cows, having a great time. When it came time to leave, John told them that they could take some corn back with them, if they wanted—that there was plenty left; just go and pick some.

"As goodbyes were being said, a good friend of John's—purple with barely contained laughter—told him he'd better come say goodbye to the young couple. There, in the back seat, was the corn that they had picked to take home—stalks, roots and all.

"One wonders how they were going to cook it."

Kathy of White Bear Lake: "This was about 20 years ago, and my friend was working on her master's degree in education. It was spring, and we would take our bikes and head east from St. Paul to the St. Croix on weekends.

"After crossing many miles, surrounded by acres of newly planted cornfields, my friend commented: 'Boy, they sure grow a lot of chives out here.' And then she asked me if I knew what all of those black birds with red wings were.

"I told her they were red-winged blackbirds—and evidently she thought I was making this up, because she said, sarcastically: 'Oh, very funny.'

"So, for the past 20 years, every time I see a new field of corn, I have to chuckle and think: 'Just look at all those chives!'"

M. of St. Paul: "I was sittin' at my house today, me and two of my friends, and we were watchin' TV, and this commercial comes on for that spaghetti where they show it growing on trees.

"My one friend, A., is sittin' in the chair and says: *'That's* how spaghetti grows?'"

Jenny of Mankato: "When my sister and I both lived at home, she was ... ohhh ... not very homemakerish, I guess you could say. I did a lot of the cooking and cleaning to help out my mom, 'cause she worked nights.

"Then my sister moved away to college, and I thought: 'This poor kid is gonna be just lost.'

"So she calls me one night and says: 'Jenny! Mom there?'

"And I said: 'Yeah. Hang on.'

"She says: 'No, no, no! I just want to ask you a question. Don't tell her!'

"I said: 'What's up?'

"And she said: 'I need some help. I'm trying to make some supper.' I don't even think Kathy could make toast, you know? So she says: 'How do you make macaroni and cheese?'—'cause my mom had bought her all this really easy food: canned stuff, a case of macaroni and cheese, you name it.

"I said: 'Kathy, you just read the directions on the box.'

"And she says: 'Well, I understand all of that—about how you add half a cup of milk and two tablespoons of butter and the cheese packet, and you mix it all up. But how long do you boil the water for?'

"I said: 'You mean once you put the noodles in? 'Til they're soft!'

"She says: 'No. How long do you boil the water before you put the noodles in?'

"Aaauuuggghhh!"

G. of White Bear Lake: "I just wanted to let you know about my sister, who married very young. She prepared her first Thanksgiving dinner, and upon going into the turkey cavity and removing the giblets and the neck, she exclaimed: 'This must be a boy turkey!'"

BULLETIN BOARD NOTES: And quite a boy, at that!

Princess Grace of Mahtomedi, with a "not-so-fond remembrance of a hospital stay I had a number of years ago": "I had my gall bladder removed, and that precipitated a seven-day hospital stay—which would have been shorter had my bowel sounds come back a bit more quickly. They didn't—which made the surgeon, who happened to be a friend of mine in residency training, a bit nervous about his expertise.

"Every few hours, a nurse with a cold stethoscope would come into my room, walk past my roommate and her many and constant visitors, pull the curtain around my bed for privacy, and listen to my lower abdomen for those important bowel sounds. I was quietly told that I could not leave the hospital until I'd had that all-important first bowel movement, so they could tell that all was well.

"Then, once they'd heard even an inkling of bowel sounds, they began asking—quite often—if I'd had a bowel movement yet. Most of the nurses asked quietly, but one nurse was quite irritating—striding into the room past all of the visitors and asking in a loud voice: 'HAVE YOU HAD A BOWEL MOVEMENT YET?'

"Now, this was B.K.—Before Kids—and I still had a small modicum of modesty, so I gathered my strength and feebly asked her to *please* respect that modesty and not ask me such an embarrassing personal thing so loudly, in front of strangers. She nodded and left.

"The next time she returned, she strode into the room, past all of the visitors and my roommate, smiled at me, winked, pulled the cloth curtain around me—and *then* hollered: 'SO, HAVE YOU HAD THAT BOWEL MOVEMENT YET?'"

Dimples of Stillwater, telling of her work as a nurse at a family-practice clinic: "Every summer, the clinic did the athletic physicals for our local high school. We averaged 25 to 30 students a morning—primarily boys. We would place their name on the counter by the nurses' station, along with a urinal for them to give us a urine sample.

"I called in a strapping 14-year-old and told him to go to the men's room and give me a specimen.

"Normally, this took five minutes. After 20 minutes, I knocked on the men's bathroom door and informed him that if he was unable to go now, we could have him try after the physical. He told me that it was all right; he was finally able to go.

"He proceeded to march up to the nurses' station and place his urinal on his name, along with a specimen—a bowel movement."

Bob Woolley of St. Paul: "An ad for Preparation H on TV today reminded me of my prankster friend, from back when I lived in Illinois.

"His sweet wife did not always catch on to his sense of humor. One time, she told him about a suppository her doctor had prescribed. He told her: 'I don't believe in suppositories. For all the good they do, you might as well shove them up your rear end.'

"Several hours later, as they were retiring for the night, she returned to this delicate subject: 'John? You know what you were saying about suppositories? Well, isn't that what you're *supposed* to do with them?'"

Norah of St. Paul: "Years ago, I had a boyfriend who had a sister who had these terrible, terrible yeast infections. She got them regularly, and they wouldn't go away. I told her that my tried-and-true home remedy is to take B-complex vitamins and to douche with yogurt.

"She said 'Thanks'—and came back a couple days later and said: 'Wow! This is really great! My infection is completely gone! And I feel great,' she said, 'but my question is: What do I do about all the strawberry seeds?'"

The Woman in the Shoe of Andover: "I was talking with my neighbor about a notice we received regarding an emergency sprinkling ban in our city. Apparently, the water towers are registering zero reserves. The city cannot maintain adequate fire protection at this level; nor can household water use be maintained.

"We can only water new sod, vegetable gardens, and new trees and shrubs. I was commenting on how I didn't want all of my beautiful flowers to die—and that if I had to, I'd buy some water at the grocery store, to use to save my flowers. Or: I had just filled up the kids' pool, the day before, and could use that water to water my flower garden and all of my hanging plants.

"She said: 'Well, I'm just going to get water from the faucet inside the house to water *my* flowers with.'

"Now why didn't I think of that?"

Dave of Eagan: "A young lady at work and I were discussing the switch from Standard to Daylight time, and she said that she always looks forward to Daylight Saving Time—because, since there's more daylight, the snow melts faster."

E.J. of St. Paul: "A woman I work with, in a smoke-free office, has to go outside to smoke. I was asking her: 'Isn't that kind of bothersome to have to always go outside?' And she said: No, it gives her a chance to get some fresh air."

Jim Johnson of St. Paul: "One winter, when my car-door locks kept freezing up, I thought I was very clever when I discovered that I could use a cigarette lighter to warm up the key, or in some cases warm up the lock directly, get it thawed out and get into my car. I thought I was also clever when I decided to use the same maneuver to thaw out my frozen locking gas cap—and I was about to apply the flame to the gas cap when the gas-station attendant said 'Are you sure you want to do that?' "

Art of Vadnais Heights: "My wife tells me that she and my mother-in-law put oil in the car—and it took 'em two hours, and they could not understand how it could take two hours, because it never takes that long at the service station.

"They'd put it in the most obvious spot: in the dipstick."

Homeless of Woodbury: "I was riding with a woman I know, and she drove through a stop sign. I called her on it, and she said: 'I can go through it without stopping because it's a four-way stop, and all of the other people will be stopping, anyway.' "

Driver Ed of St. Paul: "On my daily commute down I-94 a few days ago, I noticed the car ahead of me had a horrible shimmy in its left rear wheel. It looked for all the world like that wheel was about to fall off. It was shuddering and shaking and vibrating, and I was afraid to get close to it—for fear it was gonna pop off and cause the car to careen all over the interstate.

"The driver was going along about 65 miles an hour, apparently oblivious to the problem.

"I finally decided to be brave and what I thought was charitable. I pulled up alongside of him, rolled down my passenger's side window (fortunately, I have power windows, so I didn't have to reach way over), and gave him the universal signal for 'Roll down your window.'

"He did, and I yelled out to him: 'Your rear wheel's about to fall off!'

"He waved and smiled and said: 'I know. It's been that way for a while.' He rolled up his window and waved again—and sped off.

"I thought: 'Well, if it's been that way for a while, *why are you still driving with it that way?*'

"There's just no helping some people."

Paul Bunyan Wannabe: "My friend Ron said he was having a tree-removal party.

"I asked how many trees, and he said: 'Three.'

"I asked him what kind, and he said: 'I don't have any idea.'

"I asked why he was removing them, and he said: 'Because they have Dutch elm disease.'

"We're not gonna let him handle the chain saw."

Gubben of Minneapolis: "My sister tells of a coworker who asked her lunch group: 'Who was that ballplayer who died from Lou Gehrig's disease?' "

Bud of parts hereabouts: "I was at a health club the other night when this guy next to me asked if I knew the names of the Marx Brothers.

"That being a fairly basic trivia question, I answered: 'Groucho, Harpo, Chico and Zeppo.'

"He said: 'Oh, yeah, I couldn't remember that fourth one.'

"A couple of minutes later, he said: 'I never knew anyone else named Chico. Did you?' I said that I knew a guy in school who they called Chico, but I wasn't sure if that was his real name.

"He then said: 'He was the one who played the harp, right?'"

Spiff of St. Paul: "I recently acquired a portion of a rather, shall we say, eclectic library, and included in this collection are the writings of the Marquis de Sade. When a friend of mine discovered that I was reading some of these novels by the Marquis, she replied—with a straight face, I might add—that she didn't like the writings of the Marquis de Sade because, well, she found them too sadistic."

The Walrus: "My sister was at a meeting last week where an individual read a fairly long prayer (or poem?) to the group, then announced that it had been written by Circa in 1800."

BULLETIN BOARD NOTES: Sometime around then, at any rate.

Greg of western Wisconsin: "I used to own a little bookstore, and we once, at Christmastime, had a Bible shoplifted."

Holly of Inver Grove Heights: "Today, a lady in the lunch line ran short of money. She forgot it upstairs.

"I said: 'Oh, here's a dollar.' She owed, like, 63 cents. And I said: 'Just consider it one of those random acts of kindness.'

"So she paid for her lunch—and took the change! I thought it was kind of humorous."

Nancy Lee of Oak Grove: "I went shopping in the mall for some jeans yesterday, and I went into a store, and a cashier asked if she could help me. When I said 'Yes, I'm looking for some jeans,' she said: 'What kind?'

"I said: 'Guess?'

"She said 'Levi's?'"

Kaye of parts hereabouts: "I want to tell you what my son gave my husband, his father, for Father's Day. We decided we would buy a canvas briefcase for Father's Day, and our son Brendan decided he wanted to call the company and order it. I gave him the credit-card number, and he called this company in Dodgeville, Wis. Brendan said he was having it monogrammed.

"This morning, my husband—Jim—got a black briefcase monogrammed with the letters D . . . A . . . D, in red."

Helen of St. Paul: "This evening, I was at a certain burger, supposedly-fast-food kind of place; you'll figure out, in a second, where I was. As I'm waiting for my chicken sandwich, the girl behind the counter is standing there waiting and waiting. 'Why do they call it a BK Broiler?' she says. 'What does the BK stand for? . . . Does it stand for Burger King? . . . Oh, well, I suppose I should've known that.'"

Karla of Burger King: "I work at Burger King in Hudson; I wear a headset to take drive-through orders. Today, some nice gentleman came to my front counter.

I took his order and told him his total, then took a drive-through order and told them to drive around to the second window.

"I turned around, and the gentleman was gone. I looked behind the car in drive-through, and there he was.

"When he drove up, I asked him if he was waiting too long. 'No,' he said. 'You *told* me to drive around to the second window.'"

Elaine of Woodbury: "My friend and I were dining in a restaurant. My friend was born with only one hand, and as we were sitting there, this airhead waitress asks: 'Sir, what happened to your hand?'

"He said: 'I was *born* with one hand.'

"And she said: 'Well, you're lucky to be righthanded.'"

N.C. Horton Sr. of St. Paul: "An employee at a local supermarket used the men's room and started to walk out without washing his hands. I couldn't help pointing out a sign saying 'Wash Your Hands Before Returning To Work.'

"He said: 'I'm not going back to work. I'm going to lunch.'"

Clare of Maplewood: "My sister was very sick, and she sent her friend to the store for some items. He was standing, looking, and he said to another customer: 'Where do you find the Cream of Wheat? They've got Cream of Potato, Cream of Tomato, Cream of Chicken—everything. But where is the Cream of Wheat?'

"Needless to say, he was promptly sent to the proper part of the store."

Bubbles of Elk River: "Tonight at the grocery store, two young girls came in. They were between the ages of 18 and 22, maybe; they looked old enough to know better.

"Anyway, I'm standin' in the grocery store, back by the meat department, and these two girls come walkin' up, and one says to the other: 'Oh, hey! This looks good! We could have *this* for supper.' And she reaches her hand over and touches something on the shelf.

"And then she turns to me and says: 'Have you ever had a beef suet ball?' I thought I was gonna die laughin', but I didn't dare, 'cause I felt sorry for her. I said: 'That's for *birds*. You hang that outside in the tree for the *birds.*'

"'Oh, God,' she says. 'Well, it looked *good.*'"

Heidi of the Hills: "While at the State Fair last summer with a good pal, I suggested she try the buffalo burgers, because I think they're pretty good.

"She said: 'No, thanks. I don't eat red meat.'

"Five minutes later, she was munching on a corn dog. I wonder what color meat she considers corn dogs."

BULLETIN BOARD OBSERVES: Most of the corn dogs we've inspected closely haven't been exactly red—but something more like a blend of brown and tan and maybe just a fleck of green.

We don't recommend close inspections of corn dogs.

Tim of South St. Paul: "One of my best friends got married about two years ago—and it was a Jewish wedding, since both my friend and his wife-to-be were Jewish. I am not Jewish, and I was the only non-Jewish person in the wedding.

"At the wedding dinner that night, there was this piece of meat on the plate. And everybody was like: 'What is it? What kind of meat is this?' And I said to my friend's brother: 'I think it's a pork chop.'

"He looks at me, kinda shakes his head, and says: 'Tim, I don't think it's a pork chop.'"

The Former Voice of the Company: "When I worked as a Directory Assistance Operator for Northwestern Bell, a customer called and asked for a telephone number. I flipped the book open (in the olden days, we didn't use a computer, but huge paper directories), swept the pages, and scanned for the name he'd requested.

"I quoted the number to him, and he said: 'That can't be the right number.'

"I verified the name and address he had requested, and repeated the number. He said he had tried the number, but 'it didn't work.'

"I asked him if he got a recording when he dialed the number.

"He said: 'No, it just rings and rings.'

"So I said: 'Well, maybe they aren't home.'

"To which he replied: 'Sure they are. I can see 'em sitting on the front steps!'

"I sat there for a moment, picturing this guy calling his neighbor while watching him out the window and wondering what was wrong with the phone.

"I told him to go over there and ask him why he didn't answer the phone.

"He said he would."

Ernestine of St. Paul (not her true name, we're pretty certain): "Years ago, I worked at the telephone company—in the business office, where we handled all the service problems. One day, a customer called in and said the cord from her telephone to the wall was too long—and she wanted to know if we could pull it in from our end."

Curly Top of Le Sueur: "I was reading an article in a health magazine on Internet addicts—people who lose their jobs and lose their homes because they are so addicted to the Internet that they can't even go off to work.

"At the end of the article, they had an e-mail address to use to join an Internet-addicts support group."

Larry of western Wisconsin: "My wife and I went on vacation over the Fourth of July week. We stopped at a tourist place that gave us a pontoon-boat ride. I was sitting by three older ladies who seemed like they were really enjoying themselves.

"The guy giving this tour said: 'If you look off to your right, there's a turtle sunning himself on a log sticking out of the water.' Then he says: 'That's a painted turtle.'

"We go on for about another half a minute, and one lady says to the other: 'Was that a real turtle?'

"And the other lady says: 'No. He said that was a *painted* turtle.'"

Slick of Ashland Oil: "About six years ago, I was up fishing with my son Aaron, who was about 6 at the time. There are two docks at the lake where we were; he was standing on one dock, and I was standing on the other. The minnow bucket was in the water off his dock.

"I walked over, pulled the minnow bucket out of the water, got a minnow, set the bucket on the dock. Baited my hook, walked back to the other dock.

"When I turned around, I noticed that I'd left the minnow bucket out of the water—but my young son Aaron was standing right next to it. So I said to Aaron: 'Aaron, put the minnows in the water, will ya?'—then turned away and made my cast.

"I hear behind me the gurgling of water—and there's my young son, pouring the minnows into the water. He put the minnows in the water."

Sonja of Monticello: "I teach piano. I have a neighbor who teaches piano, too, and she had a piano student come in, and the girl was playing a song for her.

"She stopped her, and she said: 'Now, how do you think that sounded?' She was trying to get her to think about it.

"And the girl says: 'Gee, I don't know. I wasn't listening.'"

Quad P. of Eagan: "My sweetheart and I recently took a break—and took off for the weekend without our four children.

"In the typical Friday-afternoon frenzy to get ready to drop the kids off at Grandma's and so forth, we were inside busily preparing for our weekend away—putting on the timers for the lights and doing all of the typical precautions so that nobody would break in—and the kids were out playing in the driveway, like they usually do. Of course, they love this driveway chalk.

"So we jumped into the van and took off, and my sweetheart and I had a great weekend—and when we pulled back up on Sunday afternoon, we saw that in letters about 20 feet high on the driveway, in all different colors, my oldest daughter had written WE ARE NOT HOME.

"So much for trying to keep the home secure."

Stan of Apple Valley: "A friend of ours went to Chicago for a business meeting. She was sitting on the wall of a park pond in Chicago, visiting with her counterpart from Chicago, and the lady from Chicago said: 'Oh, my! Look at all that splashing out there on the pond. One duck is trying to drown another duck!'

"Our friend had to explain to this city bumpkin from Chicago that the one duck who was on top of the other duck was not, indeed, trying to drown the other duck, but had something very romantic in mind."

BULLETIN BOARD SAYS: We never imagined that romance had much to do with it.

Egghead of Blaine: "We have a Super Nintendo game called 'Wayne's World' that we recently found in the clearance bin. A not-insignificant feature of the game is the *schwing!* sound effect Wayne and Garth use—combined with a knees-locked pelvis thrust—to signify a male physical response to Heather Locklear and Pamela Anderson.

"As I said, this effect is an integral feature of the game, so our 6-year-old son imitates this sound whenever it occurs in the game. Fortunately (I guess), he doesn't quite understand its original meaning, as he usually says 'Schwing! Schwing batter batter batter . . .' in a baseball heckler's chant.

"I'm not quite ready to correct him."

Ace of Wyoming: "My wife, Judy, has had contact lenses forever, it seems. When my rather eccentric father first met her, years ago, he felt intimidated at times, and at a loss for words—but being a staunch, opinionated, thick-skulled Norwegian, he couldn't pass up a chance to give Judy his views on her contact lenses.

"In his illogical, Archie Bunker style—with his own eyeglasses in his hand, waving them in the air—he stated that if God had wanted us to wear contact lenses, he wouldn't have given us *these.'*

"She had no comeback."

Stephanie of Rochester: "Thirty years ago, when I was a Midwestern-educated, idealistic high-school English teacher, my husband and I took jobs in rural New Hampshire.

"The school where I was teaching offered only French as a foreign language. (Actually, more Canadian-French.) I was mildly proficient in Russian—the result of a Cold War education milieu and a best friend whose family spoke only Russian at home—so I naively offered to start a Russian-language course, to add some variety.

"My request for textbook funding was voted down at the school meeting—and in New Hampshire at that time, the school meeting was really like a town meeting, with everyone attending to make sure that some pinko, left-leaning, libertine, uppity city slicker didn't pollute their kids' minds with notions of independent thinking.

"My request went dead in the water when a self-righteous protector of children's rights stood up and declared: 'If English was good enough for Jesus Christ, it's good enough for *my* kids.' He was roundly applauded, and until we moved away—about three years later—my school mailbox was inundated with John Birch materials.

"How times have changed."

Grandma Up North: "My daughter called me from Chicago with this story about Halloween:

"She did a favor for a friend by going to the church in the neighborhood and helping with the Halloween party, and this mother came up to her and said: 'Isn't it *terrible* about the violence—and the *terrible* costumes that children wear? My son wanted to be one of those Power Rangers, but I wouldn't let him. I just think that it's just *terrible.'*

"And my daughter said: 'Well, my son likes to watch it once in a while, too. It *does* have a few good things—like the bad guys and the good guys and so on.'

"The funny thing about this—and I thought it was *very* funny—is that the woman was dressed as Morticia Addams.

"There are a lot of confused people in this world."

CHAPTER THREE

Come Again?

Episodes of creative hearing:

Emily's Brother of St. Paul: "What's all this I hear about budgie jumping? They say that people are jumping off of bridges and using budgies to break their fall. I think that's terrible!

"I remember my little parakeet, Petey; he was so cute. Those birds are *much* too small to support the weight of a grown man—especially when it's falling! Why, you'd *crush* the poor things.

"I don't know why people have to be so cruel to little animals. First, the gerbils; now, this. I think we ought to take the crushed bodies of those little budgies and put them up ...

"What?

"Oh. Never mind."

Big Ears of the suburbs: "I work at an elementary school where there are gerbils and guinea pigs in cages in quite a few of the classrooms.

"Recently, one of the students had asked her parents to get her one of these pets at home. She reported, at school, that she was sure her parents had a guinea pig hidden in their bedroom that they were going to give to her as a surprise—because every morning, this student could hear the guinea pig squeaking through their locked bedroom door."

My Husband's Reason for Living of rural Pierce County, Wis.: "I was sitting at the bar with some friends, and a stranger sat to my right. We hadn't exchanged words all night until a heavily—and very cheaply—scented woman leaned in between us to order a drink.

"As she walked away, the fellow said: 'She smelled like a French whore.' Being a nice girl—especially a nice girl from North Dakota—I had never heard that phrase. I thought he'd said: 'She smelled like a French horn.'

"I thought that was a rather odd thing to say, but I didn't want to appear rude and ignore him, so I replied as best I could. I said: 'Well, I hadn't thought about it, but I suppose they could start to smell if you didn't open the spit valve and blow them out once in a while.'

"Whoever that fellow is, I hope he reads this and finally understands. I'll never forget the look he gave me as he got up and walked away."

Dave of Backus: "A little while back, I was feeling pretty happy about things. Things were going good, and I was excited. I said to the wife: 'You know, honey, I'm feelin' euphoria.'

"She turns to me and says: 'You know, hon, I feel for you, too.'"

God's Favorite Cheesehead: "My wife and her mother were driving across North Dakota with her mother's cat, Hugh, in the backseat. Her mother said she was getting hungry, and my wife told her there was fruit in the cooler.

"A mile or so later, my wife asked: 'Did you get a banana, Ma?' and her mother turned to her, shocked, and asked: 'What? Did I give Hugh an enema?'"

Doodah of St. Paul: "I was sitting in the back of the class with a group of friends, having a test that I was not particularly well-prepared for. The question was: 'What structures exist in Egypt as well as Mexico?' I could not, for the life of me, think of the answer—so I turned to my friend and said: 'What's number 8?'

"She turned back to me and whispered: 'Beer mints.' I thought to myself: 'Beer mints?' I said: 'What?'

"She said: *'Beer mints!'*

"Well, I figured, I guess these things exist; they must make beer, or something along those lines, so I wrote it down. Naturally, I did not get the question correct, and the teacher, being on the ball, quickly figured out the problem, and the next day I was moved to the other side of the class.

"I've never really lived down the embarrassment of that moment, especially since the teacher, without using my name, told the story in front of the class and throughout the years to the classes of my two sisters, who were three and four years younger than me.

"I guess the moral is: If you don't know the answer, just leave it blank."

BULLETIN BOARD REPLIES: Or take a wild guess. Under no circumstances, however, should one guess: "Beer mints."

E.W.D. of Stillwater: "We had gone to San Francisco for the first time. We had our grandchildren with us . . . and we took the trolley; the kids were excited. The youngest, a little 4-year-old called John-John, got down to Fisherman's Wharf and started looking in all of the windows and the doorways, and he said: 'Where are they?'

"I said: 'Where are who?'

"He says: 'Where's the fishermen dwarfs?'"

Shannon of Inver Grove Heights: "As a Christmas gift for my mother, a friend of mine got her a sweatshirt with a picture of my kids on the front of it. She wore it to lunch with someone she hasn't seen in quite a while. Forgetting what shirt she had on, you can only imagine how red her face turned when she removed her jacket and her friend said: 'God, have *they* ever gotten big since the last time I saw you!'"

Julie of St. Cloud: "My 4-year-old daughter's been puzzling me with her references to a 'speedy God.' I asked her what she meant by that, and she said: 'You know, Mom! In church, we say: "Thanks, speedy God."'"

Dee Dee of Maplewood: "A number of years ago, I was worship chairperson for our church. Our minister sometimes had fairly long sermons, and the service would last longer than an hour.

"One day, the service ended about 15 or 20 minutes late. A few minutes later, one of our most highly respected church members approached me and suggested that I needed to do something about this. He was visibly upset, and as he talked about how the minister sometimes repeated himself and used more examples from Scripture after he'd already made his point, he was growing more and more animated and finally ended with: 'The bastard doesn't know when to shut up!'

"I was stunned. This man had always been a perfect gentleman, and I couldn't understand why he would say such a thing unless he was losing his grip. I was very concerned about him and couldn't get it out of my mind for several days.

"Finally, I told a friend about it—and as I was recounting the story, it suddenly became obvious to both of us that he had said: 'The pastor doesn't know when to shut up.'

"I was so relieved."

Mairzy Doats of White Bear Lake: "When my first child was born, all she wanted to do was eat. I was breastfeeding her, and it wasn't long before I was very, very tired—and very sore.

"After one especially tiring day, my husband was sitting with me as I rocked and nursed her yet again. She started to fall asleep. I whispered to my husband: 'I think she's going to nod off.'

"He was frantic as he tried to grab her from my arms, yelling: 'What can I do? How can I help?'

"I glared at him and said: *'What are you trying to do?'*

"And he said: 'I thought you said she was going to gnaw it off.'"

Lake Elmo Lily: "My mom lives in Wisconsin, and last weekend my adult sisters and brother and I were helping her with her fall cleaning. My sister Barb and sister-in-law Cookie were cleaning in the kitchen, and an ad for the La Crosse Octoberfest came over the radio. The announcer stated that the Maple Leaf Parade would begin at 1 P.M.—and Cookie turned to Barb, in all seriousness, and asked: 'Why would *anyone* want to go to a make-believe parade? And why would you have to be there at 1 o'clock?'

"We howled."

Victoria of Little Canada, through fits of giggling: "My friend Rick and I were watching 'Sweet Justice'; you know, the show with Laura from 'Little House on the Prairie.' And I asked him: What was the name that Michael Landon used to call her on 'Little House on the Prairie'?

"And he looks at me, in all seriousness, and says: 'Half Mind.' Not Half Pint, but Half Mind!

"And now he's mad, 'cause I'm callin' you guys."

Katelind's Mom of Rice Lake, Wis.: "About 14 or 15 years ago, when I was just a little kid, all my cousins and my sister and I would sometimes spend the night at my grandma's house.

"On one Saturday morning, my aunt came over to help make us all some breakfast. She came into the living room, where we were all playing, and she said: 'Kids, what do you want for breakfast—scrambled eggs?'

"We all mumbled something, except for my sister—and she says: 'What?'

"My aunt says again: 'So what do you want for breakfast—scrambled eggs?'

"My sister just looks at her again, and she says: *'What?'*

"And my aunt—finally, practically screaming at her—says: *'What do you want for breakfast—scrambled eggs?'*

"My sister looks at her and smiles, and she says: 'Ohhhhh! Scrambled eggs! I thought you said 'Grandma's legs.'"

Grandma of Webster, Wis.: "My 75-year-old friend was in the stall in the men's room, and he 'made some music.' A youngster and his dad were also in the men's room, and the little boy said: 'What was that? Did you hear it, Dad?'

"No comment was heard from Dad.

"The little boy then said: 'It sounded like a harmonica!'"

Wilz of Highland Park: "When I was hunting with a couple of my friends, one of them broke wind and immediately said: 'Shhhh! I think I heard a bear snort.'

"And the other one said: 'And boy, has he got bad breath.'"

Dan of Arden Hills: "A few years ago, I was talking to a friend about the magazines he subscribed to, and he said he subscribed to 'While I [Expel a Posterior Breeze].'

"It wasn't until I was at his house that I realized he subscribed to *Wildlife Art.*"

BULLETIN BOARD NOTES: *If you've seen enough wildlife art, you'll understand the confusion.*

Short Timer of Barron, Wis.: "I had told the Realtor that our bird feeder attracts all of the regular birds—and, on second thought, added that I had also spotted a cardinal there.

"Two or three days pass, and then we get our House for Sale spec sheets. Ever so nice, and every one of them boasts that we have 'spotted cardinals.'"

Chrysanthemum of St. Paul: "I was on the road today with my friend Wings, who is from Minneapolis, and we were having this wonderful heart-to-heart talk about where our lives were going, and what we wanted to accomplish, and what kinds of things we were wanting to do at this point in life that we hadn't been doing, and how we thought things were going.

"And I said that I was hoping I would write more.

"And he thought about that, looked out the window, watched the countryside go by—and then he turned to me and said: 'You know, I think Barbara wants a riding mower, too.'"

Pat of Mahtomedi: "Years ago, I worked in a secretarial pool for attorneys who dictated reports elaborating on the welfare and living conditions of beneficiaries under guardianship. The tapes were sometimes difficult to understand; compounding the problem were the limited vocabularies of the 18-year-olds transcribing them.

"My favorite report included the sentence 'The ward lives on an 80-acre farm with his paramour.' The transcribed version became: 'The ward lives on an 80-acre farm with his power mower.'

"Paints a very different picture, eh?"

CHAPTER FOUR

This 'n' That 'n' the Other

Blinded by the lyrics: Take it away, **Sara Cassidy** of parts hereabouts: "You know that song that says 'Good morning, America, how are ya? Well, don't you know me? I'm your native son.' I overheard a co-worker singing along today: ' . . . I'm your neighbors' dog. . . .' Really!"

Jess's Mom of Wyoming: "We were coming back from skating yesterday, and we had an oldies station on. The Four Seasons were on, singing 'Let's Hang On,' and Jess said to me: 'What does that line mean?' I said: 'What line?' And she said: 'That little chipmunk dining on your hand.'

"It was 'that little chip of diamond on your hand'—but I do like 'that little chipmunk dining on your hand' much better."

Egghead of Blaine: "My loving wife and our 6-year-old son like to sing along to music in the automobile. Today she realized that while she was singing 'I wanna be sedated' with the Ramones, our son was not. She asked, and he told her he was singing 'I want a piece of Danish.'"

Ruby of Arden Hills: "I was just riding in the car with my kindergarten daughter, and the song that was on the radio was 'Soul Man.' And she was singin' along, and I said: 'What are you saying?' And she kept singing: 'I was *sooooooo* mad.'"

Little Red of Cottage Grove: "I'm a child of the '60s, and my children believe that a Beatles' song says: 'I've got a chicken to ride.' That's what they're running around the house, singing: 'I've got a chicken to ride.'"

BULLETIN BOARD NOTES: And she don't care.

Name that twone! In the matter of interchangeable melodies and lyrics, here's **Cathy** of Highland Park: "My boyfriend Vince has proven to me—over . . . and over . . . and over again—that the words 'Oh, Vince, he is the coolest ever in the world' can be sung to the tune of virtually every song that's ever been written. Just ask him."

Melba of St. Anthony Village: "One of my favorite musical corruptions is singing Robert Frost's 'Stopping by Woods on a Snowy Evening' to the tune of 'Hernando's Hideaway.' When you think about it, it works very well."

BULLETIN BOARD NOTES: It works equally well if you refuse to think about it.

Joy, joy, joy? From **Nursing Nancy** of Vadnais Heights: "Our 4-year-old son, Jens, loves to sing and is developing quite an eclectic taste in music. Yesterday, after spending all day with his 20-year-old sitter, he started jamming to Ace of Base's 'All That She Wants Is Another Baby'—a funky new hit. Without missing a beat, he switched into 'Well, I got joy, joy, joy, joy down in my heart—hey!' Then, he went back to 'All that she wants'—and back and forth. Throughout the entire medley, Eleanor, his 14-month-old sister and part-time go-go dancer, threw her head and hair violently from side to side and worked at snapping her fingers.

"It was pretty delightful."

BULLETIN BOARD REPLIES: Delightful? Don't you realize, Nursing Nancy, that this is exactly how the Jacksons got their start? Get the kids a chemistry set before it's too late!

Bringing on the heaves: Thank you, thank you very much to **Shan** of Cannon Falls: "The song that always makes me want to reach for the Ipecac has gotta be that '70s chestnut 'Feelings,' by Morris Albert. If there was ever a song that was born to be sung in a Las Vegas lounge, 'Feelings' had to be the one. Every time I hear it on the radio, I always picture the same scenario:

"We're in a small lounge in Vegas—perhaps called the Boom-Boom Room, with headliner Nick Ramone. Nick has just finished his toe-tappin' version of 'Proud Mary,' and he decides he wants to quiet things down a bit. He has the lighting director put the special blue gel in the spotlight, and he stands there with a cigarette and a drink in one hand and a pair of large nylon love-pat-style underpants that were thrown onstage to him by a middle-aged woman from Cedar Rapids, Iowa.

"He takes a drink, wipes his brow with the aforementioned undergarment, looks the woman in the eye and says: 'I'd like to slow things down a bit here tonight and sing you one of my favorite songs—and I hope it's one of yours.' He gives his cue to the bandleader: 'Feelings, nothing more than feelings . . .'—and as the song builds to its swirling climax, there's not a dry eye in the house."

B-b-b-bernstein, S-s-s-sondheim: Perhaps the silliest call the Bulletin Board Hot Line has ever received (high praise, indeed!) came from **Harry Samtur** of St. Paul: "I'd like to sing a song for you [which Harry proceeded to do, with feeling—as you, too, must if you are to appreciate the depths of the goofiness here]: 'The most beautiful sound I've ever heard: Ch-ch-ch-chia! Ch-ch-ch-chia! I've just met a Pet named Ch-ch-ch-chia! And suddenly I've found how wonderful a sound could be. Ch-ch-ch-chia! Say it loud and there's music playing. Say it soft and it's almost like praying. Ch-ch-ch-chia! I'll never stop saying Ch-ch-ch-chia! The most beautiful sound I ever heard: Ch-ch-ch-chia!'"

After a very slight pause, and without further ado, Harry continued: "Away out West, they've got a name for rain and wind and fire. Away out West, they've got a name: They call the wind Ch-ch-ch-chia."

"And what are *you* this year, big . . . boy?" From **The Desk of Leonard Smalls, Stuttgart on Mississippi:** "Always a Ch-ch-ch-chia fan, Leonard feels compelled to tell you about what might be the finest Halloween costume he's ever even heard of.

"This guy went to Ragstock and bought an old suit, which he took home and soaked with water. He then smeared it with grass seed and hung it on his porch, watering and reseeding as needed until the big day, when . . . *voila!* He was a six-foot Chia Pet.

"Leonard understands that the roots, which penetrated the material of the suit, were more than a little uncomfortable."

Birds of a feather: From **Mark the Nurse** of Wisconsin: "I was on my way home from work the other night, and I stopped at a pet shop to take a look at the birds. The birds are usually way in the back, so I start walkin' back and I hear this flipping sound. I go way in the back, and in a cage under a sign marked 'White Sacred Doves of Peace' were two white doves beating the hell out of each other—pecking at each other, pulling each other's feathers out."

Mixed messages: From **The Phone Male** of St. Paul: "There is something both irritating and incongruous about being on hold for 15 minutes to a business, all the while listening to an intermittent recording come on and say: 'Your call is extremely important to us.'"

Signs of the times: From **John** of St. Paul: "A portion of the tile facade on the Wabasha side of the Schubert Apartments was removed this last week. For several years, there has been an intriguing seven-word message on that piece of wall. Neatly written in black Magic Marker, with the rounded script of a young girl's hand, it read:

"'I miss Juan
"'He is locked up.'

"I never passed that spot without wondering about the fate of Juan or his faithful friend. This life is tough on young men named Juan and their young women friends."

Anonymous woman of St. Paul: "I was in downtown St. Paul recently on a weekday, down at City Hall and some of the nearby buildings, and I noticed that you cannot go by a door to some of these buildings without going through a cloud of smoke. You have smokers stationed on both sides of the door, frantically puffing on their cigarettes—since they've been banished to the outside.

"It used to be that people put statues of lions or griffins around the entrances to these buildings made of stone. Now, instead, we have smokers—living guardians of the portal."

Sea rations: First, **The Old Man** of Maplewood: "This happened in 1942, when I was in Pearl Harbor working on raising our sunken ships. We in the military were the only ones who had such luxuries as coconut.

"I happened to be on a hot job, and it was hurry, hurry, hurry. I was on the late shift—11 P.M. to 7 A.M.—and it so happened that I had to go through the ship's bakery about eight times during my shift. And what did I spy but a 50-gallon paper barrel of coconut!

"After the baker left, all of the lights in the bakery were shut off, except the small ones on the floor. I made about eight trips back and forth and stuffed both hands full of coconut. I wasn't supposed to have it.

"At about 5 A.M., the baker came on while I was having a feast. He switched on the lights, and what a surprise: After my good luck, about 5,000 cockroaches just swarmed out of this barrel. Did I get sick, right on the spot!

"Can I say I have never eaten coconut since that day?"

Dennis of Austin: "When I was in the Navy, I was stationed aboard a refriger-ated-cargo ship delivering food supplies to Vietnam. We would spend as much as two months out to sea before going back to port and resupplying.

"We had this one sailor on there that was known to have a drinking problem, and we'd been out to sea for three weeks at least and he appeared to be intoxicated several times during the day. No one seemed to know what he was drinking or where he was getting it—until one day, he was caught in one of the cargo store-rooms drinking from a large bottle of vanilla extract.

"When he was brought to the attention of his chief, the first response from the chief was: 'Damn! I should've known what he was doin'. Every time he'd [expel a posterior breeze], it smelled like a cupcake.'"

Ah, the smell of it! Aromatic memories:

M.K. of Shoreview: "Every time I smell vanilla, particularly vanilla extract, I think of a time when I was in bed with my old boyfriend. I had wrapped some vanilla can-dles that I had brought with me on a vacation weekend with him in my lingerie *[BUL-LETIN BOARD NOTES: And how he got in her lingerie, we don't want to know!]*, and between the scent of the candles burning and the lingerie itself, it was some-thing of a Vanilla Weekend. Every time I smell vanilla nowadays, I get to thinking."

Marsha of Eagan: "After my baby was born—my first little boy, Alex—the nurse came in, and she said: 'Before I bathe your baby, before I shampoo his hair, I want you to smell him. I want you to smell that smell of a newborn baby.'

"And I smelled him, and it was the most wonderful smell ever. I mean, it was ... it was earthy ... I can't even describe it ... it was a *primitive* smell, and I just locked into that little boy. It was so wonderful. I'd urge women who are pregnant to smell their newborn children, because you'll never get that wonderful, earthy smell back again.

"When people talk about the smell of a new baby—with the baby powder and the lotion and all that—I just think: There's nothing better than the *real* smell of a brand-new baby."

Ginny of Falcon Heights: "Whenever I smell Nivea cream, it brings me back to 13 years ago, to a warm summer night, rocking in the chair, with a breeze blowing in the window, nursing my freshly bathed baby. It's just such a warm, wonderful memory; it makes me weak."

Painless Mike of Woodbury: "Every time I smell my hands after splitting fire-wood, I'm reminded of my grandfather. It's a great smell: oak and a little honest work. It smells better than most colognes. And every time I smell dead minnows, beer cans and gasoline, I think of my other grandfather and all those great summer afternoons in his boat, fishing."

Charly of St. Paul: "Every time I smell an Easter lily, I think of my grandma, who used to wear some sort of lily-of-the-valley perfume. It makes me realize how much I miss her. And whenever I smell a cherry Life Saver, it makes me think of my first kiss. Yup, we were both suckin' on cherry Life Savers."

Connie of Stillwater: "Every time I smell Lilac Vegetal after-shave, I melt. I was the only girl, with three brothers, and I used to sit on the pot and watch my daddy shave. When he was all done, he'd slap on some Lilac Vegetal after-shave, and he'd reach down and slap a little on both my cheeks.

"I'm reminded of that often because now my husband wears it, knowing the effect it has on me. Every time I smell it on him, I say: 'Oooooh, you smell just like my daddy.' And now, sometimes, he slaps it on our son, and of course I tell him: 'Oooooh, you smell just like your daddy.' Pretty soon, my daughter Laura's gonna be 2, and hopefully we'll continue the tradition with her."

Yardman of Fridley: "Every time I smell Copenhagen snuff, I think of my dad and the warm summer days on the porch when he'd be chewing Copenhagen, and we'd sit in his lap and read stories. To this day, he still chews it; to this day, my mom stills yells at him for chewing it. They've been married for 45 years."

Marian of Inver Grove Heights: "Yesterday, it was kinda cold and fall-like, and I smelled a cigar, and it reminded me: Back when I was a little kid, my father always used to sit down on Saturday afternoon and smoke his cigars. He would listen to the Gophers' football game, and he would draw on a piece of paper and move the football back and forth as they would progress, or regress. But when I smelled that cigar yesterday, it brought back all the memories of when I was a little kid and I used to sit in his lap and watch him smoke that cigar and listen to the Gophers. Long time ago. TV wasn't even in."

Crazy Connie of Hastings: "The smell of new-mown hay always reminds me of my father. Long after we had tractors, my father liked to mow the hay with the team of horses, Sally and Dan. They were big old things, Percherons, and whenever I smell new-mown hay or grass, I can see Daddy out on the old mower, with Sally and Dan in the harness. Sally was a real easy-goin' horse, and Dan was kinda feisty. He would always speed up as he got closer to being done with the work, 'cause he knew he was ready to head to the barn."

Throw the cow over the fence some hay! Beginning with **Mommy** of White Bear Lake ("I used to have a real name; it's just been so long since I've heard it; we'll go by 'Mommy'"): "My grandpa always said you could tell a good German from Wisconsin because they always turn their sentences around. You know, something like switching the object with the prepositional phrase, as in 'Throw the cow over the fence some hay.'

"Well, my step-grandmother—a good German from Steubenville, Ohio, by the way—came to visit one summer and, on our way to a picnic, reminded us to take a few lawn chairs in case there was no place to sit in the trunk.

"She's the same woman who, when asked if she needed a ride home, said: 'No, that's OK. Ralph will run me over with the truck.'"

Norse Steve of Forest Lake Township: "In an article Friday—not in your paper—about female financial traders in Britain, there's a sentence that goes: 'Female recruits must routinely shrug off suggestive remarks and leering requests to show their breasts or remove their panties from male colleagues.'

"I thought that was ridiculous—but after all, it *is* Britain."

Crazy Aunt Helen of St. Paul: "I'm looking at the 'Parenting' column in your paper: 'In her bedroom at my house, my daughter has a photograph of our two cats pinned to the side of her night table.' Yowwwww!"

T-Bone of Andover: "There's a woman I went to school with, and she claims that her mother would call the family to the dinner table in this way: 'Your father's already half-eaten! Come to the table and eat yourselves!'"

We are what we eat (and drink): And isn't *that* a frightening thought—except, of course, to **The Snackmeister** of St. Paul: "I was aghast the other day at the grocery store when, mixed among the Ho Ho's and Ding Dongs, I saw a Hostess Oat Bran Muffin. This from the company that's famous for bringing us Twinkies and Fruit Pies and Sno Balls!

"I was really getting worried that the Nutrition Police were getting out of control. But my faith was restored today. I saw an item in a magazine that listed the top five food items by total value of grocery-store sales in the United States: No. 1: Coke. No. 2: Pepsi. No. 3: Processed cheese. No. 4: Campbell's soups. No. 5: Budweiser.

"Is this a great country, or what?"

Department of good questions: Bemusements:

Dr. Ogre: "I was just talkin' to somebody about frog legs, and I asked 'em why they ate 'em, and they said: 'They taste just like chicken. They're good.' Well, if that's the case, why don't you just eat chicken legs? If you're eating frog to taste like chicken, why not just eat chicken to taste like chicken?"

Ms. Linda of Eagan: "A few days ago, I was driving along Eagan's scenic Cliff Road when I passed the local water-treatment facility. What caught my eye was this: There is, in front of the water-treatment facility, a little circle of benches—courtyard-style, almost like a picnic area—with a little water fountain in the middle.

"Are people out there saying to each other: 'Honey! It's a beautiful day! We've had so little time together. How 'bout a little cheese and vino down at the Eagan water-treatment facility?'

"Maybe so, but I'm not going to be drinking out of the water-treatment water fountain any time soon."

Spooge of Oak Park Heights ("boasting the greatest maximum-security prison in the United States"): "I have a gripe—or a displeasure. You guys are professionals; you can decide. *[BULLETIN BOARD NOTES: Feel free to laugh out loud here; we did.]*

"It's when I go into a public restroom—be it at a sporting event, a mall, or even where I work, which is a large place. I'll go in and do my business, and there's eight or 10 or even 20 stalls in there. And lo and behold, somebody else comes in—and instead of going three or four or 10 stalls away from me, they've gotta come and sit *right next to me* to do *their* business.

"What's the deal? Are they lonely?"

Fear and trembling: From **Rebecca** of St. Paul: "I've got an unreasonable fear: I think it's Pee Shyness, or something—because every time that I go into a public bathroom, I sit down on the porcelain throne and try to pee . . . but if somebody comes in and sits down next to me, and there's silence in the room, I can't go to the bathroom. I don't know why—because I know this person cannot see my face, and they have no idea who I am.

"Oftentimes, I'll find that the other person just sits there with her pants or her skirt around their ankles, and they don't pee, either! I think this is a common fear."

Mary J. of White Bear Lake: "When I get up in the morning, I'm afraid when I come downstairs that I'm going to find an alien from outer space, dead, on my living-room couch.

"I don't know what to do about that. Maybe you could help me out."

BULLETIN BOARD REPLIES: Sorry, but we're not qualified. We're not certain anyone is.

Kurt of St. Paul: "My simple pleasure is waking up in the morning and finding out that the dead alien on my couch did my dishes before he passed away. Aliens—you've just gotta love 'em."

P.Y. of St. Paul: "One day, my ex-husband (before he was an 'ex') told me about a fear that he couldn't get over. He was afraid that when he stuck his hand in the mailbox to get the mail, another hand from inside the box would grab him and try to pull him in. I told him that was the most ridiculous thing I ever heard. *[BULLETIN BOARD NOTES: Keep in mind that this is the same woman who wrote the next paragraph.]* But ever since, I feel uneasy about sticking my hand inside the mailbox without first looking inside, in case 'something' is there.

"Another one of my weird worries: I just recently have owned a garage, for the first time in my life. Every time I go to the garage, before opening the door, I have an uneasy feeling that the whole place is covered with millions and millions of woodticks. They are crawling all over each other and cover everything: ceiling, floor and walls. The car is just a shimmering, crawling silhouette. Then, they get on my feet and start up my legs. I try and try to brush them off, but they stick like barnacles. Then, my hands are covered, and they spread over my body. I'm encrusted like an armadillo and can't move. Finally, I fall down and become part of this horrible undulating woodtick-sea.

"It sounds like a nightmare, but I never dreamed it. It's just a stupid irrational fear. I feel so relieved each time I open the garage door and there's no woodticks inside."

John of Woodbury: "I can't get on escalators with people—especially obese people. Here's why:

"Where I work, the escalators are really narrow. One day, as I was going down, I heard this wheezing right behind me. There was this extra-large woman having a major coughing attack. A really morbid thought occurred to me: Assuming she fell, she'd land on top of me—and pretty much stay there. There we'd be, this fleshy person holding me down as I met my fate at the escalator-turned-meat-slicer, slowly descending to death. Not a pretty picture.

"Now, before you corpulent citizens phone in your outrage: This is an *irrational* fear. I do know better. But that image of turning into cold cuts always gets the best of my sensibility."

Muggsy of West St. Paul: "I'm a corpulent person who has an irrational fear of falling on a skinny little bony person and being skewered like a shish kebab."

M.P. of Woodbury: "One of my unreasonable fears: going to a drinking fountain. I have to look behind me because I'm afraid that when I go down to take a drink, someone's gonna come and mash my face right into the spigot there."

Andrew of St. Paul: "It happens whenever I'm in a department store or a restaurant or the gas station, and I go up to pay with my credit card, and they run the card through the machine, and you're standing there for the next 15, 20 seconds while this machine is calling some weird place like Hoboken, N.J., or New York City or who-knows-where, and you're standing there waiting for this machine to approve you, and I have this fear that the machine is going to print HA-HA-HA-HA-HA across the screen."

Shelly of Woodbury: "I'm an X-ray tech, and I work the midnight shift, and sometimes we have to go down to the morgue to take X-rays of . . . well, dead people. Now, I know these guys and ladies are dead; doctors have decided they're dead, and they know dead. But my most unreasonable fear is that one day when I'm putting a film under some dead guy's head to take a picture of his skull, he's going to flip his eyes open, grab my wrist, and scream at me: *'I'm . . . not . . . dead!'*

"And that'll do it; I'm gonna have to either find a different job, clean my pants, or just drop dead on the spot."

Eileen's Sister of St. Paul: "I have this fear that whenever I open my trunk for the carry-out boy to put the groceries in, there will be a dead body in there. There's no *reason* there should be a dead body in there, but I feel relieved just the same."

M.G. of St. Paul: "My unreasonable fear is walking through a parking lot, when you walk between two cars facing each other; I'm afraid they're gonna somehow start up and smash my kneecaps.

Amy of Fridley: "I have an unreasonable fear: It's when I go to start my car, that it'll blow up—like in one of those Charles Bronson movies. It's strange, but sometimes I get that feeling when I turn the key that it just might go KA-BOOM!"

Roxie of South St. Paul: "I have an ungodly fear. When I'm painting a room and I have to take the electrical socket covers off, I'm always afraid when I go to put the screwdriver on the screw that the screwdriver's gonna slip off and go into the socket and I'll get electrocuted. Thanks. Have a nice day."

Amy of Minneapolis: "My strange fear is clowns. I've been afraid of clowns ever since I had a horrible dream when I was 4 that Ronald McDonald kidnapped me on a bus. I suppose this is kind of irrational, and this doesn't overtake my life or anything and make me a babbling fool, but if I were alone on a dark street and a pack of clowns approached me, I would cross the street to avoid them."

Brian A. of White Bear Lake: "I was about 2 or 3, and I got a G.I. Joe for Christmas—and it just scared the hell out of me. My sister picked up on that right away, so she took the thing—and I'd always find it hiding in my dresser drawers, or else I'd be taking a nap and see G.I. Joe on the outside, tapping on the window.

"I still feel a little uncomfortable around G.I. Joes—*and* my sister."

Celeste of Burnsville: "Last Thursday, my mother was with me during the rainstorm, and she shared with me one of her most irrational fears. She's 75 years old—well, she will be 75 this year—and she told me that she has always been afraid that during a storm, a tornado will come and pick her house up and blow it across the lake that she lives on, and she'll fall out and fall into the lake and drown!

"Now, I wish that she had never told me that, because last night during the thunderstorm, I woke up—and I happen to live alongside a lake, too—and I couldn't stop thinking about what she had said. Now I'm afraid that that might happen to me."

BULLETIN BOARD ADVISES: Two words: swimming lessons. One word: psychotherapy.

Cautious of St. Paul: "One of my constant fears is that my underpants will fall down in public someday. This dates back 30 years, to when my very elderly high-school English teacher lost her drawers in class. She was standing there lecturing, and all of a sudden, down around her ankles was this mass of peach-colored fabric. Her bloomers had bit the dust! No joke.

"Well! She gingerly stepped out of them, bent over, picked them up, walked over to her desk, opened the drawer, threw them in, shut the drawer and stood there, red-faced, while the class absolutely died. We were rolling in the aisles—and in a flash, the news was all over the school. Poor woman.

"To this day, whenever I wear a skirt or a dress, I don't feel safe unless I've got my underwear hooked with a safety pin."

K.S. of Minneapolis (echoed, in essence, by **Becky** of St. Paul—who concluded: "I know you guys feel the same way, too"): "I'm afraid everybody I've ever known who has died is watching me whenever I'm doing something immoral or not quite right. Not that I'm doing anything wrong, but . . . oh, I don't know . . . *sex,* you know. Kinda watching me while I'm doing that. That bothers me."

Aimee of the Midway: "My unreasonable fear is brushing my teeth in the morning. Don't you ever wonder if there's bugs or something crawling over your toothbrush? Gross."

Lisa of Mendota Heights: "Before I tell you about this fear, I think I had better explain its origin:

"A couple of years ago, a friend told me about two acquaintances of hers who had traveled to Jamaica. While on this vacation, the couple returned from breakfast one day to find that their hotel room had been ransacked. Nothing valuable had been stolen; mostly, stuff had just been thrown around the room.

"When they got home and developed the film from their trip, however, they came across some *very* unusual pictures, which the vandals had taken using the couple's camera. In several of the photographs, it was obvious that one of the vandals had placed the travelers' toothbrushes in his . . . um, butt.

"The couple had, most unfortunately, continued to use these toothbrushes *after* the hotel room break-in and until they saw the photos. *[BULLETIN BOARD NOTES: Then they stopped.]*

"I later learned that this story was just that: a 'story,' made up by an obviously twisted mind. But it was too late for me; the fear had already been planted in my brain. So now, whenever I travel (or even if I need maintenance work or something done in my apartment, and I'm not going to be there), I feel compelled to hide my toothbrush for fear that it will otherwise end up in someone's butt. (And when I say 'hide,' I mean that Sherlock Holmes, Ellery Queen, Jessica Fletcher and 10 blood-hounds together couldn't find the thing if they had all day.)

"When I tell my friends, even the ones who were present at the original telling of the 'Jamaica story,' about my toothbrush fear, they look at me as though I have lost my mind. Perhaps I have, but at least I know that *my* toothbrush is safe at all times."

Deanne of Rosemount: "Being that I'm an ex-dental assistant, and having seen grown men and women cry and even faint, and having seen others head for the door when they saw the dentist coming into the room, I developed a fear of my own—so I decided that I would work for an oral-surgery group. This way, while I was helping to work on the patients, they were peacefully asleep and didn't feel a thing.

"With this one group I used to work for, believe it or not, we used to play this game: If any of the assistants caught the teeth as they came sailing out of the mouth, we gained points—which were redeemable for muffins on Friday. I ate lots of muffins.

"And as for going to the dentist: I'd rather pass out first. I brush, floss, rinse three times a day—and, thankfully, sleep peacefully."

Games people play: Says **The Husband** of St. Paul: "My wife and I have a new game now. It's even more fun than Rug or Not a Rug [in which the object is to guess whether a man's hair is all his own].

"I suppose this is a game that everybody who starts looking for a house to buy learns to play. We call it: What's Wrong With *This* One?

"You look through the homes-for-sale ads in the newspaper, and you come across one that says: 'Large, 4-bedroom, 3-bath. New carpeting throughout. Lower-level walkout to ⅓-acre private back yard.' And then the price: $95,000.

"What's wrong with that one? Is it (a) next door to a crack house; (b) missing a roof; (c) blessed with a toxic-waste dump in the back yard; or (d) looking right down Runway 3 of the Minneapolis/St. Paul airport?"

'Tis the season? Reported **Debbie** of Inver Grove Heights, on November 8, 1994: "I was driving by a cemetery on Friday, and they're already putting the Christmas wreaths up on the graves. I thought: Even when you're *dead*, you can't get away from someone tryin' to rush the season on you."

Say "Cheese!" Heck, say *anything!* From the frontiers of documentary photography comes this dispatch by the deeply amused **Julie** of St. Paul: "I was talking to this old lady where I work, and she just started volunteering information—and wanted to show me a picture of her husband, who happened to be deceased. She pulled out her wallet—and, sure enough, showed me pictures of him in his *coffin!*"

Ashes to ashes: On the lighter side of cremation:

The Odd Fellow of North Branch remembers a gentleman who "wanted his ashes scattered over his favorite lake. Following his death, he was so reduced, and his spouse made arrangements with a pilot.

"As they were flying over the lake to scatter the ashes, the pilot told the lady to open the window. She did so—and the wind blew the ashes all over the cabin of the airplane.

"Understand the poor devil ended up in a vacuum cleaner."

Sue of Hastings: "I've always said I wanted to be cremated and put into an hourglass. I don't want to just lie there for eternity; I want someone to pick me up and roll me over once in a while."

Patrick of Woodbury: "When I die, I want to be cremated—and my ashes, put in an Etch-a-Sketch."

Patricia of St. Paul tells of a dream she'd had: "I was talking to my three daughters, and we were planning my demise. In the dream, I told my daughters that I wanted to be cremated, and they asked me: What should they do with my ashes? In a very matter-of-fact way, I told 'em: 'Divide them up, sprinkle them on your cereal, and eat me for breakfast.'"

Jon of Highland Park: "I feel that cemeteries are a tremendous waste of land. If everyone who dies gets buried, someday cemeteries will take over the landscape. I plan to be cremated—and instead of being stuck inside a non-biodegradable casket and buried under six feet of dirt, I have decided that whatever remains of my bodily matter should reenter the nutrient cycle, as it was intended.

"Therefore, my wishes are to have my ashes placed in a hole, and then to have a white pine planted on top of my remains. As the tree grows, the roots will absorb what was once me and incorporate my molecules into its cells. I might reside in the branches of this majestic tree for a hundred years or more.

"And who knows? Someday I may even end up—once again—as a stud in someone's house."

BULLETIN BOARD NOTES: We have never been more surprised to stumble upon a punch line.

A day in the life: From **The West Side Grouch,** on Election Day: "I just came down to breakfast today and found a list. My wife always makes out these lists, and the last three items on her list for today are:

"Clean out the cat box.

"Vote.

"Throw out the garbage."

The Lowest Common Consumer: Notes from the Department of Duh:

Ms. Linda of Eagan: "I went out today and bought a new Day Runner—the little organizer book with the different kinds of calendars, and the address book, and the little place to put your spare house key, and the special place for everything.

"I love these books, because they give you this wonderful false sense of control. It's a great prop! You can look in it when someone asks you to do something—and pretend you have a social life. You can write things down in it to delude yourself into thinking you're going to do them. It's like you think: 'Hey, I need to make that dentist appointment!' So you look in your little book, and there it is: 'Make dentist appointment.' And you think: 'No problem. I am *on* it.'

"So, anyway, I bought a new one today, and I opened it—and tucked in the front was an owner's manual. Honest! It says: 'Owner's Manual.' This surprised me, because I would have thought that even with my limited technological know-how, this would be a machine I could operate without assistance of any kind.

"Are they worried that I'm really confused? Do they think that I'm opening the Velcro flap, putting bread in, and wondering why toast doesn't come out?

"It turns out that the Owner's Manual contains helpful tips—such as: 'The four-year calendar is useful for checking dates and long-range plans.' I'm doing that V8 forehead-slap, thinking: 'I was *wondering* what that was for.'

"I think I've just about mastered it now."

Hiflyer of Bayport: "As I was doing my heavy-duty intellectual reading this morning (including Bulletin Board), I noticed the front of the Kellogg's Crispix cereal box. Gosh, in the picture on the front of the box, the spoon is as big as an Army mess-line serving spoon—and each piece of cereal is as big as my fist.

"Does the box really need the caption 'ENLARGED TO SHOW TEXTURE'? Has truth in advertising gone too far?"

Doctor Friendly of St. Paul: "For some reason, I read the warning on the side of some D-cell batteries that I just bought. Among other things, it says: 'If swallowed or lodged in ear or nose, see doctor.'

"Frankly, if you can lodge a D-cell battery in your ear or nose, you shouldn't be seeing *me;* you should be seeing a promoter."

The Queen of the Tin Palace: "My friend and I went to northern Wisconsin bass fishing over Labor Day weekend.

"Because of the really warm weather, the fish weren't biting. So, being the stubborn Finn that I am, I resorted to trying everything in my tackle box. Still no luck.

"The next morning, we stopped at a bait shop where a display of something called Smelly Jelly caught my eye. Upon further investigation, I discovered this is a concoction that you spread on your lure, worm, leech, etc., to attract fish. It came in about 30 flavors—sort of like a Baskin-Robbins for our gilled friends. They had Eau de Corn, Salmon Roe, Mayfly Madness; I chose Crayfish Anise because I know the bass really like the little buggers.

"We get out on the lake; I open the box, take out the little tube, unscrew the lid—and the smell about knocks me over! Like a million dead and rotting shrimp. Right there on the jar, in bold, black letters, I see: 'NOT FOR HUMAN CONSUMPTION.'

"Dang! And I was just reaching for the box of Ritz crackers."

The Husband of St. Paul: "We just got a new dishwasher. One of the warnings, in a whole page of consumer warnings, is: 'Do not allow children to play in the dishwasher.'

"Hey, you kids! Get out of that dishwasher . . . *right now!* . . . Yes. . . . Yes, it's fine. . . . You can play in the oven."

What's in a name? Says **Patti** of Inver Grove Heights: "I was flipping through some ads and clipping coupons, and I came across an ad for 'Permanent Makeup': eyeliner, lip liner, beauty marks, eyebrows, full lip color, camouflage, electrolysis.'

"The name of the shop is . . . Natural Image."

The ring of tooth: Reports **Sodbuster** of Columbia Heights: "When I had my wisdom teeth pulled, one of 'em came out all in one piece. A friend of mine was a jeweler. He cut the roots off—and it was like a big white stone. He mounted it on a ring for me. It was beautiful.

"And then one day, I was goin' down the road on a motorcycle and a bee flew up my sleeve, and I was shakin' my arm to try to get the bee out of my sleeve—and the next thing I knew, my ring was gone. Could not find it.

"That's a helluva way to lose a tooth."

The road to ruin: From **Little Ann** of Falcon Heights: "My husband and I were driving south on Highway 51 the other day, and I saw this crumpled-up little step stool sitting on the side of the road. I said: 'Oops, somebody lost their stool.'

"We were driving a little bit longer, and my husband said: 'Oops, somebody lost their raccoon.'"

There oughtta be a law! A "modest proposal" from **Bill** of Maplewood: "Let's require all vehicles to be built so that the four-way flashers go on whenever an in-car phone is in use. Seems like a win/win situation: Other drivers are alerted to distracted motorists, and distracted motorists get more of the attention they seem to crave.

"Plus, it wouldn't really matter that the flashers make the turn signals inoperative, because phone-talker drivers never signal, anyway."

Street smarts: Says **John** of Inver Grove Heights: "I was taking a cab from Lake Street in Minneapolis to St. Paul, and I learned that the cab driver had a degree in psychology.

"I said: 'That must be pretty interesting.'

"He said: 'Yeah, it helps me understand why people cut me off in traffic, or are lousy drivers in general.'

"I said: 'Really? Why's that?'

"And he said: 'Because they're jerks.'"

Know thyself: Says **Fred** of Highland Park: "I saw the following sticker in the back of a van in England: 'Designed by a computer. Built by a robot. Driven by a moron.'"

Know thy shoes: From **J.P.** of Oakdale: "I knew it was time for me to get a new pair of work shoes when my folks came for a visit one day and came in the side door where the shoes were, and my dad asked: 'You guys havin' sauerkraut for dinner?'

"I got up and threw 'em out right away."

The many charms of Iowa: From **Mari** of Mounds View: "Today in the Minneapolis paper, there was an advertising insert for Iowa—and on the cover, they've got a picture of . . . a mime! Like people are gonna go to Iowa if that's all they can offer—a mime!"

BULLETIN BOARD REPLIES: Excuse us, sir? Which way is it to Minnesota? Sir? Yeah, you! We're talkin' to you, pal! We wanna get the heck outta here! SAY SOMETHING!

Oh! Canada, eh? Reports **Ann** of Fridley: "My son and husband go to Canada fishing, and they usually come back discussing the 'eh?' at the end of sentences.

"My husband says that's how they named Canada. They didn't know what to name it, so they put all the letters of the alphabet into a bag. They pulled out the 'C' and said 'C, eh?'

"The next letter was 'N, eh?'

"And then 'D, eh?'

"And that's how they named Canada."

Ask Bulletin Board: (1) **James Lola** of Rice Lake, Wis.: "I was watching 'Jeopardy!' the other day. The announcer introduced 'Jeopardy!' as 'America's favorite answer-and-question game show.'

"Must be—but is there another one?"

BULLETIN BOARD REPLIES: We're so sorry, but your question must be in the form of an answer. Next?

(2) **Gooney** of Across the River: "I recently had a disconcerting thought which I can't get out of my mind: It occurred to me that maybe everyone thinks *I* am the weird relative at Christmas dinner. I mean, do weird relatives know who they are?"

BULLETIN BOARD REPLIES: No. That's their charm. Next?

(3) **Judy** of Como Park: "Just feeding my dog, and I see on the label where it says 'Now has a new, meatier taste,' and I'm wonderin' where they find the folks to check it out."

BULLETIN BOARD REPLIES: On major airlines everywhere. Next?

(4) **Dr. Ogre:** "The wonderful woman I'm seeing—the woman with fabulous babernacity, who is, by the way, The Movie Trivia Goddess—took me to see a movie. We went to see *In the Army Now.*

"I wanted some popcorn, but I didn't want as much as they had in the small popcorn, so she said: 'Well, get one of those little kid packs!' And I sorta felt silly, 'cause it was a Little Rascals thing; they give you this cute little pop and this little thing of popcorn—which turned out to be just exactly the right amount.

"And you're also supposed to get a little surprise.

"Well, we're sittin' there in the movie, and I'm eatin' my popcorn and drinkin' the pop—and come to the end of the meal, and there's . . . there's no surprise! No, no, there was absolutely no surprise.

"I mean, I was not happy—not because I didn't get the surprise, 'cause, you know, I figured it'd probably be a Gummi Bear or something, but gosh darn it, if you're going to advertise a surprise, give me the surprise!

"You know, granted, I'm an adult, but I do have a little brother and a little sister who are 2 and 4—and they might enjoy the surprise.

"But no! There was no surprise! Can someone please give me some feedback on this? What was the surprise?

"Pet peeve. Gosh darn it, that was buggin' me."

BULLETIN BOARD GIVES SOME FEEDBACK: Let's review the facts here: They promised a surprise. You expected a surprise. There was no surprise. Surprise! Case closed. Next?

(5) Al B. of Hartland: "If there is more than one answer for each question, how come there are more questions than answers?"

BULLETIN BOARD REPLIES: Do you mind if we answer that with a question?

How do we know for sure? Wonders **Polynomial:** "How do we know for sure that Samuel Pepys' last name was really pronounced *Peeps?*

"After all, this was the 17th century we're talking about. He couldn't very well go on Leno or Letterman and natter on about how he gets so steamed that people are always calling him *Peppys,* when any fool knows it's *Peeps.*

"For some reason, how to pronounce his name is one of those little facts that I have known forever, but the recent letter on the topic got me wondering. Could this be an actual *oral transmission?* And if so, just like in the old game of Telephone, where one person of a group sitting around a table whispers a phrase into her neighbor's ear, who whispers into the next person's ear, and it continues around until it comes back to the starting point wildly distorted, maybe it really started out as *Perps,* or *Pups,* or *Peps . . .* or maybe even *Peppys,* and just got twisted along the way.

"How do we know?"

When cultures collide: From **The Dartman** of Dinkytown: "When I was 10 years old, we had an exchange student living with us who was from Egypt. His name was Hossam.

"Right after my mother had spent a long day waxing and buffing and polishing the parquet floor in the little dining area off of our kitchen, during dinner Hossam elbowed a full, uncapped, gallon bottle of milk off the table. It hit the floor on its side and gushed at least half of its contents across the floor.

"My mom's jaw just dropped—and Hossam was really excited, because he had learned this new English idiom and had the opportunity to use it. He said: 'Well, there's no use crying over spilt milk.'

"My brother and I looked at each other, and we looked at Mom, and I know my brother and I were thinking the same thing: that any minute now, we might just have a dead Egyptian on our hands."

The highfalutin pleasures: From **Doctor Friendly** of St. Paul: "In the office today, I was seeing a woman who is visiting from Japan. She had a problem with her hand, but her English vocabulary was not good enough to come up with the right word to tell me what the problem was—and I couldn't figure it out from her gesticulations.

"When we were both seeming a bit perplexed about how to proceed, her husband whipped out of his shirt pocket a tiny, palm-sized computer. He turned it on and entered a word in Japanese, and on the screen the word 'anesthesia' showed up. Just to make it all the more interesting, he pressed another button, and the voice synthesizer on the computer spoke 'an-es-the-sia!'

"I was pretty sure I understood what she was talking about, now, but 'anesthesia' wasn't quite the word that one would normally use in English. So, to double-check that my understanding was correct, I took it from him and typed in 'N-U-M-B ENTER.'

"The screen lit up with a bunch of Japanese characters, which he showed to his wife. Her face lit up, and she said: 'Yes! Yes! That's it!'"

Bob Woolley of St. Paul: "There's a great little program called Kaboom that you can add to your home computer, so that instead of making ordinary, boring beeps when some event happens, you can put in other, more interesting sounds. I now have my computer set up so that when I insert a disk, I hear Bart Simpson saying 'Eat my shorts!' When I eject a disk, I hear Ronald Reagan saying 'Go ahead, make my day.' And, best of all, when I try to delete something, it warns me, with Ricky Ricardo saying to Lucy: 'Ohhhh, no you dunt.'"

Before the beep: Says **Rob** of Cottage Grove, a student at St. Olaf: "Right now, our answering machine says: 'Hi! You've reached Rob and Aaron's room. This is not the answering machine; the answering machine is broken right now. This is the refrigerator. If you could leave a message, I'll just stick it to myself somewhere.'"

Carl of Bayport: "Our phone message says: 'Hello! You've reached our residence. Due to the recent change to Daylight Savings Time, we're a little bit confused—so we answered your call an hour ago. Please leave your name and number after the tone, and we'll get back to you as soon as we get things straightened out.'"

Darrell Pangborn of Inver Grove Heights: "I think mine's kinda neat. It says: 'For a transcript of this recording, please leave your name and number.'"

After the beep: From **Deb** of White Bear Lake: "I work for Northwest Airlines, in the reservations department, and in bad weather I get pulled to work on a desk called Canceled or Delayed Flights. So now, picture this: We've got bad weather; we've got a plane that's supposed to leave Minneapolis for Los Angeles at 5 P.M.; it's noon. We've got 200 people to call, so we start dialing like mad.

"What do we get? We get people's answering machines. We get things like: 'Hi! It's the Joneses! I'm Jenny! . . . I'm John! . . . I'm Julie! . . . And this is the baby, Janey! And this is our dog, Jack.' Bark, bark—and we have to wait through all this to tell people: 'There's a 3 o'clock flight. We've canceled the 5 o'clock, but there's a 3 o'clock.'

"We get answering machine after answering machine, and they're long and they're tedious. The worst one was the lady who said: 'I'm sorry I'm indisposed right now, but I'll be available in a minute'—and then we heard the toilet flush.

"One of the funniest ones was the lady who said: 'I'M SORRY! I CAN'T HEAR YOU! PLEASE CALL ME BACK!'—and it was a plane landing. It was really very funny; we all had to call and listen to that."

Betty Boop of Blaine: "I can't believe the stupid messages people leave on their answering machine, and I'm sick of 'em—so now, when I get a long-winded message, all I do is say: 'Please stay on the line for Publishers' Clearing House.'"

Howdy, mayhem: From **Dan** of Rosemount: "When you're walking through the airport, at the little security station, I've always wanted to wear something that's gonna make the alarm go off—maybe a heavy belt buckle—and then, just before they have a chance to pull me over and say 'Put the contents of your pockets on this tray,' I'd like to just grab my bag off of the X-ray machine, tear down the runway and scream, 'You'll never take me alive! Never!'—just to see what kind of attention we could get."

BULLETIN BOARD NOTES: Do not read this item aloud (or even think about it—just to be safe) as you're passing through those security gates, unless you want more attention than you've ever cared to get.

The merry pranksters: From **Leonard Smalls:** "I had a friend who was an employee at the international airport who got reprimanded because he'd get on the intercom late at night and say: 'Attention, please. At this time, we'd like to ask all Northwest passengers who have not done so to please do so immediately.'"

The unkindness of strangers: Here's a call that reached us in the last week of March 1993, from a young St. Paulite named **Jean:** "I was at Rainbow the other day, shopping, and a lady came up to me and said: 'You look like my daughter!'

"I said: 'Oh, really?'

"She said: 'I sure do miss my daughter. Would you call me Mom?'

"I said: 'Uhhhhh . . . I really can't right now.'

"'Oh, please, please, please,' she said, 'would you call me Mom just one time?'

"And I was kinda . . . 'Bye, Mom!'—and ran down the aisle.

"I went to check out, and there she was—two people in front of me in line. When it was my turn to pay, the lady looked at me and said: 'Oh, your mom said *you'd* pay for the groceries.'

"And I said: 'That's not my mom'—and I told her everything that the lady had said.

"She said: 'You'd better go out to the parking lot and get her!'

"So I ran out to the parking lot, and she was just going into the cart corral, and I pulled on her leg—just like I'm pulling yours.

"April Fool!"

'Tweren't necessarily so: From **Mary** of Blaine: "When I was a kid, I knew three men who were in the Rotary Club: my grandfather, my uncle and a family friend—and they all, by coincidence, had an artificial leg. For years and years, I thought that Rotary was a club for men with only one leg."

Rules to semi-live by: From **Walter** of Apple Valley: "I'll never pull off more than three squares of toilet paper at any given time. I figure you can do the job with a little bit, and it really bugs me when my wife or my son pull off more than that."

BULLETIN BOARD MUSES: We can only speculate that Walter once persuaded his family to abide by his rule—until Walter insisted that they shake on the deal.

Said **The Bogey Man** of Anoka, "a true conservationist": "Walter could save even more by using both sides of 1½ sheets."

The second time around: From **Queen Bee** of Lino Lakes: "Talk about recycling! I reuse my chewin' gum! When it loses its taste, I put it on the end of an 18-inch crochet hook and pick up lint off my bedroom carpet with it.

"I'm in a wheelchair, so it saves me from fightin' with the vacuum cleaner more than once a week. I use that same crochet hook to put my slippers on, as I can't reach my feet.

"It just goes to show you that necessity *is* the mother of invention."

What is love? Says **Bashful** of Burnsville: "Never having experienced the mad, passionate, heart-clinging, head-dizzying euphoria of Love, I looked into my lover's eyes today, across the small restaurant table—there with the light shining off his balding pate, his thin-lipped, chipped-tooth grin smirking behind his new, $250 no-line bifocals, and I declared, out loud: 'I don't see my soul shining out of your eyes.'

"And we both cracked up in hysterical giggling.

"I said: 'I see bloodshot eyeballs.' He said it was probably the wrong angle of the reflection of his eyeglasses.

"Love is *really* when you're willing to clean up after them when they're sick, and going to work for the past 10 years to allow them to seek their dream of being self-employed (which, as most people know, is not the same as earning a living). After 25 years of marriage, love is sacrifice, support, companionship and romance.

"That is: in it for the long haul."

Gypsi of New Brighton: "You'll know it when it happens. It's kind of like being in labor. That's what I told my friend Nicole [who gave birth to Ashley on March 1, 1994, with Gypsi assisting]: When it's the real thing, you'll know it.

"It's wonderful, and it's painful, and it's exciting, and it's anxiety-ridden—all at the same time. It *is* a lot like labor. Wow!"

BULLETIN BOARD MUSES: And one more thing: There's a time to push, and a time not to push—and if you know which is which, you'll be a lot happier along the way.

The things we do for love: Says **Mary** of Mahtomedi: "I knew I was a mom when I found myself eating a sandwich with one hand and cleaning up vomit with the other, and it didn't even bother me."

Poetic justice: Says **A Teacher:** "We were talking about our kids at school, and how they play with hamsters, and the school psychologist—this wonderful woman—said that the only way she can stand to watch children play with hamsters is that she looks at these hamsters and thinks: 'Well, maybe they were child abusers in the last life.'

"If you've ever had a hamster and a 6-year-old, you'll understand."

Requiem for a lightweight: Says **Merlyn** of St. Paul: "Another fall ritual begins: Each warm fall afternoon, at the warehouse where I work, I throw open the windows to enjoy the breeze—and in buzzes a mud dauber. I don't know if this is what they're *really* called, but that's what I call the bees with the long tails who inhabit the exterior brick and mortar of my building.

"The first time one entered, I panicked—but now, I know these are the old guys. They've lived for a season outside my window and are looking for a nice warm place to die. Drawn to my fluorescent lights, they buzz as they fly, slowly, back and forth under the fixtures. It's almost like those people who have near-death experiences who say they're drawn to the light at the end of the tunnel. My fluorescents are their light.

"The morning after they enter, they're dead. I find their spent bodies on the floor of my place.

"I've come to think of this as The Funeral Ceremony of the Mud Dauber—a harbinger of the fall, as predictable as frost or falling leaves."

Day for night: From **R.J.** of Hammond, Wis.: "Normally, I grumble about Daylight Saving Time for a while when it first comes—as I just hate getting up in the dark, and I deeply resent the loss of even one hour of much-needed sleep.

"But this morning was different. I went out to do chores shortly after 5. The garage cat shot outside as I opened the back door, and a bunny in the back yard streaked for cover. It was just such a treat to watch the night merge with the dawn and then be melted away by it.

"It was so still outside, and though there was frost on everything, the ground was still somewhat soft underfoot. The quiet sounds of the cows chewing their cuds were soon replaced by the horses' rustling their hay and the young stock getting up and stretching and groaning and jostling for their grain.

"An owl called repeatedly to his lady friend, who answered in a higher voice. (I don't *really* know which was which.) A big yellow crescent moon hung over the lightening eastern sky, and that changed from midnight-blue to a dusky purple to an ever-deepening rose color as I worked.

"The killdeer, with their frantic cries, woke up first, in their usual utter confusion. (Those poor dumb birds must spend 90 percent of their lives in chaos.) The robins were next—first calling with strident chirps, and then gradually beginning their lovely morning trills. Pheasants began clucking out in the fields. The owls fell silent, and the red-winged blackbirds and the song sparrows and all of the others began greeting the day.

"Sounds kind of silly, but just pausing to watch and listen—and see something that I wouldn't have seen without Daylight Saving Time—was just a neat present to myself this morning."

Now I pray me down to sleep: From **RCA Walt** of Apple Valley: "I'm an ordained minister—and when I was in seminary, part of our training, of course, was to practice preaching. *[BULLETIN BOARD WONDERS: How many thousands of times do you suppose seminarians have joked among themselves about practicing what they preach?]* In that class, we had to speak in front of a group of other students, and they also videotaped our sermons—so we could watch it and find any ways to improve.

"I decided one day that I would watch the videotape of myself preaching, and I put it in the machine and sat down to take a look . . . and promptly fell asleep. I woke up sometime later, long after the tape had run out, and just started laughing at myself. I remember that story whenever I need to keep from taking myself too seriously."

Three little words: A pair of very fine examples of verbal economy, from **Bev** of Hudson, Wis.: "I have two most beautiful phrases: 'Your baby's perfect'—and from my own personal experience: 'It is benign.'"

Bad haiku: Three lines at a time/Syllables: Five, seven, five/Very, very strange:
(1) **Pippi** of North Branch: "He sits there—*reading!*
"I'm dancing in the hallway.
"'You 'bout done in there?'"
(2) **Oops, Sorry:** "Intestinal gas!
"Gazpacho and garbanzos.
"I should know better."
(3) **The Clover Kicker**—with a found Bad Haiku: "Push button. Rub hands
"Slowly under warm air. Stops
"Automatic'ly."

What *is* that thing? Here's **Norm** of Minneapolis, remembering his first day of ground school: "The instructor got up in front of the class, and he showed us a drawing of a single-engine airplane, and he asked us what that little twirly thing was at the front of the airplane. A few of us ventured some guesses; we said it was a propeller, or an air screw, or something like that.

"He shook his head at every one of those things. Finally we gave up, and he said: 'Well, you know what it really is? It's a fan to cool the pilot.'

"We laughed a little bit at that, and he says: 'You don't believe me, huh? Just wait 'til it quits turnin', and see how quick you start to sweat.'"

Who *are* those guys? Here's **Still Single** of the East Side: "I was at this softball game last Sunday night. I was sitting in the stands by third base.

"The other team was up to bat. I didn't know the name of the batter—but, well, I didn't feel so bad, because neither did his coach.

"He yelled out, trying to encourage him: 'Go, Brian . . . or Matt . . . or whoever the hell you are!'"

Where *is* he? From **Theresa** of St. Paul: "One of my cousins was married to an FBI agent. He was involved in investigating Jimmy Hoffa's disappearance. In the course of the investigation, he ended up in San Bernardino, California, where he visited my aunt and uncle and beloved Irish grandmother. When the subject of Hoffa came up, my grandmother announced briskly that she knew exactly where he was.

"'You do?' said the agent.

"'Yes,' answered my grandmother, smiling sweetly. 'He's in hell, dear.'"

Could, like, you, like, check again? Writes **Janet** of Summit Avenue: "A friend was telling me about a radio program that dealt with a topic germane to Generation X. Ellen was amazed at how the X'ers being interviewed seemed incapable of speaking an entire sentence, or even two or three words in a row, without using 'like': 'It was, like, unbelievable, how often, like, you know, they said "like."'

"This led me to relate to her a recent encounter I had across the counter of my local video-rental store. I knew that *Like Water for Chocolate* had been released on video and wanted to know if this store had a copy. The conversation went something like this:

"**Me:** 'Hi. Do you have *Like Water for Chocolate?*'

"**X'er:** 'Just a second. I'll check. No, it's, like, not here.'

"**Me:** 'Are you sure?'

"**X'er:** 'Yeah, there's, like, nothing even close to that.'

"**Me:** 'Can you check again? It's *Like Water for Chocolate.*'

"**X'er:** 'There's, like, no movies that start with "Water."'

"**Me:** 'The movie is *Like Water for Chocolate.* It's under *L*, not *W.*'

"**X'er:** 'Really? *Like Water for Chocolate?*'

"**Me:** 'Like, really!'"

Annals of self-repudiation: Says an **anonymous woman:** "My 15-year-old son is filling out a job application, and it asks about special qualifications for the position. He wanted to know if it would be appropriate for him to put 'Honor Roll Student.'

"I said: 'Yeah. That'd be a good idea.'

"And then he asks me: 'Is honor spelled H-O-N-O-R?'"

The terrorists: Says **Jeff** of St. Paul: "I want to give you a definition of Sheer Terror. I'm sitting in my dentist's chair yesterday morning, from 8:30 to 11:30. *Three . . . hours.* I'm getting two crowns, which means filing off the teeth—and in the middle of it, the dentist decides that I need a root canal. Two crowns and a root canal. The bill is going to be $943. And what happens? From behind my back, as I'm lying in the chair with a bib over me, drooling out of my mouth, I hear the dental assistant saying: 'How do you spell cavity? Is it C-A-V-A-T-Y or I-T-Y?' Now, *that's* terror."

What's in a name? Says **Kay** of White Bear Lake: "A friend of mine, years and years ago, taught school up on the Iron Range, in a small town. A boy came to school, and the teacher asked him what his name was, and he said: 'Gooey.' She said: 'My, that's a strange name. How do you spell that?' He said: 'I don't know.'

"The next day, his mother came, and the teacher said: 'That is a strange name your boy has. Where'd you get that name?' And the mother said: 'Out of a book.'

"And the teacher said: 'How do you spell it?'

"And the mother said: 'G-U-Y.'"

Nobody's perfect: One **J.D.** of parts hereabouts sent us the following recent **Correction** from "our county paper": "There were errors in last week's article 'Dog bites three at Hamlet Park.' The person who was named as receiving a citation for allowing the dog to run loose was correct, but she was a 27-year-old woman, not a 38-year-old man. The 10-year-old boy bitten in the hand, was actually 4 years old and was not the grandson of man bitten in the forearm."

J.D. adds: "And maybe it was a different park."

This town's not big enough for both of us, you . . . you skunk: Here's one that **Skippy** of Winona spotted in the "Goodview Police blotter" of a local newspaper: "11:00 P.M.—Citizen complaint of a large skunk around dumpster. Skunk left at officer's request."

BULLETIN BOARD NOTES: And didn't even make a stink about it.

Wanted: Dead or Alive! The Sloppy Joe Gang! From the blotter of **Amy by the Graveyard** of St. Paul: "Recently, I bought a bag of groceries for a party I was throwing—but as I was briefly absent from my car, somebody stole my bag of groceries.

"All they got was about 10 cans of Manwich sauce and a big jar of pickles.

"My advice to everybody in St. Paul is: Keep an eye on your hamburger."

That's pathetic! And **Debbie** of Inver Grove Heights—having just finished filling out her Publishers' Clearing House entry—didn't need to be told so: "I was trying to put all of the little stickers on the right places, and after a few minutes, I laughed—'cause I actually was spending some time deciding which color Jaguar I wanted, and how I wanted my $10 million delivered.

"And I thought: I've *gotta* get a life.

"I'm actually sittin' here *debating* if I want my $10 million delivered in weekly, monthly or yearly payments!"

Ask a silly question . . . : Reports **The Big Sis** of Stillwater: "My little sister was running for Miss New Richmond, and the judges were doing their interviews with all of the candidates, and they asked them what fruit they wanted to be.

"All of the other girls were saying, like: 'A banana—because it's not what's on the outside that counts; it's what's on the inside.' You know, answers that they thought the judges would want to hear.

"And my little sister said: 'A cantaloupe.' And they asked her why, and she said: 'Because it's orange on the inside.'"

Try to remember: From **D.H.** of Lino Lakes: "Way back when, I developed a mnemonic device for *hemorrhage, diarrhea* and *hemorrhoids*—how to keep all of those consonants in the correct order. I realized that they all Really, Really Hurt."

Hmmmmmmmmmm: From **Sue** of Woodbury: "In the '70s, I worked at a local discount store, and they sold a shampoo called Placenta Plus. I always wondered: If they openly advertised the Placenta part of the shampoo, it makes you wonder what the Plus part was."

June of Blaine: "I noticed a book called *Women Who Do Too Much.* It seems to me that if you have time to read a book with that title, you have too much time on your hands."

BULLETIN BOARD MUSES: Next—Women Who Read Too Much.

Open mouth, insert foot: Here's **Babs** of parts east, "on the eve of my due date, hanging on to my sense of humor by a thread": "As I walked through the grocery store with my 4-year-old last week, we got all the way around the store in about 45 minutes—and by the time we got to the deli case, I was feeling a little warm, a little sweaty around the face.

"I looked at the ladies behind the deli counter, which is about chin-high, and asked them if they thought it was a little warm in the store. One of them looked at me and said: 'Perhaps you're going through menopause.'

"I said: 'Wait just a minute.' Stepped five feet back from the counter. She looked down, saw my belly, looked up and said—to make things worse: 'Oh! All I could see was your face.'

"So I'm calling with a there-oughtta-be-a-law about having a 50-year-old face and looking nine months' pregnant. Included in that would be: You shouldn't be able to have any of these conditions at the same time: pimples, pregnancy and gray hair. I'm only 34—and I've got all three.

"I also wanted to give some notes about pregnancy; I've been thinking about these for nine months now and have finally gotten around to calling. I wanted to say: When there's any doubt, the only two things that are appropriate to say to a pregnant woman are 'Congratulations!' and 'You look great!' If in doubt, be quiet and smile."

Famous first words: From **Elaine** of Mendota Heights: "I was preparing supper, and our 9-month-old son was in his high chair. My husband, returning from work, opened the door—and our son put out his arms to his dad and shouted his first word, joyfully: 'Mama!' Took us *weeks* to change his mind."

Uncle Frank of Hastings: "A few years ago, my niece brought her 2-year-old over to our house on his first Halloween. All painted up, he held out his plastic pumpkin to my wife, and she dropped in a couple of pieces of candy. He looked in his pumpkin and then came over and held out the pumpkin toward me. I reached in my pocket and took out my change. I dropped it into his pumpkin.

"Again he looked into the pumpkin, and then he held it toward me and said: 'More money.'

"How is that for a cute first sentence?"

BULLETIN BOARD REPLIES: Well, it may not be quite a sentence—but it's cuter than heck—especially seeing as how he'll likely be saying the same thing to various other authority figures for the rest of his life.

Our living language: A few entries for our dictionary-in-the-making:

June of Blaine: "Ever notice the women/girls with what I call *HBO Hair?* You know, the kind teased and ratted up so high that they are picking up the movie channels?"

Diane Currie Richardson of North St. Paul: "Over 20 years ago, when I was starting my career as a teacher of deaf children, I used to share stories with a college friend, Andi, who was also starting out in the same line of work.

"She was teaching preschoolers—an adorable age replete with special communication challenges. Andi would routinely ask the children what they'd eaten for dinner the night before, using that as an opportunity to teach food vocabulary, among other things.

"One day, a child told her that he'd eaten *window cake* for dinner. As a teacher of deaf children, one feels an extraordinary obligation to make sure all misunderstandings are cleared up, so Andi had no choice but to call the little boy's mother to find out what they'd had for dinner.

"I still prefer his term—*window cake*—for Jell-O."

Peabody of St. Paul: "With Thanksgiving and Christmas coming up, I'd like to coin a new word: *'Do-Goader.'*

"You generally find one or more Do-Goaders at every Thanksgiving or Christmas dinner. Shortly after the meal is served, the Do-Goaders take over: Care for some more turkey? Are you sure? Try the peas and carrots. They're good. Sure? If you don't see something, ask for it. Remember, there's more dark meat out in the kitchen. You've had enough potatoes? Sure?

"On and on this goes throughout the meal, until a person has to be almost rude to keep on saying No Thank You. How much nicer it would be to eat well without being goaded."

Our live-in language: From **Cheryl** of Columbia Heights: "I can't figure out why there isn't a good word for your . . . partner, when you live together.

"You don't want to call him your *lover;* that's tellin' people too much. He's not a *friend*—although that's part of it. We need a nice word to describe . . . your partner, when you live together. And *partner* isn't a good word, either; it sounds like a cowboy word."

The Monster of Tangletown: "My girlfriend's parents refer to me as *Amy's current boyfriend.* That's how I was introduced all day at her sister's open house."

Don of Eagan: "We've tired of *roommate; paramour* is too stilted; *friend* is inadequate. So now we're introducing each other as *my prisoner.*"

Our times: From **Diana** of Mounds Park: "When my two sons were 5 and 7, they were playing with their cousin; she was 6. They had gone upstairs to play House, and a little while later, my older son came down looking rather mad.

"I asked him why he wasn't playing House with the two other kids anymore, and he said: 'They always make me be the ex-husband.'"

Beth of White Bear Lake: "One of my daughters, Rachel, who was about 4 at the time, said she knew the difference between boys and girls. I thought: 'Uh-oh. Here it comes.'

"I said: 'Well, what is it, Rachel?'

"She said: 'Well, girls wear two earrings, and boys only wear one.'"

The Shooter of Mendota Heights: "I was putting my young son to bed with a book one night, and after I finished reading him the book, I said: 'What would you like to be when you grow up? Would you like to be a doctor—like your mother?'

"And he said: 'No.'

"And I said: 'Why not?'

"And he said: 'Because, Dad. Only *girls* are doctors.'"

Egghead of Blaine: "My wife won tickets to the Hootie and the Blowfish concert this summer. It was a fabulous afternoon at the show!

"One of the more interesting items for sale were single condoms packaged in paper matchbook-type covers. We bought one and sent it to a friend, whom I'll call Mike, along with his birthday gifts.

"Mike recently told us that the neighbor kid (not yet a teenager) saw the condom lying on the table and asked innocently enough: 'What's that?' That is when Mike began to sweat out a dilemma. He didn't want to lie or evade the question. Neither did he want to invite a new series of questions best answered by the kid's parents. So Mike told him the simple truth: 'Well, that's a condom.'

"The kid's reaction took Mike completely by surprise. Using his best I-can't-believe-you-think-I'm-still-a-child voice, he said: 'I know *that*. Why does it say "Cover Your Hootie"?'"

Oh, and was her face red! From **A Former Bennie:** "I was a resident assistant in a freshman dorm. While helping the new students move into their rooms, I noticed that one woman was having difficulty assembling her loft. She, her father and I tried—in vain—to force the metal pieces together. As we were about to give up, I said: 'Oh, put a little K-Y on that, and it'll slide right in.' You should have seen the look on his face!

"And mine—when I discovered one of the more conventional uses for K-Y."

Virgins among us: An **anonymous woman,** in reply to a young B. Boarder who'd wondered if anyone ever waited anymore: "Yes, there's some virgins out there getting married. I was a virgin, and my husband was a virgin. And my daughter just got married four weeks ago, and she was a virgin—and supposedly, so was her husband. So there you have it: at least four in the whole state of Minnesota."

BULLETIN BOARD MUSES: There's acres of room for smart-aleck commentary on this particular call, but we'll settle for simply this: Isn't that "supposedly" just priceless?

For men only? A story recorded by **Jeff** of St. Paul (which, when we played it for several male colleagues, prompted immediate and uproarious laughter—but elicited rather tepid and a-few-seconds-too-late appreciation from female listeners): "A couple years ago, a bunch of us were sitting around talking about sex, and I mentioned that I knew this woman who was involved in a *ménage à trois.*

"My brother-in-law got real interested; he said: 'You did? Really!?'

"And I said: 'Yes, I did.'

"And he said: 'Well, did she like it?'

"And I said: 'Yeah, I guess so. She thought that being in bed with two men at the same time was pretty exciting.'

"And he goes: 'Two men? That's *disgusting!*'

"I guess what's good for the goose is not always good for the gander."

For better or for worse: Here's **Linda W.** of Eagan, passing along a joke that her husband told her: "There's two guys, and they're talking, and the one is saying: 'I just celebrated my 35th wedding anniversary, and I've been happily married for all these years.'

"And the other guy says: 'How do you account for this long, successful marriage?'

"And so the guy says: 'I let my wife make all of the small decisions, and I make all of the big decisions, and it just works out.'

"And the other guy says: 'Well, what do you mean? Give me some examples.'

"And the guy says: 'Well, my wife, for instance: She made all of the decisions about where we were gonna live, and the style of our home and decorating, and where we were gonna work, and what careers we were gonna pursue, and how many children we were gonna have, and where they were gonna go to school, and the kind of car we're gonna drive. Things like that.'

"And the other guy says: 'What kind of big decisions did you make?'

"And the guy says: 'There haven't been any yet.'"

Keeping your ears open: Says **J.P.** of Lakeland: "I was just biding my time in the Group Health lobby this afternoon, at the clinic on Plato Avenue, and there's a phone there. I'm sitting there, and this woman makes a phone call, and as she's chatting away, I overhear her say: 'I have a fever of 101.5 degrees. I have a sinus infection. And my stove is broken. And you're asking *me* what's for dinner?'"

What is wrong with SM/SFs? Quite a pair:

Adventure Woman: "I have a gripe: Sometimes I read the Personal Line, and what angers me is that so many men look for a woman who is slim. Here we've got 'slim,' 'slim,' 'petite,' 'petite,' 'petite,' 'slender,' 'slim,' 'slender.' They must want underweight women—which I think is just pretty sick.

"So I wonder: Are we talking matters of attraction or control? How many women list a man's weight in their top criteria?

"And here's the ultimate irony: These men are pigs!"

Jack Straw from Wichita: "Just readin' here about Adventure Woman, and she's got a problem with these men lookin' for these slim gals. She says: 'How many women list a man's weight in their top criteria?'

"So I just turned the page around and looked at the Personal Line this mornin'. It seems like if it ain't 'slim,' it's 'athletic' and 'physically fit' that women demand. Let's see. Here we go: 'physically fit,' 'athletic,' 'athletic,' 'physically fit,' 'athletic,' 'athlete,' 'healthy,' 'healthy,' 'trim' and 'desirably fit.'

"That's just a few of 'em—but, you know, here's the ultimate irony: These women are pigs!"

Faint praise: From an **anonymous woman** of Wisconsin: "It's a good thing I have a sense of humor. I've been married 18 years and have three children—and while my figure is still pretty good, I don't look like I'm 20 years old anymore.

"I recently bought a black Slimsuit—one of those bathing suits with control and uplift in all the right places. As I modeled it for my husband, he cocked his head to one side and grinned, saying: 'That's *amazing!* How do they *do* that?'"

Trina of Isanti: "I'm a teacher, and my students recently were deciding which biographies of great people they would send up in a space capsule, if they had that choice. They took a class vote, and they voted for me! I was so pleasantly surprised, and I felt so good.

"And then Nancy Kerrigan came in a close second."

Short Timer of Barron, Wis.: "A recent reunion took me back 30 years, so to speak, to the friends I grew up with during my first 10 school years.

"A classmate sympathized with me by speculating on my feelings, way back when, at having to move away and leave a school team destined to come within a whisker of a state championship.

"'You,' she exclaimed definitively, 'deserved to be on *our* bench!'

"So much for my fantasy."

Jeff of Woodbury: "The first time I met a woman that I later became very close friends with, I was at a bar with a group of friends. She asked why I didn't have a girlfriend.

"I responded that I guess women just weren't very attracted to me.

"She looked at me and in all sincerity said: 'That's not true. I think you're attractive, and I'm not even that drunk.'"

What's a nice boy like you . . . ? From **L.** of St. Paul: "When I was in my early 20s, me and a bunch of my girlfriends were at a bar, and all night long, guys would come up to the table and ask girls at the table to dance. They'd always ask me last— so when they got to me, I always said no.

"Finally, as the night was gettin' on—at about midnight—another guy came up, and he went right around the table again. Asked me last—and I said to him: 'You know, if you would've asked me first, I would've said yes—but I just don't like to be asked last all the time.'

"So that was that. He went away.

"A little while later, the lights came on; it was bar close time, and we were all shufflin' out, and that same guy came up to me and said: 'Would you like to go to bed with me? I asked you first!'"

1658 of St. Paul: "I'm an MTC bus driver, and one night I had a guy comin' on to me in the bus. He was really weird, and nothing I could say would shake him off.

"Finally, he said: 'Hey! You spend one night with me, and you'll never want to spend a night with another man.'

"And I thought: 'Yeah. You're probably right. One night with you, and I'd swear off men completely.'"

CHAPTER FIVE

Immutable Laws of the Universe

Lionsmane of Minneapolis: "Have you ever noticed that the more a man thinks that he is God's gift to women, the less likely it is that he is?"

Al B. of Hartland: "An unwanted guest never feels unwanted."

W.W.J. of Minneapolis: "When two people sleep together, the person who snores will fall asleep first."

Bob of St. Paul Park: "The only person who likes channel-flipping is the person with the remote."

Murphy of St. Paul: "The week after you rent an old movie from the video store, it will show up—for free—on broadcast television."

Bob Woolley of St. Paul: "If you watch a TV show only twice in one season, the second time you watch it will be a rerun of the episode you saw the first time."

Captain Kirk of Minneapolis: "The time of day when you're sittin' at your desk and you put your hands behind your head and lean back in your chair, tossing paper clips in the air, is the time when your supervisor walks by."

Linda of West St. Paul: "The chance that someone's watching you is directly proportional to the stupidity of your act."

Murphy's Lawyer of Northfield: "The other line always moves faster."

Bill of Hastings: "The other line always moves faster—until you get in it."

Gail of Eagan: "The call you are waiting for will come in as soon as you leave your desk."

Steve of Shoreview: "The moment you take a humongous bite of your food is the same time the phone rings."

Kathy of Cottage Grove: "When nature calls, so does everybody else."

Mr. Mars of St. Paul: "Whenever you tell a waiter that you need just one more minute to make up your mind before they take your order, they disappear for 15 minutes."

Angel of Rosemount: "How many people are left after closing is directly proportional to how bad you want to go home."

MDW of St. Cloud: "Whenever you go through a yellow light really late and feel a little guilty about it, knowing you could and should have stopped, at least one car behind you will also go through."

The Chemist of Como Park: "The number of stoplights where you hit the red is always directly proportional to the amount of time you're running late."

The Graduate of Ham Lake: "The only place you're never going to see a deer on the highway is where it says 'Deer Crossing.'"

Garibaldi of Stillwater: "The mountain-like bump in the road that ruins your shocks and knocks the fillings from your teeth never has a BUMP sign by it."

Skitter Marie of St. Paul: "If the directions to the place say 'You can't miss it,' you will."

B.K. of Brooklyn Park (echoed by **The Assistant Editor** of Shorewood and by **Jammy** of River Falls, Wis., whose British friend has confirmed that it's true on either side): "The windshield wiper that doesn't work will always be on the driver's side, and the smeariest part will always be right in the middle of the driver's field of vision. Never above it, never below it."

Brad of Little Canada: "The biggest, juiciest bug will always splat right in the driver's line of vision."

Maureen the French Teacher of St. Paul: "Whenever you see a man and a woman riding a motorcycle, the man will be driving."

Murphy of St. Paul: "When you're driving on a long trip and you finally find a radio station that's playing something you want to hear, you'll drive out of that station's range within one mile."

Q.T. of the East Side: "As soon as you're backing up in your car blindly, a commercial will come on the radio with horns honking and scare the crap out of you."

BULLETIN BOARD OBSERVES: Which ought to teach you, sooner or later, not to back up blindly. But we know what you mean.

Driver Ed of St. Paul: "Whichever insurance coverage you don't buy is the insurance coverage you will need."

Auntie Bee of Inver Grove Heights: "The more inclement the weather, the closer the guy behind you is on your . . . shall we say, bumper?"

Spunky Buns of Roseville: "As soon as you make enough room for a safe distance in front of yourself on a busy highway, some jerk will squeeze in ahead of you and take it."

Driver Ed of St. Paul: "The shortest distance between two points is under construction."

Bogart of Woodbury: "The time it takes your car to warm up in the winter is *precisely* the amount of time it takes you to get where you're goin'."

Rob of the Midway: "Drivers who forget to turn off their lights when they park always remember to lock their doors."

The Three Stoogettes of Hastings (who sounded like teenaged girls—or, we should say, young women), called with their Top 10 Rules of the Universe. We particularly liked a pair of them:

"No. 7: The haircut you wanted the most is the haircut that looks the worst on you.

"No. 3: The minute you buy an outfit is the minute it goes out of style."

Homeless of Woodbury, passing along a formulation by **The Woodbury Pelican**'s husband: "If you have one boy with you, you get one boy's help. If you have two boys, you still only get one boy's help, because when two boys are together, they each do only half a boy's work. If you have three boys to help, don't plan on getting any."

Blazer of St. Paul: "The times that you get home on time, your parents are never home. But the *one . . . time* you come in late, they're waiting for you at the kitchen table."

J. of Stillwater: "The day before the class picture, you get a big pimple on your face."

The Procrastinator of Forest Lake: "The degree of injury inflicted upon oneself while in the act of shaving is directly proportional to the importance of the event one is shaving for."

Lala of St. Paul: "When it rains, your umbrella is always where you are not.

"When you're driving to work, it's at work. When you're driving home, it's at home. When you're walking out to your car, it's *in* your car."

"It never fails."

Neb of Eagan: "With the weathermen promising—for the past *week*—that it's going to rain, and it hasn't, I finally broke down and put the sprinklers out. I have 'em runnin'—and what happens? We're gonna have rain. Figures."

Marie of the East Side: "No matter how long you keep the puzzle with the piece missing, you will find that piece a week after you throw the puzzle out.

"Bert's head was under the refrigerator."

The Clicker of St. Paul: "Of 10 objects equally spaced throughout a room, your baby will unerringly go to the most disgusting one of the bunch."

Wendi of Lauderdale: 'You always know exactly where something is until you need or want it. I hate that."

Grandma Up North: "You'll never find those instructions. *Ever!*"

Shan Carson of Eagan: "If you know that a repairman's coming 'sometime today' and you have to leave for 15 minutes to go pick up your son, that's the 15 minutes he'll be there."

Sofia of parts hereabouts: "The minute the maintenance person walks in the door is the minute the problem fixes itself."

The Domestic Goddess of Lakeville: "Whenever I have to set the alarm to get up early in the morning, the kids always sleep in late. And on days when I can sleep in late, the kids are up early. It never fails."

Vertically Challenged: "When you go somewhere with a child—the one you couldn't get to take a nap earlier—they will always fall asleep a minute and a half before your destination."

Mrs. Kanga of West St. Paul: "The amount that a toddler will dawdle is directly proportionate to the fullness of his mother's bladder."

ABBA of Highland Park: "If you buy clothes with extra buttons, you'll never need one."

Al B. of Hartland: "If it would look really good on you, it doesn't come in your size."

Katie of Stillwater: "One size does *not* fit all."

Lucy of Little Canada: "Buy something that's a little too big for you, and you think: 'It'll shrink when I launder it.' It won't shrink one iota.

"Buy something that fits perfect. You can count on 10 percent of it being gone after laundering."

Kinky of parts hereabouts: "Exercise clothes only fit the kind of people who don't need to exercise."

Grandma Up North: "The things that you take out of a box will never fit back in."

Champ of St. Paul (in response to **Lionesse** of St. Paul Park, who said: "Saran Wrap (a) will stick to itself when you do not want it to; and (b) will not stick to itself when you want it to"): "There's a much more basic Immutable Law of the Universe—and that is: Inanimate objects aren't."

Kris, Mom of 2 of Stillwater: "No matter which way you hang an ornament, it will first face backward."

Michael Donovan of Minneapolis: "If you drop an object onto the floor or ground, that object—even if it is square—will roll to a place where you will have to lie on your stomach in order to retrieve it."

June of Blaine: "After you rip off the sheets you need to do the job, the clean roll of paper towels will roll/fall/drop into whatever unspeakable glop it is you're trying to swab up."

Victor of Hugo: "An extension cord, regardless of its length, is always a foot too short."

Dennis of Austin: "You have a long extension cord, which you carefully coil up and neatly hang on its peg. The next time you go to use it, it will have a minimum of three knots in it."

Nancy of St. Paul: "The more you want a piece of information, the higher the probability that the only person in the organization who has that information is sick for the day."

Stacked of St. Paul: "The one back issue of a magazine for which you are looking in a library will be the only issue missing."

Sheilah of Maplewood: "By the time you become proficient in the skill required to complete your current project, the project will be finished.

"By the time you are called upon to use said skill again, you will have lost your mastery of it and have to relearn it."

Piper-to-Be of St. Paul: "If you've got something really smelly on your fingers, you will keep smelling them—no matter how stinky they are."

The Chemist of Como Park: "If there's a song on the radio that you don't like, and you turn off the radio, that awful song will keep going around and around in your head—so you might as well leave the radio on."

CHAPTER SIX

Please Release Me!

The music that won't let go:

M.C. of St. Paul: "One of life's greatest small annoyances is having a song or melody fixed in your brain which repeats itself without control.

"For several days, I have been humming 'Itsy Bitsy Spider' and 'Little Rabbit Foo Foo,' whose melodic themes are quite similar. I don't know why this happened. I have no contact with small children. I do not watch 'Sesame Street.' Yet Foo Foo constantly hops through the forest, 'scoopin' up the field mice and boppin' 'em on the head,' while I.B. Spider perseveres against the forces of nature and 'climbs the spout again.'

"Is there some significance to account for it? Could it reflect unresolved social issues?

"Foo Foo exhibits overt aggression toward smaller creatures. Mother Nature threatens to turn her into a goon if she does not desist, but gives her 'three more chances.' Foo Foo ignores the warning and meets this horrible fate. Bye-bye, Foo Foo.

"In contrast, Itsy Bitsy attempts to 'climb the water spout,' but is washed out by the rain. Undaunted, the feisty arachnid bides her time and, against all odds, succeeds.

"Why did the bunny and the bug turn out so differently? Were Foo Foo's parents at fault? Did they continuously tell her how cute and adorable she was, so that she thought fuzzy ears and a snowy-white tail exempted her from the consequences of her behavior? Or did she have so many siblings (Fee Fee, Fo Fum, etc.) that she didn't get enough attention—and, ignored and unloved, took it out on the field mice? Why did she ignore Mother Nature? Was her metamorphosis merited? (Three strikes and you're goon!)

"In contrast, perhaps Itsy Bitsy received quality time from her leggy parents, who sent her into the world prepared to pull herself up by her bootstraps (which, for a spider, is no small accomplishment).

"I don't know the answer, but pondering these questions has driven the tunes from my mind. Uh-oh! [Singing:] 'You picked a fine time to leave me, Lucille.'"

Highlander of St. Paul: "I was raised in a very musical household, thanks to my mom. She sang opera for 20 years, then retired to teach, and wound up teaching world music to elementary-school kids for 15 years. Now she composes music for children.

"You would think I'd have a fair shot at getting a Puccini aria or some fabulous Senegalese drum pattern stuck in my head. But noooOOOOOooooo! I get 'Copacabana' by Barry Manilow. And on a really bad day, that alternates with 'My baby takes the morning train' and several television-commercial jingles.

"Obviously, I have some seriously bad karma to work off here."

Scott of St. Paul: "I'd just like to let **M.C.** and **Highlander** of St. Paul know that the stupid songs stuck in your head are nothing until you have had a Barney cassette in your house and you wake up singing 'I like to eat, eat, eat apples and bananas' or 'If all the raindrops were lemon drops and gumdrops.'

"They don't know what hell really is."

The Hazel-eyed Girl of St. Paul: "All of you people have got it wrong. I live with kids, too, and what's worse than Barney, worse than Winnie the Pooh, worse than all of those is the Lamb Chop and Shari Lewis song [singing now] 'the song that ever ends. It just goes on and on, my friend. Some people started singing it, not knowing what it was. Now they'll keep on singing it forever just because it is the song that never ends . . .'

"You got it?

"In my head, all the time. Really bad."

Wendy of Vadnais Heights, who lived to tell the tale—and who sounds, amazingly enough, as sane as the next person: "I'm calling because you made me have one of these stupid songs get stuck in my head: 'It's a Small World (After All).' That song is something that, since 1972, I've hated—through half my life.

"We went, as a family, to Disney World. It had just opened. We all went in, riding in our little boats, in the 'It's a Small World' little ride thing full of all of these ethnic, animatronic dolls bobbing back and forth and singing this obnoxious song.

"Well, the boats broke—and so we're all trapped in this little river, going through the world with all these children singing 'It's a Small World.' It felt like we were in there for an hour—but they never turned off the sound! These kids are singing this song for an *hour,* and finally some guy had to come slogging through in boat shoes and drag us out with a hook.

"It's a fear and loathing; it's been something that I've had nightmares over. The last couple years, I've been back to Disney World twice and can't even walk by the place without shuddering."

Hestia of Eau Claire, Wis.: "I think it would be even worse to be sitting in that display having those dolls bob up and down . . . and no sound at all."

The Sheltie Lady of Energy Park: "A friend is continually bemoaning the fact that one fellow employee seems to be on break more than he's at work. They have developed their own version of 'The First Noel' to kind of soothe themselves, or provide amusement, while he's gone, and it does a little number on the supervisors.

"The guy's name is Al. So what do they sing? 'No-Al, no-Al, no-Al, no-Al'—and then they repeat it: you know, the first four words of the chorus of 'The First Noel.' The supervisors now are taking note of every time they sing 'No-Al, no-Al, no-Al, no-Al' and logging this for future action as they discover that he really isn't present most of the time. The *supervisors* are even laughing about it; *they're* even singing it now.

"It's probably as contagious as some of the rest of those songs—much to Al's detriment in the future."

BULLETIN BOARD OBSERVES: It's our experience that the "future" imagined by The Sheltie Lady's friend and her fellow worker bees never arrives. Here's what really happens: Al gets a big promotion.

Pippi of North Branch: "In case you didn't know, the only sure-fire way to rid yourself of a bad song is to sing it to someone else and give it to them.

"My husband is the king of torturously bad songs. He waits until I'm drifting off to sleep at night, puts his arm around me, kisses my ear gently, and then softly sings: 'Timothy! Timothy! Where on Earth did you go? Timothy! Timothy! God, why don't I know?'—or some other equally bad lost classic. Then he rolls over and goes back to sleep.

"But, hey, thanks for letting me get that 'Timothy' off my mind, because that's one downright painful song."

Frisco of San Francisco, "the band playing out at Lakewoods Resort in Cable, Wis.": "We've decided that we've been nice long enough—and that you actually *deserve* the worst song of all time: 'Imagine me and you, I do, I think about you day and night, it's only right to think about the one you love, and hold her tight, so happy together. Bah-dah-dah-dah dah-de-dah-dah de-dah-dah de-dah-dah-dah!'—et cetera, et cetera.

"Peace and love."

The Artful Dodger of White Bear Lake: "I just had to call Roto-Rooter. Try to get *that* jingle out of your head!"

Petie of Oakdale: "I need to be released from the Meow Mix song—where all the cats go 'Meow, meow, meow, meow' *[BULLETIN BOARD NOTES: and that's just the start of it]*. Once you start it, it does not stop; you will go around singing 'Meow, meow, meow, meow' all day long."

Glitter of Maplewood: "The absolute truly worst song that you can have going around in your head—and it goes around and around and around and never stops—is: 'I feel like Chicken Tonight, Chicken Tonight.'"

Marge of St. Paul: "My boss came up with a way to get songs unstuck. What we have found is that if a song is stuck in your head and you sing it the way Bob Dylan would sing it, it gets unstuck! Of course, Bob Dylan doing 'Little Rabbit Foo Foo' might erase more than the song; it'll probably erase your entire brain. But it's worth a try."

BULLETIN BOARD REPLIES: Iiit's a smaaaaaaall world, aaaaafter alllllll. Iiit's a smaaaaaaall world, aaaaafter alllllll. Iiit's a smaaaaaaall world, aaaaafter alllllll. Iiit's a smaaaaaaall, smaaaaaaall wooorld.

Only one problem with this method: You could get Dylan stuck in your head—and then you'll be wishing, desperately, for "Little Rabbit Foo Foo."

Barbara of Highland Park: "Try walking around all day with 'You like milk and it shooooowwws. It does a bahhhdy gooooood. You like milk and it shooooowwws.'

"It's *horrible.* Horrible, horrible experience.

"But thank you, Bulletin Board, and carry on the good work."

Anna of St. Paul: "I don't think I've ever heard, like, Bob Dylan sing, so I don't know how to get songs out of my head that way. But for anybody else who hasn't heard him sing: You can just think about the way Eddie Vedder sings; he sings like he's, like, singing while he's eating or something; you cannot understand a word he's saying. It's just, like, all jumbled together and everything."

BULLETIN BOARD REPLIES: She's never heard, like, Dylan sing? The tiiiiimes, like, they have a-chaaaaaanged.

Much later, we heard from **Vaughn's Godmother** of St. Paul: "I was driving in the car with my nieces, Halley and Roxanne, who are 9 and 5, and a song by Bob Dylan came on the radio: 'Tangled Up in Blue'—which is one of my favorites, so I turned it up and was kinda jammin' to it. The kids were silent for about a minute, and all of a sudden, Halley pipes up and says: 'What *language* is this?'"

An Average Joe of St. Paul: "About a year ago, I had a Bulletin Board experience which I have resisted calling in—for good reason:

"One day, just as I arrived at work, I changed radio stations and heard the song from hell. So obnoxious was this song that even today, it maliciously rears its ugly head if given the opportunity and relentlessly plays on and on in my brain.

"Being a loyal reader and a generally good guy, I kept that experience to myself, rather than inflict it upon my fellow Twin Citians. But for the past couple of weeks, the 'Please release me!' sections have sent loyal Bulletin Board readers into a frenzy of trying to cope with weird and unrelenting songs that other, less sensitive people have called in.

"Well, enough is enough. You've opened Pandora's box, and I'm about to tell you the absolute worst song of all time. So bad that Barry Manilow's 'Copacabana' sounds like Mozart compared to it.

"You've been warned. Stop reading now if you know what's good for you. Well, here goes:

"'I'm Henry [for you young'uns: That's pronounced *EN-ery]* the eighth, I am. / Henry the eighth, I am, I am. / I got married to the widow next door. / She's been married seven times before. / And every one was an Henry—*Henry!* / She wouldn't have a Willie or a Sam—no Sam! / I'm her eighth old man, I'm Henry. / Henry the eighth, I am.

"'Second verse, same as the first'—a little bit louder and a little bit worse.

"Well, I warned you! Damn that Herman and his Hermits. Damn, damn, damn."

The Music Man of St. Paul: "I wish I could call in something erudite-sounding, such as: 'I just can't get the theme from the scherzo of Bruckner's Fourth Symphony out of my head. It's driving me nuts! I bet *everybody* has that problem.'

"Unfortunately, my particular involuntary mental musical obsession today is a little more run-of-the-mill: 'Tie me kangaroo down, sport. Tie me kangaroo down.' And: 'Tan me hide when I'm dead, Fred. Tan me hide when I'm dead.' And, of course, the famous 'Play your didgeridoo, Lou. Play your didgeridoo.'

"I tried imagining it as Bob Dylan would sing it, but somehow it came out sounding as if it were Marlon Brando—and that just made it worse.

"I sort of brought this on myself. Last night on a long trip home from a friend's house, instead of listening to the classical music station, like I usually do, I hit the button for the oldies station. That's a sure-fire recipe for getting *something* stuck in your head—because all they play, all day long, is songs that already have their echoes and shadows dormant in your brain, just waiting to be reawakened by one more playing of the song."

Your Faribault Connection: "The song I get into my mind and can't get out is 'Waltzing Matilda.' Anything Australian . . . Mel Gibson's *name* will bring the song to my mind. And I can't get it out. It will stay with me all day! It goes over and over.

"I love it, though."

BULLETIN BOARD REPLIES: As do we.

Meet us down by the billabong, mate, under the shade of a coolibah tree.

Diane of Springfield, Mo.: "Something happened a couple weeks ago that really touched my heart.

"It was the seventh anniversary of my mother's death, and I was feeling real blue that day. I turned on the TV in the middle of the day, and the movie *Out of Africa* was on, and I'd never seen it before.

"There was a real beautiful scene between Meryl Streep and Robert Redford. They were out on the plain during a safari. They were eating a meal near the light of the fire, and he turned on a Victrola. What played was an instrumental version of a song that I hadn't heard, or thought of, in many, many years.

"My heart started beating a little faster, and I began to cry—but I began to sing every word of the song. It's called 'With Someone Like You.' My mom used to sing it to my dad, and her dad used to sing it to her mother.

"Today is the third anniversary of my dad's death, and I would give just about anything if I could have them back again.

"I'm very, very grateful that that song has not been released from my memory."

CHAPTER SEVEN

This Ain't Butterin' No Parsnips

Family talk:

Kate of St. Paul: "When I was a kid, it was very standard to say 'This ain't butterin' no parsnips' when you meant: It's time to get up and go to work.

"It was when you were sitting around the kitchen table, drinking coffee, . . . just kind of, you know, goofing off in the morning, and then somebody would say: 'Well, this ain't butterin' no parsnips.'

"I thought it might be kind of interesting to hear what other B. Boarders have to say about family sayings that are sort of a tradition."

Al B. of Hartland: "My mother used to tell me: 'If you can't say anything nice about someone, let's hear it.'"

Gus the Grouch of West St. Paul: "My Uncle Frank had a saying that he'd holler out to people who would speed past him in the car. He'd holler out: 'Go, you damned fool! Hell's only half full!'"

Kathy of Vadnais Heights: "My dad had a saying: 'Don't borrow a jack'—which basically meant: Don't assume the worst is going to happen. There was a story to illustrate it, which he had to tell each of us only once—and the short version is basically this:

"A man got a flat tire in the middle of the night. He had no jack in his car, and the only house for miles was a farmhouse up the road.

"On his walk to the farmhouse to ask if he could borrow a jack to change his tire, he wrestled with the necessity of having a jack versus the possibility that the farmer would be very angry at being awakened in the middle of the night.

"He finally gets to the door and knocks on it. And when the farmer answers it, the man says: 'You can keep your damn jack'—and walks away, without ever knowing the farmer's reaction.

"So if you're ever worried about something and assuming the worst is going to happen: Don't borrow a jack."

Missy of Mahtomedi: "I was gonna have a birthday party for my daughter's third birthday, and I was cleaning the house and trying to get the balloons ready and getting all set up for it. I went out in the living room—and my husband had a bucket of water with soap in it and a washcloth, and he was scrubbing down my stepper. You know, an exercise stepper—making sure that my stepper was clean . . . which is *very* important before a birthday party.

"So now, any time that men do dumb things, my sister and I say: 'He's cleaning the stepper.'"

Edgar of Coon Rapids: "My granddad was a railroad engineer. He had a saying:

'The steam that blows the whistle never turns the wheel.' He applied it when he was hearing some politician talk about what he was gonna do for the country.

"That saying comes to my mind every time my company's gonna have another productivity meeting."

P.A.T. of Menomonie, Wis.: "My wife and I were at her mother's for Christmas. My wife's uncle came over to visit. He's a cute octogenarian whom I had met only a couple of times.

"As we were sitting around talking about little or nothing, there suddenly appeared one of those lapses in conversation that seem to last way too long. Feeling the vacuum building in the air, Uncle says: 'I still have all my teeth.' We stifled our laughter until after he left.

"That one simple statement has become our filler for the occasional pregnant pause."

Herbie's Mama of St. Paul: "As my grandma and grandpa aged, my grandma became more and more domineering, and Grandpa said less and less—and just sort of sat and smiled. At one family dinner, one of the grandchildren passed Grandpa a bowl of peas—and Grandma leaned over and snatched that bowl of peas out from in front of Grandpa and said: 'Alf doesn't like peas.'

"So whenever my husband or I would overstep our bounds a little bit and speak for the other spouse, we would just lean over and say: 'Alf doesn't like peas'—and we would get the message."

Auntie of Hastings: "Years ago, my mother gave my father a rear-view mirror for his birthday. However, it was to go on *her* car. Since then, whenever someone does something for someone else which is obviously for their own benefit, we refer to this as a rear-view mirror."

Must Be Getting Old of the East Side: "When I'd be talking too much to my mother, she'd tell me to give my tongue a sleigh ride. As a kid, I always thought that was the dumbest thing to say to somebody.

"I just had a birthday on Friday. I'm 32. And yesterday, my son was talking too much to me, and I was trying to have a conversation on the phone—and I put the phone down for a minute, I looked over at him and said: 'Would you please give your tongue a sleigh ride?'

"I just could not believe that came out of my mouth."

Daddy John of St. Paul: " 'Give your tongue a sleigh ride' was part of the original slogan for selling ice cream at the St. Louis World's Fair, in about the year 1900 [1904, to be precise]. That's the fair that 'Meet Me in St. Louis' was about.

"My mom and dad were born in 1891 and 1890, respectively, and they both first heard of ice cream from the St. Louis World's Fair. My dad was born and raised in Missouri. (That's Missou-*rah,* not Missou-*ree*—according to him.) He was actually taken to the fair and tasted ice cream for the first time.

"I wasn't born until 1927, and when I was little, my mother still made real old-fashioned ice cream—and if I wanted any, I had to help turn the crank. And let me tell you: It was worth whatever effort it took to get some.

"When it was all frozen, my mother would open the freezer and take out the dasher inside, and she would run her finger down one of the vanes and lick it off. Like all really great cooks, she was always the first one to taste everything she made. And her wonderful smile would spread across her face; her whole face sort of beamed and twinkled at the same time, and she would say: 'Freeze your teeth, and give your tongue a sleigh ride'—and would hand me the dasher to lick off.

"Gee, I can feel it now. It's like deja vu. It's like going to heaven for a short time."

Don Alfonso of Pig's Eye Palisades: "Half a century ago, seven of us kids growing up in St. Cloud got this financial advice from our dad, whenever we were tempted by bargains: 'If battleships are a nickel, we don't need any.'"

Pat of St. Paul: "My dad said: Don't ever do business with a man who has nothing to lose."

Bulgy's Youngest Kid: "My late, great, often-quoted daddy used to say: 'Statistics show that there are more horses' asses than there are horses.'

"I don't have the numbers to back it up, but I believe it to be true."

Dean Bunn of Brooklyn Center: "When something was very obvious, and also very bad, my father—God rest his soul—would say: 'It's pretty hard to hide a dead skunk.'"

Ann B.: "My family owes one of its phrases to our slightly off-center, but dearly loved, mother.

"We all gather for one weekend a year on the North Shore, taking up four cabins very close to the edge of Lake Superior. We were all sitting around the campfire one day, and someone made a comment about hiking near the lake. Mom looked a bit confused and said: 'What lake?'

"There was dead silence, then uproarious laughter.

"We use that phrase whenever someone is missing something very obvious to everyone else."

The Kansan of Woodbury: "When I moved up here four years ago, my husband's kids explained to me that the Northern Lights were only in picture books; they didn't exist, because certain young eyes had never viewed them.

"Well, last summer, my husband and I were treated to a *glorious* night of Northern Lights—but it was too late to wake the kids up. I vowed I'd notify them when they happened again.

"One night, I walked out my door about 9:30—and there they were, dancing across the sky. Never mind that it was the southern sky—and a cloudy evening. I raced inside to call them and have them experience this wonderful phenomenon.

"The 13-year-old sighed and informed me that the lights were from an Inver Grove Heights car dealership.

"So now, whenever we pass a store with a spotlight in motion, the kids say: 'Hey, look! The Northern Lights!'"

Ivan's Youngest of Lake Elmo: "When someone told my dad that his barn door was open, he said: 'If the cow can't get up, the cow can't get out.' Dad has been gone for two years now—and boy, do I miss his quick wit."

Pastor Dave of St. Paul: "When my great-grandmother was resorting to house-cleaning shortcuts (like sweeping dirt under the rug), she used to say: 'Who lost their cow won't look *there* for it.' I have found that saying all too useful over the years (much to my discredit)."

Cyndi of Mounds View: "Years ago, my husband—who happens to be His-panic—was the kitchen manager for Guadalaharry's, and it was his job to train in all of the new help.

"He had one gentleman who just didn't seem to *get* it; he kept asking questions, over and over and over . . . and usually during the lunch or dinner rush, when my husband had no time. So my husband would yell out: 'I'm busy! I'm busy!'

"The gentleman finally got so frustrated that he walked out, and the last thing he yelled to my husband was: '*I* don't *know* what *ambeeshee* is! *I* . . . don't . . . speak . . . *Spanish!*'

"So now, whenever we are busy and don't have time—which is very often, since we have a 4-year-old—we just yell out: '*Ambeeshee! Ambeeshee!*'"

The Gymnast of Roseville: "My sweet daddy has lots of interesting sayings. Like, whenever he burps, he looks around and says: 'The mallards sure are flying low today.'"

Denise da Nurse of Woodbury: "My maternal grandfather and three succes-sive generations of family have used the following expression to comment on fash-ion fads and peer pressure: 'Why don't you just paint your butt green and run with the *rest* of the ducks?'"

Gramma Barb of St. Paul: "Back as far as I can remember, when my mom was asked 'What are you doin'?' and she was doing something obvious, like washing dishes, she would answer: 'Milking a duck.'

"Yes, now I say it, too."

Liz of Grand Avenue: "When my mom would be on her hands and knees, scrub-bing the kitchen floor, and I would say 'Hi, Mom. What're you doin'?', she would say: 'I'm moving the piano to Chicago.'"

The New Bill of Shoreview: "When I was a kid, my dad—who grew up in cen-tral Wisconsin—had a saying for anyone who was pouting excessively. He would say: 'You can go from here to Oshkosh on that lip.'

"I thought that was pretty strange, considering that we lived in Utah."

S.O.B. (Sweet Old Bill) of Maplewood: "My dad—the original S.O.B.—used to have a saying when people had a stroke of great luck, or just something went their way more than anybody would ever expect. His saying was: 'The dumber the farmer, the bigger the spuds.'"

Terri of Cottage Grove: "When we were kids, my great-grandfather would al-ways ask us: 'What do you know for sure?'

"We'd always say: 'Nothin'.'

"And he'd say: 'Well, it takes a big dog to weigh a ton.'

"I guess he was right."

Butch of St. Paul: "I grew up in the country, and we'd have city kids come out, and you'd tell 'em things like 'Oh, don't go there; that's poison ivy'—and invariably they would walk in there. Of course, we'd get hollered at for lettin' 'em walk in there.

"And my grandfather used to come up, put his hand on your shoulder and say: 'You can't argue with stupid.'

"You know? It's true. You can't argue with stupid."

The Seagull of Coon Rapids: "My dad would sometimes become upset with the work of a so-called expert whose creations proved to border on the ridiculous. He used to say: 'The guy who came up with *that* idea ought to walk in the water 'til his hat floats.'"

Monte Cristo of St. Paul: "I have a friend who, because he subscribes to that newspaper across the river, feels unworthy (and rightly so) of contributing to Bulletin Board. As his representative, I would like to share the wise words of his uncle, who, when he means that it is too late to avert a disaster, says: 'Well, the goat's on fire and it's headed for the barn.'

"This friend also reports that in Montana, when the locals are describing someone who is all show and no substance, they say he is 'all hat and no cattle.'

"Odd, isn't it, that hats appear so frequently in our lives as a bad sign?"

Deb of Highland Park: "My grandfather's favorite saying was '*Chicheh yedjish dalshe budjish*'—Polish for: 'The slower you go, the farther you'll get.'"

The Minnesota Nightingale of Ogilvie: "After a large meal, my Norwegian daddy would say: 'I wish all my friends were as full as I—and all my enemies, twice as full. Then they would burst.'"

Debbie of Inver Grove Heights: "My grandmother always had an expression . . . and she would say it in Dane, and it might have lost something in translation . . . but when a particular food didn't have flavor to it, she would say: 'It tastes just like stickin' your tongue out the window.'"

Jim Bob of Merriam Park: "My dad's expression for something worthless is 'not worth a hoot in a whirlwind.' I figured out much later that 'hoot' is a euphemism for, uhh, posterior breeze.'"

BULLETIN BOARD REPLIES: Wait a minute! "Posterior breeze" is the euphemism—for [posterior breeze]!

Dicky-Do of Woodbury: "My dad used to tell us that 'any old horse can [expel a posterior breeze] first thing in the morning, but it takes a mighty good horse to [expel a posterior breeze] after a hard day's work.' This was, of course, most often said in the evening—and always with a very proud smile on his face!"

BULLETIN BOARD REPLIES: We're not certain that was pride you were seeing.

Debbie of Inver Grove Heights: "Whenever someone had a posterior breeze, my grandmother would say: 'I think I hear someone coughing in their pants.'"

Bri of Wyoming (echoed by **Wendy** of La Crosse, Wis., and **Deirdre** of Cottage Grove): "My ma calls them 'barking spiders.'"

Rex of Highland Park: "My old rough-and-tough Irish grandmother used to break wind frequently, wherever and whenever—although she didn't call it that. She always said: 'Better out than a doctor's horse at the door.'"

Skinny Dipper of Oakdale: "When somebody had stomach pain, my father used to place the blame on a [posterior breeze] caught crosswise."

T. Coin from The Dungeon of St. Paul: "In regard to posterior breezes: I've heard my father-in-law say: 'If they don't pay the rent, you've gotta kick 'em out.'"

Jonny Quest: "When I was a kid, whenever we'd come into the house and ask my dad where my mom was, he'd say: 'She went to poop, and the hogs ate her.' It went over my head until I realized, as I got older, that my dad grew up on a farm without any indoor plumbing."

Ol' Virginny of Cottage Grove: "My Norwegian grandmother, usually quite circumspect in her speech, blew the socks off us with this little shocker:

"Watching a female relative smoking, she said: 'When you smoke, your mouth looks like a bull's a— in a hailstorm.'"

Lolo of Maplewood: "When Papa wanted us to get moving, he'd say: 'Don't just stand there batting your eyes like a toad in a hailstorm.'"

Grandma Mary Kay: "My father's mother—my dear old Grandma, long since gone—used to say, when someone yawned: 'Shut your mouth. I was born in a cave, and you make me homesick.'"

Dennis of Austin: "My father, who is 78 years old, has a thing about chewing gum in general—and female gum chewers in particular. He says: 'The only difference between a girl chewing gum and a cow chewing its cud is the intelligent look on the cow's face.'"

The Mug Lady of Crystal: "When we'd say 'What are we having for dinner?,' my mom would say: 'Tripe and trolley bags.'

"Boy, it took a long time for me to finally figure out what tripe was. The trolley bags? Never have."

Pathfinder of Shoreview: "'Trolley bags' is what we used to call a 'motorman's friend'—which, in case you're not familiar with it, is what a motorman wore strapped to his leg and other portions of his anatomy because they weren't allowed to take breaks during their work day—and they still had to take care of business.

"So that's what a trolley bag is. Hope I haven't ruined your meal."

Kay of Apple Valley: "Whenever I asked my mother what day it was, she'd always say: 'Today is the day they give babies away with every pound of tea.'"

El Gringo Antiguo of North Oaks: "You guys printed half of a couplet that just screams to be completed: 'Today is the day they give babies away with every pound of tea.'

"The last half of that is: 'If you know any women who want to have babies, just send them around to me.' *[BULLETIN BOARD NOTES: Hearing this, one of our colleagues—unaware of what El Gringo Antiguo would say next—said it sounded like a sailor's ditty.]*

"If you were a plebe at the Naval Academy, years and years ago, and you were contentedly munching your breakfast, an upperclassman could say 'Mister, what day is it today?'—and if the plebe was able to report this little couplet, why, he could go on munching his breakfast. But if he said something stupid like 'Today is Monday, January 16th, 1995,' then he was told to 'Shove out!'

"What this means is: He drops his chair onto its back and shoves it under the table—and then has to crouch at exactly the same height as he was before, when he was sitting on the chair, and finish off his meal that way.

"This sort of tended to give us pretty strong leg muscles."

Weas of the Midway: "I found this in the book *Irish Proverbs*, illustrated by Karen Bailey: 'Soft words butter no parsnips but they won't harden the heart of the cabbage either.'"

Sherry of Merriam Park: "Imagine my surprise when I was reading *Vanity Fair* by Thackeray and ran across the first page of Chapter 19, apparently asserting that fine words butter parsnips as well as anything else.

"Since Mr. Thackeray can't fax this to Bulletin Board, I remain his faithful amanuensis,

"Sherry from Merriam Park"

BULLETIN BOARD NOTES: Here's the passage in question:

"Who was the blundering idiot who said that 'fine words butter no parsnips'? Half the parsnips of society are served and rendered palatable with no other sauce. As the immortal Alexis Soyer can make more delicious soup for a half-penny than an ignorant cook can concoct with pounds of vegetables and meat, so a skilful artist will make a few simple and pleasing phrases go further than ever so much substantial benefit-stock in the hands of a mere bungler. Nay, we know that substantial benefits often sicken some stomachs; whereas, most will digest any amount of fine words, and be always eager for more of the same food."

Marsh Weed of Highland Park, in the fall: "I guess I'm feeling a little contemplative this evening. My folks are getting ready to leave for warmer climes, and I guess I'm already starting to miss them a little bit.

"My mother says and does a lot of things that annoy me—petty little things that get repeated every day. Sometimes I think she does some of them on purpose, just because she *knows* they annoy me.

"But now, as I am doing something in the kitchen that she occasionally does—but without making the same annoying comments she always makes when she does it—I'm hearing her voice in my head making that comment.

"At first, it just makes me grin, realizing that that comment is now so built into this task. Then I realize that someday—God willing, a very long way off—I will no longer hear her make that or any other annoying comments. All I will have is that echo of her voice in the back of my head.

"Realizing that now, I guess I'll not only tolerate, but also cherish those remarks that I know she'll make from now on, because I'd much rather have her around making them than just the echo of her voice.

"I love you, folks. Go safely, and return safely in the spring."

CHAPTER EIGHT

All in the Family

Entries of many sorts in the Permanent Family Record:
Darlene: "Dear Bulletin Board,
"This is my first Mother's Day with no mother to whom to send a card. I wrote this letter for my mom and hope you will find it worthy of publishing. If not, I think she'll get the message, anyway. Thanks. . . .
"May 1, 1995
"Dearest Mother,
"It's your hands I remember the most. I can close my eyes and envision your long, thin fingers, curved slightly with arthritis. The hands of an artist. The hands that never failed me. . . .
"You hands were that of a legal secretary when you were a young woman. If only you had been born in a different era, yours would have been the hands of the lawyer. You took painting classes and discovered your talents in landscapes done in oils. I look at the walls of my living room and marvel at the beautiful paintings you did before I was born. Your soul shines through each one.
"Your delicate hands curled my ringlets when I was young. And when it came time to get those ringlets cut off, only you were allowed to cut them. Each birthday cake I had was lovingly baked and decorated by your hands. I always begged for a 'store-bought' cake, thinking they were much more special. How foolish I was.
"Your fine-boned hands sewed my clothes, bandaged my knees, typed my term papers, made the veil for my wedding gown, held me when my twins were still-born, and crocheted a special afghan for each grandchild. Your hands supported me through the stages of my life.
"Your beautiful hands tended the lovely flowers in your garden. I never had the time to learn the difference between a weed and a tender shoot, so I never had to help. I called Dad this weekend. He said the stone is in place with your name on it. He wondered which side to plant the flowers on. I don't know. I never paid any attention before.
"Your graceful hands were finally stilled by a stroke in September. Then it was my hands holding yours, stroking your hair, caressing your cheek. I remember you telling me the story of how your mother died. You had been keeping a long vigil by her sickbed at home. Finally, you fell asleep, exhausted. That was when she died. It seemed you felt guilty that you weren't awake with her at the end.
"I, like you, tried to stay awake. Several days of seeing you in a lifeless coma was so hard. I, too, fell asleep. But in your last act of selfless mother's love, you waited

for me to awaken, take your quiet hand, and sing your favorite hymn. It was a privilege to be with you as you breathed your last, peaceful breath. I kissed your cool hand and placed it gently down.

"Your strong hands have sustained me in this difficult year, Mom. Whenever I find myself sad or alone, I put my hand on my shoulder and feel your fingers caressing it. I know when my time comes, I'll find you with hands outstretched, waiting for me. Thanks for always being there for me. Happy Mother's Day.

"Your loving daughter,

"Darlene"

Judy of Woodville, Wis.: "My mom was blind for over 40 years of her life—but the lady raised six kids, cooked, kept the house clean, and took good care of my dad.

"She also had a wonderful sense of humor. Sometimes she would bump into a wall—and say, in a puzzled voice: 'I used to walk through that wall.' She got that line from Aunt Clara of the TV show 'Bewitched.' Aunt Clara was a witch losing her powers, but was still trying to walk through walls.

"I miss my mom, and I wish she were still here—trying to walk through walls."

Ellen of St. Paul: "When I was little, I invented a little creature by the name of Tommy. Tommy was about three feet tall, and he did everything that I told him to do. It was wonderful. He came to dinner every night, and Mom set a place for him, and we played all day long together.

"One day, Mom and I were going to the store, and she almost smashed Tommy in the car door—so I held out my thumb and smashed my thumb instead. Mom wasn't too happy with that.

"When Tommy went away one day, Mom set the table for dinner as usual, and I said: 'Oh, Tommy won't be here today.' And she said: 'Why?' And I said: 'He went away.' She told me later, when I grew up, that she almost felt like she'd lost a child, because Tommy never came back."

Axman of Mondovi, Wis.: "When I was 7, I kept pestering my mother to get me a jack-in-the-box. Dumb thing to want, of course, because at that age I could have been surprised by it only once—and not even once if I knew what I was getting.

'Mom wouldn't say it was dumb, but she refused to get one, anyway, explaining it wouldn't be worth the trip to town (26 miles) or the money (which we didn't have). I still wanted one, and finally she told me she would just make me one if I would go into the other room and not peek.

"(We lived in a two-room tarpaper cabin at the time. I'm not making this up.)

"A few minutes later, she called me in and handed me a cigar box. I was breathless. I started to raise the lid, then chickened out. I reached for the lid again, braced myself, and drew back again. Mom said: 'Oh, just go ahead and open it!' She seemed so impatient that I went ahead and very cautiously raised the lid.

"In one corner of the box sat one of my sister's jacks.

"Despite my disappointment, I saw the point of the joke and laughed, though somewhat weakly right then. Later on, I considered it very funny and treasured the memory of it. Mom, however, felt guilty for years.

"I know she did, because 30 years later, she said so and gave me a real store-bought jack-in-the-box that plays 'Pop Goes the Weasel' when the handle is turned. She made a point of presenting it to me before my wife and I had our first child so I would know it was for me and not the baby.

"Naturally, I did not keep it entirely to myself; I shared with that child and the other one we've had, too. I would let them turn the handle, but I always made them let me hold the box."

Toni of St. Paul: "There was definitely a nip in the air this morning. It was the kind of morning that made me want a nice, warm, mushy breakfast—even though I don't eat breakfast (mushy or otherwise) anymore.

"Ah! But I used to! Every day before school, my mother (Sweet Rose of I.G.H.) would make breakfast for me. And on cold mornings: Malt-O-Meal! Not just regular, but *chocolate*. And not just chocolate: The only way I'd eat my Malt-O-Meal was with marshmallows.

"My mother would use mini-marshmallows and make a big smiling face right there in the middle of my bowl. And two raisins for the eyes. If she didn't have any mini-marshmallows, she'd use the regular ones, but cut them up with the poultry shears (no easy task, as I've found out since then). What a special way to start out a day!

"I tried making Malt-O-Meal for myself once. Even put marshmallows in it. But it just didn't taste the same. I think my mother put something special in it: an ingredient called *love*.

"I love you, mother. Have a nice, warm, mushy day, fellow B. Boarders."

Frodo of Shoreview: "When I was a kid, I absolutely hated macaroni and cheese. Now when my older sister, who's 14 years older than I, was baby-sitting me one night, she said that I had to eat all of the macaroni and cheese on my plate before I could go out and play.

"Well, I grumbled and griped—and she finally relented and divided the plate in half. She put half of the noodles on one side and half of the noodles on the other, and she said: 'You can eat half of it. If you eat half of it, then you can go out and play.'

"So I struggled and groaned and gulped and washed it down with milk, and finally got half of that macaroni and cheese eaten. I called my sister; she came into the room, and I said: 'Look! I got it down! Can I go out and play now?'

"She looked at my plate, and she said: 'Oh, noooo! You ate the wrong half!'"

Anonymous woman: "Back about eight years ago, when my children were 6, 8 and 9, they were playing outside our home. The oldest boy has retardation, and his younger brother and sister were very protective of him.

"So they were all out playing together, and a group of boys came along, and they were teasing my son. He was trying to talk to them; he's just very outgoing, very friendly. And they said: 'Hey, retard! What are you trying to say? What are you trying to say, retard?'—which was horrible, but his brother, who was 6 at the time, said: 'Well, I'll tell you what my brother's trying to say. He's trying to say: "I would rather be a retard than a dumb son-of-a-bitch like you."'"

"Although ordinarily I do not let my children speak like that, I thought: God, that was the best comeback I've ever heard."

Jeff of Hastings: "A long time ago, when I was quite young, I asked my father if I could buy a pocketknife. When he asked me why, I said: 'Well, I want it to carry to school, so I can protect myself.'

"He went out into the kitchen, came back, handed me a Hershey's bar and said: 'Here, carry this instead.'

"I looked at it and said: 'Well, why?'

"He said: 'It tastes so much better when they're shoving it down your throat.'"

Jan of Oakdale: "I was a senior at Harding, and I was a decent student; I didn't really have any troubles or anything. My dad had trusted me with my fairly new license and his brand-new Buick LeSabre hardtop—a car that he really loved—and I, in my youthful naivete, decided to teach a younger friend how to drive.

"Well, her foot froze on the accelerator, and as we clipped off a telephone pole, I reached over with my foot to hit the brakes. Luckily, the car stopped about 30 feet from a brick-fronted house—and we realized later that had the pole not been an old one that easily broke on impact, or had the car not been a big V-8, we surely would have been severely injured, or worse.

"I called my dad. When he arrived, we stood there looking at his beautiful car that was smoking and ruined, and I turned and said to him: 'Dad, your new car.'

"He turned and looked at me, and he said: 'The hell with the car, as long as you're OK.' He didn't say anything else; he seemed to sense that I understood just what could have happened, and I did.

"I ended up having some consequences related to that, involving going to juvenile court and the suspension of my driver's license for six months.

"I'm 45 now. I'm a mom. I've been a teacher for 24 years in Minneapolis. I've never forgotten my dad's face, or the way he handled that very large teenage mistake of mine. It's affected countless interactions with my son and hundreds of interactions with my students.

"I guess he taught me one of life's most valuable lessons—at least the most valuable lesson in my life—that day, which I've never forgotten: that I, as his child and daughter, was his most valuable possession.

"When I received my driver's license back from the state six months later, that day my dad gave me the keys to the repaired Buick. No lectures. No warnings. I could feel the trust in me that he had. I guess I would wish that every teenager could have a dad like that.

"And I would really wish that teenagers could just understand how difficult it is for parents to start to let go."

"At this point, Rosie interrupted: 'Sounds like your mother parking her car.'"

The Husband of St. Paul: "The mother-in-law called today. She wanted to tell us that they've just acquired a family burial plot in a cemetery in their hometown, and that there's room for them and their children and their children's spouses.

"Ma wanted to be sure that I didn't feel any pressure to join them—that if I had other arrangements, that would be fine, and there would be no offense taken.

"So now I have a decision to make.

"Do I want to spend eternity lying in peace next to my lovely wife? Certainly. Absolutely.

"Do I want to spend eternity in what I understand is a charming, well-maintained cemetery? Sure. Who wouldn't?

"Do I want to spend eternity lying in rest next to my wife's family? Well, yeah. They're great people! Why not?

"But here's the kicker: Do I want to spend eternity in Iowa?

"Hello? Cremation Society?"

Chuck's Daughter of Mahtomedi: "Several years ago, after my father died and was cremated, my brothers and I gathered in his workshop and built a box to contain his ashes for burial.

"For the construction, we chose pieces of scrap wood left over from various favorite projects of his over the years: a bit of cedar siding from the home he built, some knotty-pine tongue-and-groove paneling from a room he loved, oak from a special bookshelf.

"The result was a beautiful and meaningful tribute to his life and death. The building of it allowed us a much-needed opportunity to grieve together.

"Upon presenting the completed (and filled) box to my mom, my older brother stated that we had all had a hand in the project—except for Dad, who had both hands in it.

"It was only because we had grieved so much that we were able to laugh so long. Dad would have appreciated both the joke and the tribute."

Merlyn of St. Paul: "I've told Bulletin Board of my only brother, David, and how we were a matched pair of kooks. I remember going to Dudley Riggs' [comedy theater, in Minneapolis] with him—and deciding, for that evening, we would speak only Norwegian. Never mind the fact that, between us, we knew, on the outer limits, 200 words of the language.

"How bizarre we were together.

"Then he died of a brain tumor and left me like a fuzzy mitten in a world of Aris Isotoner gloves.

"Two years after his death, my only son was born. We named him David, in honor of his uncle he'd never know—and, strangely enough, he's very much David. Early on, I'd look at family photos and see my brother in my son. And he's interested in the same things—helping me feel my loss a little less deeply.

"Today, I opened the laundry chute to throw down my dirty clothes, and from my son's bedroom in the basement, I heard his computer singing 'Fish heads! Fish heads! Roly-poly fish heads! Fish heads! Fish heads! Eat 'em up! Yum!'

"What a surprise to hear my brother's and my favorite silly song coming from my son's room—and to know that my brother's goofy sense of humor is alive and well in my son."

Judy of Bayport: "Two of my Aunt Dot's daughters-in-law were named Kit and Sharon.

"One time when Dot was introducing them to some of her friends, she accidentally introduced them as S— and Karen. From that day on, the two of them had an ongoing argument as to which one was Karen.

"Finally, Sharon thought of a way to solve the dilemma. She decided to get personalized license plates that said KAREN.

"My wonderful Aunt Dot has died, but her memory lives on in stories like these."

The Queen's Mum of Vermillion: "At a recent family reunion, the tables were sagging under the weight of showy displays of the relatives' finest cooking. It was obvious not all would fit, so—fool that I am—I thought some could be added as containers were emptied.

"One of the first to come through the line was my husband's 94-year-old Aunt Margaret. (We won't even change the names to protect the innocent.) She's some inches shorter than five feet, and less than shy about voicing her opinion.

"'*Where's my Jell-O? I brought Jell-O, and it's not on the table!*'

"Indeed, she had, complete with fruit cocktail and covered with whipped topping—true Minnesota-style, to ensure that no color could be seen.

"'It's in the fridge, Auntie, and as soon as I clear a place, I'll be sure to get it.'

"Twenty minutes later, she pushed herself in front of the people still in line. With her heaving bosom of indignation resting about table-height, she once again demanded: '*Where's my Jell-O? I asked Mary Ellen if she had some, and I want to know why it's not out! I brought Jell-O, so where is it?*'

"I made a dash for the kitchen, got her Jell-O, made the next three people take some—'and please, please report the fact to Margaret.'

"About that time, Mary Ellen came around the table to give me a hug and whispered: 'You know, I've always *hated* Aunt Margaret's damn Jell-O.'"

Debbie of White Bear Lake: "This happened about 10 years ago, just before Halloween. We were telling our relatives how much we liked White Bear, except that we got our pumpkin smashed every Halloween. We thought this was really a low-life kind of activity. Then some of the relatives piped up and said that, well, in *their suburb* this *never* happened. Why, not only had their pumpkin never been smashed, they had never even *seen* a smashed pumpkin in *their* neighborhood.

"Well, my husband and I looked at each other and thought: It's just like they were *begging* us to come and smash their pumpkin at Halloween. So, after the kids got done trick-or-treating, we had an errand to run. We badly wanted to go and smash their pumpkin, but we didn't want to set a bad example for our kids, who were little at the time.

"So we were driving to the store, and we looked in the back seat and the kids were sound asleep. We thought: This is just God's *permission*. So we drove to their house and gleefully smashed their pumpkins. We were hoppin' around like a couple of college kids, just having this great time. We got back in the car—and out of the darkness, one of our children said: 'You know, you guys could get arrested for that kind of stuff.'"

Nothing Surprises Me Anymore of the East Side remembers "a couple of incidents that happened during one of the most joyous holiday seasons I've ever had": "On the day before Thanksgiving, a chance of flurries had turned into a blinding snowstorm, and having deserted my hopelessly buried car at work, I walked home— only to find my first-grade son sobbing uncontrollably. It seems that the Pilgrim and the Indian princess that he had painstakingly spent weeks coloring in order to be the centerpiece at our Thanksgiving table had been forgotten in his desk, due to the excitement of the blizzard.

"So there is old Dad, head down into the wind, walking up the middle of the snowbound street, heading for school.

"All of us, including the Pilgrim and the Indian princess, had a great Thanksgiving. And you know what? If our house caught fire right now and my family was safe, I know what I would go back in to save.

"A few weeks after this incident, my son and I went to pick out our Christmas tree. The trees were sorted into areas based on their size and shape. There was a $35 area, and a $30 area, a $25 area, a $20 area—and there was also a $5 area of deformed trees and broken branches that could be cut up and used for wreaths.

"After 15 to 20 minutes of searching, my son came running up to me in breathless excitement. He had found the perfect tree. He grabbed my hand and, sure enough, dragged me to the $5 area and pointed out his prize. Its trunk weaved back and forth like a mountain road. On one side of the trunk, the branches were no more than 2 feet long, while the branches on the other side stretched 4 to 5 feet. Finally, a fork about four-fifths of the way up the trunk gave this masterpiece two distinct tops.

"My son seemed to sense my reluctance and looked up at me with the saddest eyes I have ever seen and said: 'Dad, if we don't buy it, nobody will—and it will have such a sad Christmas.'

"Well, with a little bit of engineering, I did get it to balance in the tree stand, and with a lot of trimming, it almost resembled . . . well, no, it never really did . . . but, anyway, the tree and the rest of us had a very happy and unique Christmas. And I think we probably had even more visitors as word got out about our happy Christmas tree."

Cuckoo Mama of Burnsville: "Last weekend, while grocery shopping, I encountered an elderly woman in one of the aisles. It was obvious she'd had a stroke; her left arm dangled helplessly at her side, and she dragged her left foot behind her as she pushed her cart with the right side of her body. It broke my heart to see her struggle so with her cart.

"While unloading groceries at the checkout register, I noticed the same woman in the next lane. She was paying for her groceries at the time. And I saw a girl about 12 years old approach this woman, and she said: 'Excuse me—but could I help you bag your groceries and take them to your car?'

"The woman nodded.

"The cashier smiled.

"And I wiped tears of ecstasy from my eyes. You see, that compassionate, precious little girl was my daughter.

"Hear? I'm gonna cry just telling this story. What a priceless memory."

Bud of Eagan: "On New Year's Eve, my daughter, Holly, was part of a foursome in a movie ticket line.

"She saw that the cashier was being slowed down in her work because of a young man who kept asking questions and wanted to see a movie, even though he had no money. It was clear from his manner of speech and naivete that he was not blessed with the mental capacity most of us take for granted.

"After she was inside for a couple of minutes, she came back out and found that the situation had not changed, so she plunked down $7 in front of the cashier and said: 'He's with me.'

"The man said in astonishment: 'Are you paying for my ticket?'

"She took his hand and urged: 'Yes. Come on!'

"During the movie, the man reacted emotionally (and sometimes vocally) in all of the right spots, and a good time was had by all. Afterward, she contacted the local authorities, who agreed to get the man home safely.

"Do you see why I love her so much?"

Mary Ann of Mac-Groveland: "I need to tell you a Mom Story.

"My mother was a very, very modest woman. 'Sex' was not a word that one used with her. And one didn't use the word 'pregnant'; one said 'expecting a child.'

"So about the fourth pregnancy that I had, I was kind of bitterly complaining about three little kids—'I'm tired, and I'm this and I'm that.' And my mother said to me: 'Listen, dear. You made your bed. You should have slept in it.'

"I thought that was *wonderful!*"

M.B. of White Bear Lake: "My husband is one of 12 children, and the first Thanksgiving after we were married, we were all seated around the dining-room table, enjoying our dinner—and my mother-in-law always said what was on her mind. After grace was said and everyone was quietly talking, she said: 'Mary, is he good in bed?'

"It sort of put a stop to the conversation, and everyone looked at me. I turned about 30 shades of red and choked on my turkey, and she said: 'Well, I was just wondering—'cause his dad sure was.'"

BULLETIN BOARD NOTES: Obviously.

Camobund of St. Paul: "Our daughter was married recently. At one of the events preceding the wedding, the bride and groom and the family of the bride were huddled around the dinner table with Grandma, my mother. She's 82.

"The bride and groom asked for her advice on how to make their marriage a success, and they all looked to her dewy-eyed, thinking they were going to get some grandmotherly thing. And she said: 'Pull the shades. Do what you want. And tell the neighbors to go to hell.'"

R.J. of Hammond, Wis.: "When my husband and I announced our engagement at a family dinner, my grandmother, who was 77 at the time and sweet-faced, white-haired, short, plump—just the epitome of a grandmother—stood up and announced a toast. She said: 'Here's to the bride who dresses in black. When she dresses up, she never looks slack. And when she kisses, she kisses so sweet . . . she makes things stand that have no feet.'

"My mother was just absolutely mortified—but now, my mother is that age, and I'm beginning to think she's getting to be a lot like Grandma."

BULLETIN BOARD SAYS: Better late than never.

The Dreamer of Maplewood: "Our 21-year-old son has been home from college on vacation, and for the last week, his girlfriend's been staying with us as our houseguest.

"Last night, we all went out to have Chinese food, and when we opened the fortune cookies to read our fortunes, somebody brought up the old 'Say *in bed* after it'—and we laughed a little, and we forgot about that . . . well, obviously didn't *forget* about it, but we didn't *do* it.

"When the girlfriend read hers, her fortune was: 'You will be rewarded for your accomplishments.'

"Nobody said anything for a couple of seconds.

"My husband turned to her and said: 'Not in *my* house, you won't.'

"She turned every shade of red, poor girl."

Princess Grace of Mahtomedi: "Every Saturday morning for years, the three of us daughters were allowed to watch cartoons on a big black-and-white TV for as long as we wanted, with very strict instructions not to disturb my mom and dad unless there was a fire or one of us was dying. They informed us that they wanted to sleep in.

"Years later, when I was a long-married adult, my dad let slip that he and my mom would lie in bed, quietly giggling and . . . how should I say this?—quietly enjoying each other's company while we obliviously watched cartoons in the next room.

'Well! Talk about nerve! Talk about naive kids! Talk about your great ideas! . . .

"And one more thing: Here's how I used to get through those long, dull Missouri Lutheran services of my youth:

"In a proper Missouri Synod church in Michigan, the hymns are played as slowly and mightily as the organist can possibly render them. So in an effort to stay awake, I would do one of two things: I would either sing the *next* verse ever so quietly, or I would try to sing the words from the hymn on the facing page—and often the words would fit, and my sister would hear me, and we would get giggling, and our shoulders would be heaving until the one with the misfortune of being closer to Mom would really get it.

"Without moving her eyes from the hymnal, Mom's hand would slowly move over one of our knees, and then a gloved hand would come down and squeeze—with an iron grip.

"I hope my reminiscing has not led any of today's children down the path of wickedness."

BULLETIN BOARD REPLIES: Not to worry—though that first item may have given their parents a wicked idea or two.

Bernie of Burnsville: "On Thanksgiving a few years back, 15 of us—our extended family—were gathered together for that traditional Thanksgiving feast. After the meal, I was kinda stretched out on the couch watching the usual football game when my sister-in-law Nancy's daughter, about 4 years old at the time, crawled up on my chest and laid down.

"I thought nothing of it until she blurted out: 'This is how Mom and Dad sleep.'

"We all turned to Nancy, who was six shades of red already, and Nancy said, with a shrug: 'We got caught.'"

Lemmy of Minneapolis: "At a family gathering recently, a couple of my cousins were in a bedroom, and one of them was breastfeeding her child. In walks a third cousin of mine and says: 'Whose kid is that?'"

West Side Mom: "One time, my college-age brother walked into the room as I was nursing my young son. He just looked at us and said: 'Enjoy it, kid. There's a long dry spell.'"

Vicki of Lakeland: "When we were kids, my two older brothers and I would go up into our attic and play Mass. One brother would be the priest, and one brother would be the altar boy; I would be a nun—a visiting missionary—and I would give the sermon. They wore vestments made out of old curtains; we used bunk-bed ladders for the altar railings.

"We would always have to quit when the brother who was the altar boy wanted his turn to be the priest, and a fight would break out, and our mom would come up and make us close down shop for the day."

Dave of Shoreview: "Now that Vicki of Lakeland has broken the ice, I suppose all of us Catholic kids can come out of the closet and admit that many of us did this.

"I remember doing it in the living room: setting up chairs in rows to make pews. The best part was: We took Wonder bread and took the crusts off and rolled it out flat with a rolling pin, and then punched out circles with a cookie cutter to make Communion hosts.

"They were just about as tasteless as the real ones."

Auntie Boo-Boo of Woodbury: "In our family, we have this game we like to play—and keep in mind that these are adults:

"You take the game of Hearts—regular game of Hearts. To embellish the game, we take a squirt gun or a spray bottle, and the person who gives you the queen of spades and sticks you with 13 points—you get to give them one squirt. It's a lot of fun.

"If someone shoots the moon, everyone gets to give them a squirt. Adds a whole new dimension to the game.

"There's nothing so heartwarming as seeing your mother, with that gleam in her eye, as she gets to squirt your dad."

Linda of St. Paul still plays this game with her five fully grown (if not unreasonably mature) siblings: "It's a napkin-eating contest. What we do is: We take a paper napkin, unfold it all the way; you stick one corner of it onto your tongue, and then—without using your hands—you have to get the whole napkin into your mouth.

"The first one with the napkin in their mouth wins. There's no prize or anything, either—but it's a pretty hysterical sight."

BULLETIN BOARD REPLIES: That's easy enough to imagine, once you've tried it—which, strictly in the interest of research, we did.

Chopper: "Today, my 6½-year-old daughter, Miss B, lost her very first tooth. She's been waiting for this moment ever since her first friend lost a tooth, way back in preschool, and I think I've been just as anxious.

"We've been working on that tooth for six weeks; in fact, the new tooth is already halfway in. Last night it was hanging by a thread, but Miss B wouldn't let Daddy or me pull it. She wanted to have Molly, the Tooth Fairy (whose real job is teaching kindergarten), pull it at school today.

"I was thrilled to see her run out of school with a big, toothless grin on her face! She was so proud of herself.

"When we got home, she put her little tooth in her special Tooth Fairy jar and wrote a note for the Fairy saying 'Dear Tooth Fairy, Please leave tooth.' *[BULLETIN BOARD NOTES: Miss B is a kid who's going places, we can tell. We'd never heard of a kid bold enough to ask for the prize without expecting to surrender the tooth. Can't you hear the Tooth Fairy now: "Whattya think, kid? I'm handin' out cash for nothin'?"]*

"As we were getting ready for bed, Miss B wanted one last look at her little tooth, and she dropped it. We searched the room high and low, but no tooth.

"I've rarely seen her so sad, nor had such an ache in my heart. She changed her note to read 'I'm sorry I lost my tooth.'

"I know far worse things can happen to a child, but it's the everyday triumphs and tragedies that touch me so deeply and make this job so bittersweet.

"Today my Miss B lost her first tooth. . . ."

Billy O. of Little Canada: "About 50 years or so ago, I was courting a girl that I thought I would like to marry, so I brought her home to meet my mother.

"We were sitting around the kitchen table having coffee and doughnuts, and suddenly my mother turned her head to the side and, without having a chance to get her hand up to cover her nose or her mouth, she let out a horrible sneeze. The pressure of the sneeze made her crack her wind—and at the same time, her dentures flew out of her mouth across the kitchen floor, under the refrigerator.

"Without saying a word, she got a yardstick and fished 'em out from under the refrigerator, walked to the sink, rinsed 'em off, popped 'em back in her mouth, sat down, and picked up the conversation where we had left off—as though nothing had happened."

The Railroad Widow of St. Paul: "Back many years ago, when my dad first got dentures, he was having some trouble getting adjusted to 'em. He had sores in his mouth, so sometimes he would take the dentures out.

"One night, he drove up to the grocery store and took the dentures out on the drive home. A little while after he got back, he remembered the dentures and went out to the car to get them. They weren't there, so drove back to the grocery store, thinking maybe they fell out of the car in the parking lot.

"In the meantime, me and my mom tore the whole house apart, lookin' for 'em. I mean, we were lookin' places you wouldn't ever think they'd be—but we were lookin' everywhere.

"My dad got back, and he hadn't found 'em, and we hadn't found 'em, either. So we're standin' there discusssin' where we should look next, and my mom just jokingly looks at my dad and asks him: 'They're not in your *mouth*, are they?'

"He got the goofiest look on his face—and sure enough, there they were: in his mouth, the whole time.

"To this day, he still gets that look on his face whenever anybody brings it up. And boy, do we."

Char of Bloomington: "My brother, who's a CPA, was having a new deck put on his house. To get the old one torn off, he asked the carpenter how much it would cost, and the carpenter said: 'Oh, about $150.' So to save this $150, he decided he would take it off himself.

"So he arms himself with a crowbar and goes out and sits on the deck and proceeds to try and pull the nails, etc. on the deck. And while doing this, the crowbar flings loose, hits him in the face, breaks his tooth; it ends up costing him a thousand dollars at the dentist."

The Blondie of White Bear Lake: "It was a cold night. I was with my mother, and we were going to go out. After fumbling for her keys for some time, she exclaimed: 'I wish I were a cow!' She couldn't find her keys; I was practically rolling in the snow, I was laughing so hard.

"She went inside to find her keys, and when she came back out, I had to ask her why. This is what she said—and she went on and on:

"First of all, she wanted to be a Wisconsin dairy cow. If she wasn't a dairy cow, her whole purpose in life would be death. But if she were a Wisconsin dairy cow, she could sit all day in the middle of nowhere, hanging out with all of her friends. She said that when you get tired, you just have to find a shady tree and you can plop down and fall asleep. If you get hungry, all of your food is lying right under you. You don't have to prepare it; it's just there.

"Then she said: When there's a storm coming or it's cold, a handsome farmer brings you into a big, cozy red barn. As she went on, she hesitated and said: 'Then, once a day—*every*day—a handsome man comes to you and plays with your breasts.'

BULLETIN BOARD REPLIES: The Blondie's mother certainly has given that farmer the benefit of the doubt—but that's her business, isn't it??

Mary of Woodbury: "My husband wonders why The Blondie of White Bear's mother would want to be a cow, when the farmer quits right after the foreplay."

Rene of St. Paul: "When my son was 2 or 3 years old, he asked me where all the milk came from. I told him we had a little tiny cow that lived in our cupboard.

He believed me—but when he got a little older, he wanted to know why he never saw the cow. I said: Because the cow was really shy and only came out at night, filled up the milk carton and then went back into the cupboard again.

"He was probably 5 years old before he started to suspect, perhaps, that Mother wasn't quite telling the truth."

Sandy of Maplewood: "When we were kids and would ask our dad for something, like money or whatever, my dad would tell us that we could have it 'second Tuesday next week.'"

Marie of Roseville: "I grew up with two brothers. When I was little and someone asked my dad how many children he had, he would always say: 'Three—one of each.' I grew up always worrying what that meant."

Nancy of Northfield: "When I was 12 years old, my father turned the lawn-mowing chores over to me—along with the push-type mower we had. (It was the '50s, and there weren't many power mowers yet.) My dad explained that he was doing me a favor, because regular use of the mower would develop my bust.

"I used the mower for three years, and it worked! Then I passed the mower to my younger sister upon her 12th birthday, with the same words of wisdom.

"When our brother turned 12, Dad bought him a power mower.

"About then, I figured out the truth."

Endless Miles of Minneapolis: "My father used to tell my sister and I that if we peed in the swimming pools in the local parks, they'd put a special chemical in there that would turn it a bright color, and it would embarrass us. So we never peed in the swimming pools.

"The other thing he told us, which I believed until I was about 12 years old: Years ago, little old ladies used to take brandy bottles and fill them with different-colored waters and put them in their bathroom windows. He told us that people could [expel a posterior breeze] in the bottles and it would turn different colors, according to what they had eaten. And I actually believed this until I was about 12 years old!

"And people wonder why I'm strange now, you know. But these myths that my parents told me, that I believed, were actually triggers for a great imaginative world. And it was fun!"

La-La of St. Paul: "Easter dinner, we were all sitting around the table reminiscing, and someone brought up one of my favorite stories of my mom and dad's courting days.

"My grandmother was not very fond of my dad. My grandpa, on the other hand, was one of the kindest people to ever walk the earth.

"Well, one time my grandma and grandpa had gone to bed, and Mom was late getting home with my dad. When Dad finally got Mom home, they sat down and started talking. Grandma was already mad because they were late coming home, and she was growing more irate by the minute—listening to them in the other room, talking—so she kept poking my grandpa, saying: 'Ed! Go in there and talk to that boy!'

"He wouldn't do anything.

"A little while later: 'Ed! Go in there and talk to that boy!'

"Well, finally Grandpa gets up, goes into the other room, says to my dad 'Hello, Bernie!'—and goes back to bed. I don't think that's what Grandma had in mind, but I think it's a great story.

"It's been over 10 years since my grandpa died, and I still miss him. Just thinking about him is, for me, one of life's greatest simple pleasures."

Pepper of Stillwater: "When I was growing up in Minneapolis, Sunday dinner was always considered something special at our house—and almost always was a chicken dinner of some sort. A carryover from the Great Depression, I suppose.

"My mother made homemade chicken soup and homemade noodles from time to time, which was always a family favorite. She would begin the early-Sunday-morning dinner preparation by putting all of the ingredients for the soup into a large pot, setting it on the stove, turning on the gas, and then heading off to church to attend Mass. She could then finish the cooking and noodle-making uninterrupted after returning from church. Because my father sang in the choir, he went to Mass later in the morning and tended the pot while she was gone. Or so I thought.

"A few years before my father died, he confided in me something about those Sunday chicken-soup mornings. He explained a bit guiltily that while my mother was away at church, he would remove all of the onion from the simmering chicken soup. He truly didn't like onion in the soup. She never noticed—assuming it just boiled away, I imagine—and he never told her. He didn't want to hurt her feelings.

"They were married 43 years when he died. It wasn't until sometime after his death that I told her of his deep, dark secret. 'That stinker!' she exclaimed, and on her face was the most touching expression one could behold. It was a mixture of: the surprise at the discovery of 43 years of chicken-soup sabotage, the girlish blush and smile of an adored sweetheart, and the heartache for her missing lover.

"Seems like the world needs more homemade chicken soup and noodles, doesn't it?"

Kathy H. of Eagan: "From the time I was 6 months old until close to the age of 5, I lived with my grandparents. I don't remember when I actually got my 'blanket,' but I remember that it was pink and violet and had pretty white butterflies flying all over it. It also had a satin border that I loved to feel against my cheek before I went to bed. I never took a nap or went to bed without it.

"Over the years and through many washings, the blanket became worn and frayed. So when I was about 5, my grandmother set out to 'cover' the blanket. We went to the store and picked out a pretty pink flannel with tiny white rosebuds on it. And for one entire afternoon, my grandma measured and cut and sewed a cover to put over the blanket.

"While she was doing this, I was about a foot away, asking all the typical 'why' questions that a 5-year-old would ask. Having now two children of my own, I realize how trying this can be for an adult. But Grandma never seemed to mind my questions and very patiently explained exactly what she was doing every step of the way.

"When she was all done, I had a new blanket, complete with a new satin border. It wasn't long after that that my dad married and I went to live with him. There were many changes in my life at that time, but the one thing that always stayed constant was that my blanket was always there, almost as a symbol of my grandma's love.

"I still have the blanket to this very day. In fact, when I took it out of the trunk today and held it up to the light, I could still see the silhouettes of the butterflies that are underneath. My grandmother passed away two years ago, and I still miss her very much. She was a very special lady, and I was lucky to have her as my grandma."

Connie of Highland Park: "Being a grandparent is *so* much nicer than being a parent.

"When my sons were young and they colored on the wall, I had a *project:* to get it off and repaint the wall. And there was disciplining that had to be done.

"Well, this past weekend, I had my darling granddaughter, Miss Megan, and after she left, I went in my bedroom and noticed beautiful pink coloring all over my bedroom wall.

"I decided to frame it."

The Great Gonzo of Oakdale: "I realized I was a parent after our first son was about 5 years old.

"We had moved into our new house, and we didn't have a bed for our 5-year-old—so my mom and dad gave me a twin bed that I had slept in. I realized I was a parent when, one day, I was walking by the bedroom and I looked in and saw my wonderful, sweet little boy, Topher, bouncing on the bed—gettin' some great air.

"There was this moment of . . . indecision, where the one side of me said 'He could fall off of there and get hurt' and the other side of me said 'God, I remember how much fun that used to be.' And in that moment of indecision, I thought: 'Hurt . . . fun . . . hurt . . . fun'—and I looked at him with all of my wisdom and said: 'Be careful.' And walked on.

"I walked into the other room and realized: 'Oh, my God, I'm a parent.' "

Bob Woolley of St. Paul: "When I was about 10, my parents decided to widen the driveway so that two cars could be parked side by side.

"The new concrete had to be poured right up to the foundation of the house. I was too young to be of much real help, but my dad went out of his way to give me a job. There was a strip of black rubber-like stuff that had to go between the new concrete and the foundation. In retrospect, I suppose that its purpose was to allow for heat expansion of the concrete without cracking the foundation. My job—and Dad stressed how important it was—was to hold that rubber strip up against the foundation while the concrete was being poured.

"He had hired several strapping young men to help spread the concrete quickly and evenly. I was scared of getting in their way, and just couldn't get in to where I needed to be. When they were essentially done, I finally worked up the nerve to confess that I hadn't been able to get my little task done. Dad was very put out, since they would have to redo much of what they had just finished. In his frustration, he blurted out: 'I knew I couldn't trust you with anything important!'

"I ran to my room and cried for a long time. He had never said anything like that to me before. In fact, the reason this story is so etched into my memory is that my parents were *always* kind, giving, devoted, and patient with us kids.

"I'm sure his outburst was just that—a product of momentary tension and frustration, which he quickly forgot. I've never had the heart to tell him how long it has stayed with me, because it would pain him to know it.

"I am not yet a father myself, but I keep telling myself I'll never make such a mistake. Unfortunately, deep down I know that it is inevitable that even the best parents, sooner or later, unthinkingly say hurtful things to their children. I guess the best we can do is hope that the kind, loving, encouraging things we tell them the other 99 percent of the time make up for those failings. They sure did for my folks, despite my telling this tale on ol' Dad."

Mrs. Romance: "Last week during a walk in the woods, with leaves floating down around me, I was reminded of a similar walk many years ago with the Little Romance who announced the leaves looked like 'rainbow drops.' She thought it would be really neat if the rainbow drops landed on her and turned her all of the different colors.

"This was at the height of her Rainbow Years, when her hero was Rainbow Bright and we hung crystal prisms in her window so she would wake up to rainbow-covered walls. You get the idea.

"As they tend to do at such times, my thoughts wandered on—and now the Little Romance is at the edge of those years of contradictions known as adolescence. We are discussing boys, bras and body changes, yet the first thing she packs for an overnight is her blanket.

"The visual rainbow has been replaced by the mystical dream catcher.

"For my part, oh how I wish that sending her safely into these years of change were as easy as hanging prisms and dreamcatchers in her room.

"Enjoy your babies."

R.J. of Hammond, Wis.: "They grow up *so fast.*

"Yesterday, I had one of those moments of reckoning. I left work and went to my son's school to watch the Halloween parade, only to discover that the sixth-graders are too old and sophisticated to take part in the Halloween parade.

"My son has multiple disabilities, and he was coming in from recess with some of his buddies. He uses a wheelchair. I waited inside the door. When they came inside, the other boys said hello to me—and he just kinda sat there and eyed me, coldly, for a minute, and then turned around and zoomed off down the hall with his friends.

"I was left standing there, feeling like I'd been slapped in the face with a wet fish.

"Every parent of a child with special needs *wants* this to happen; this is a *good* thing, right? But I have to confess: I got back in my car to go back to work, and I shed a few tears on the way.

"So let your kids be kids—as long as they want to."

CHAPTER NINE

WARNING!
Cute Kid Stories Ahead!

B.A. of Apple Valley: "We were sitting at dinner the other night with some friends, and we were talking to our 2-year-old about his baby brother or sister that's coming.

"Our friend said: 'Well, Taylor, are you looking forward to having a brother or sister?'

"And he said: 'Yes.' And then he got this look on his face and said: 'I know, Mommy! Wouldn't it be a great idea if the baby came out now and you dropped it in the soup and the soup splashed all over the table?' . . .

"Kids do say the darnedest things, I'll tell ya."

Overwhelmed Mom ("with cellulite") of Hudson, Wis.: "One *hot* day last summer, I had just showered and was getting ready for work. My bored, restless 6-year-old, Katie, was jumping on my bed, which had just been made. Wrapped in my towel, I walked into my bedroom from the bath area and scolded her for messing the bed, then returned to continue getting ready.

"Katie came running in a few minutes later, wanting to show me what she'd done. She led me back to my bed and explained that she'd put the pillows back where they belonged and had walked around the entire (king-size) bed to 'smooth out the wrinkles' in the comforter.

"She was so proud, and naturally I complimented her and told her I was proud of her for being such a big helper.

"Then, in her most serious way, she asked: 'Don't you wish I could do that to your butt, Mommy?'"

Jeanne of Little Canada: "A coworker's little daughter was in church one day, and the minister called all of the little children to the altar to sing a song. But before they did, the minister said to the little girl that he admired her dress.

"She said: 'Oh, thank you. But my mom says it's a bitch to iron.'"

Bill of Maplewood: "Our 5½-year-old daughter was lookin' at the family Bible the other day, and she says to me: 'So this was written around the time Jesus was alive, right?'

"I says: 'Yeah. You know: some of it before, some of it after—but, yeah, around that time.'

"She's turnin' it over and lookin' at it, and she says: 'Boy, we've really taken good care of it.'"

The Purple Dragon of Stillwater: "A few months ago, when my grandson

Christopher was only 3, his mother was explaining to him and his sister that their Aunt Mell was very sick. She suggested that they all pray for her.

"Christopher thought about it a minute and then said: 'What Aunt Mell needs is a big hug and kiss.'

"Christopher's much older and wiser 7-year-old sister lectured: 'Christopher, Aunt Mell is really sick. She doesn't just have a little owie like you and I get that Mommy can kiss and make all better.'

"After a long pause, Christopher said: 'What Aunt Mell needs is a Pooh bear.' Another pause. 'But not my Pooh bear.'"

Grandma Jan of Cottage Grove: "I was talking to my sweet little granddaughter Rachel on the telephone last week, and I reminded her that she had a birthday coming up next month.

"I said: 'I've already got a present for ya.'

"She said: 'What is it?'

"I said: 'Well, I can't tell you—because when it's your birthday, you won't be surprised when you open it.'

"She said: 'Well, can I guess?'

"And I said: 'Sure.'

"She said: 'Is it Rollerblades?'

"I said: 'No.'

"She said: 'Is it a game?'

"I said: 'No.'

"She said: 'Is it clothes?'

"I said: 'No.'

"She said: 'Is it a Barbie doll?'

"I said: 'Well, maybe—and maybe not.'

"And she said: 'Could you go look?'"

Lovely Rita of Shoreview: "I was outside yesterday enjoying some of the most beautiful weather, shucking sweet corn—the last of the season—when my funny little 3-year-old came up, wanting to help. When we got down to the silk, she asked me if we could save the Barbie hair. I thought it was really sweet."

Mimi of Vadnais Heights: "We were watching the news one night, and the sports segment came on. They were showing some horse racing. My 4-year-old was staring at the screen with great intensity when he turned to me with a puzzled look on his face and asked: 'Why are those horses wearing underwear on their heads?'"

Maureen of White Bear Lake: "I have a 6-year-old daughter, Jessica, and I was getting dressed, and I lifted up my arms—and I hadn't shaved under my arms for a couple days. Kinda forgot to do that.

"And my daughter said: 'Oh, Mom! Something terrible has happened!'

"And I said: 'What, Jessica? What happened?'

"And she said: 'You've got a million slivers under your arms!'

"I tell ya: I thought I was just gonna die."

D.H. of South St. Paul: "Last night as my 8½-year-old son was getting ready for his shower, he was looking at himself in the mirror—totally naked. He gets very dark brown during the summers from being in the sun, except for a very white area on his body where he wears his shorts.

"He was admiring his tan when I walked in, and he started slowly turning in a circle and said: 'Look, Dad, I'm a twist cone!'"

Lainie of Lakeland: "I was out in Seattle this summer, baby-sitting for four kids under the age of 10—none of which were my own (and don't even ask how I got into doing that).

"The older kids were making a park out in the back yard—pretending it was a state park—and they wouldn't let the youngest one, Evan, be part of the park, so he would sit in the living room just pouting and crying.

"I told the other kids that they *had* to let him be part of the park.

"About 10 minutes later, Evan came back into the house, and he sat in the same spot where he was sitting before—but this time he was all happy; he wasn't pouting or anything.

"I asked him: 'Did they let you finally play in the park?'

"He said: 'Yes. They *hired* me! I'm gonna be a tour guide.'

"And I said to him: 'Then what are you doing in here?'

"And he said: 'They gave me the day off!'"

Terry B. of St. Paul Park: "Every morning and night, my black Lab and I would walk around the schoolyard—and try as I might to clean up after her, I often missed some. So once in a while I'd go there in the afternoon to finish the job.

"One time, some kids were there, and a young girl asked a boy what that lady was doing. He said: 'I've seen her before. She collects dog poop.'"

BJ of Apple Valley: "While visiting with a friend one evening, somehow we got on the subject of dogs and their disgusting habits (taking off with panties left on the floor, digging everything out of the trash, etc.).

"I told my friend how my dog Cody had gotten ahold of my new Girbaud jeans and chewed a huge hole in the crotch when Jayce, my 7-year-old son, piped up and said: 'Geez, that must've hurt!'"

Sandy of Lakeville: "A few weeks ago, we got a new Sheltie puppy, and our children just think this puppy can do no wrong. Our 6-year-old daughter, Elizabeth, was playing with the puppy, and we noticed . . . we thought the puppy was nipping at her nose, and we were concerned that he was gonna hurt her, so we asked Elizabeth: 'Did Kirby bite you?'

"She said: 'No. He just stuck his tooth up my nose.'"

Grandma Yellow: "Last Saturday, I was frying some liver for my cat when my 6-year-old grandson, Spike, and his mother came for a visit.

"Spike said: 'Grandma, I'm hungry.'

"I teased him, saying: 'Oh, I bet the kitty would share her meat.'

"Spike responded: 'I don't eat meat. . . . I'm a vegetarian."

"Surprised that he even knew the word, I said: 'Oh, I didn't know that. When did you become a vegetarian?'

"Spike said: 'When you offered me that meat.'"

The Nanny of Stillwater: "I am watching 3¹/₂-year-old twin boys this summer. Their names are Will and Alex.

"Yesterday, we went to pick beans for lunch. I wanted Alex to try one, but at lunchtime he wasn't so sure about that—so I asked him if he'd ever read the story *Green Eggs and Ham.*

"He looked at me for a minute and then said: 'If I say yes, does that mean I have to eat it?'"

Chris of the West Side: "My 3-year-old daughter was begging us for some kind of a treat the other day. She said she just had to have a treat.

"So I said: 'Well, you can have some grapes.'

"And she said: 'No, I want something with sugar in it.'

"And I said: 'Grapes have sugar. There's lot of sugar in grapes. Natural sugar.'

"And she said: 'I don't want that. I want something that'll make me sick to my stomach.'"

J.C. of Eagan: "My daughter had kindergarten orientation last week, and the teacher was showing them how you could fold a piece of paper in half and cut out a circle—and you get two circles.

"The teacher exclaimed that that was magic.

"One little girl pipes up and says: 'My grandma is magic. She can turn tuna into tuna casserole.'"

Jane Doe of the Twin Cities: "My 5-year-old doesn't get to see his grandparents too often, and sometimes he gets them mixed up. While he was working on a Mother's Day card for my mother-in-law, I reminded him that he was making a card for Daddy's mother.

"'Is she the one with the white hair?' he asked.

"I said: 'That's right.'

"So he said: 'I'll make a picture of someone with white hair. And I'll need to make a black mustache.'

"'But Grandpa doesn't have a mustache,' I told him.

"'I know,' he said, 'but Grandma does.'"

Garden Lady of the Midway: "I went out to the alley, and there were two little girls on their bicycles, standing there. I have a little flower bed there, and they asked me what the flowers were, and I explained—and then one whispered to the other: 'Should I ask her?' So I asked: 'What do you want to ask me?'

"'Could we have a flower?'

"I said: 'Sure—but come on in the yard. That's where the best flowers are.' They couldn't see the yard, beyond my garage. They came around the corner, and they immediately zoomed in on my biggest pink tulips. Two little girls, and two big, big tulips—and they looked so wistful, I gave them each one.

"And they said, very politely, 'Thank you'—and walked away. And as they were leaving, one little girl turned around and said: 'You are the nicest gal on the block.'"

Jason's Mom of Rosemount: "I'm calling to tell you about my son Jason—and what a dear heart he is.

"When he was about 4 years old, which wasn't very long ago, he didn't like to go to day care. It wasn't that he didn't like his day-care mom; he just wanted to stay home with me, instead. So, frequently in the morning, we would have to talk about how I had to go to work to earn money to pay for our food and clothes and house and so forth.

"One day, he asked me why he couldn't go to work with me. I said that there wouldn't be anything for him to do. There'd be no toys. There'd be no friends, no TV, no snacks. And I said: 'What would you do all day at work with me?'

"And he thought for just a moment before he said: 'I would hold your hand.' I really love that kid, and I know I'd have better days at work if he could hold my hand every day."

Jeff of Maplewood: "I have a 3-year-old, and a couple of months ago I was talking to him about how big he was getting. I told him: 'You're gettin' to be a big boy, and you're gonna keep getting bigger and bigger.'

"And he said: 'Yes. And you're gonna get bigger, too, Daddy.'

"I said: 'Well, no, I'm done growing.'

"And he looked at me, kinda curious, and he said: 'No, you're teasing me. You're going to get bigger, too.'

"And I said: 'No, I'm all done growing.'

"And then he looked a little concerned, and he said: 'Well, you're going to get a *little bit* bigger, aren't you?'

"And I said: 'No, I'm as big as I'm going to get. I'm all grown up.'

"Then he looked *real* concerned, and he said: 'But you'll get a *little* bigger.'

"I said: 'No, really! I'm all grown up.'

"And at that moment, he burst into tears and said: 'Aren't you even going to have *one more* birthday?'"

Sandy S. of Oakdale: "When my son was 8 years old, he was concerned about my dying someday. He talked about how much he would miss me.

"One evening before he was going to sleep, we talked about this. I told him not to worry because I would always be watching over him—even after death.

"Well, he became quiet. He slowly looked around his semi-dark room and then nervously said: 'OK—but just don't come at night.'"

Kelly of Balsam Lake, Wis.: "About a month ago, my husband's grandmother died. She was cremated, and the entire family gathered at the cemetery to bury her remains.

"As my mother-in-law walked up to the plot with a small, eight-inch by eight-inch box, which now held Grandma, a 5-year-old member of the family ran up to her and said, matter-of-factly: 'That can't be my grandma. She was much taller.'"

Scott's Happy Wife of St. Paul: "My friend Cindy was talking to her son, Alex, who was almost 5, after he spent a weekend with his dad at his dad's house. Alex said he had flushed a little toy down the toilet, and his daddy got mad.

"Cindy asked: 'What did he do?'

"'He put me in a time-out.'

"She said: 'Oh. Did he yell at you?'

"And he said: 'Yeah. Did you hear him?'"

Peggy of St. Paul: "This morning, my 3-year-old son is driving me crazy. He's goin' 'Mommy, I want the squirt paints! . . . Mommy, I want the squirt paints! . . . Mommy, I want the squirt paints!'

"Finally I thought: 'I can't stand it anymore'—so I started singing The Rolling Stones' 'You can't always get what you want. You can't always get what you want. But if you try sometime, you just might find you get what you need.'

"He looks at me, and he goes: 'Mommy, I *need* the squirt paints! . . . Mommy, I *need* the squirt paints! . . .'"

Brian of Forest Lake: "Last Monday night, my wife and I accompanied our 4-year-old son, Benjamin, to the local nursing home. He was with his church choir, and the kids sang about 20 minutes for the older folks there—the standard Sunday-school songs, church songs. *[BULLETIN BOARD NOTES: You read that right. When he's not listening to oldies radio, Benjamin is in a choir for kids age 3 through second grade.]*

"As we left the nursing home to walk back to the church, my son turned to my wife and said: 'We should've sung "When a Man Loves a Woman."'"

The Straw Boss of Apple Farm Acres: "I am a teacher of preschool children in a Bible-study program, and we just had our first time together yesterday. As part of the morning, we teach the children the Pledge of Allegiance. And every year when I do this, I'm reminded of when my daughter first learned the pledge.

"She had been in kindergarten for a few weeks, and we attended a school event of one of my brothers. They asked the audience to stand up and recite the pledge. My daughter stood up so proud, because now she could recite with the audience.

"We said the whole pledge and got to the last line, 'with liberty and justice for all'—and you could hear one lone, little voice saying: 'Keep standing if you want morning milk.' That was my daughter.

"Every year when I teach the pledge to new children in my class, I'm reminded of this—and it always brings a smile to my face."

B.A. of Apple Valley: "Yesterday at lunchtime, I was trying to encourage my 2-year-old son to do a little bit more praying. He usually says: 'Dear Jesus, Thank you for my food. Amen.' And I said: 'Taylor, you need to say "Dear Jesus, Thank you for my food"—and thank Him for one other thing when you pray today.'

"So he obediently bowed his head and said: 'Dear Jesus, Thank you for my food and one other thing. Amen.'"

Robin of Cottage Grove: "I was in line with my daughter, who is not quite 3, at Target, and behind us in line was another lady with her two daughters. My daughter turned around to the mom and said: 'What's her name?'

"And the lady said: 'Ask her.'

"So my daughter said: 'Hi, Asker!'"

Karen of Grant Township: "I asked my son if the Stillwater schools were giving the Iowa basic skills test to third-graders.

"He said: 'Iowa basics test? Boy, I hope we don't get that. I'd flunk.'

"I said: 'Why?'

"He said: 'Because I don't know *anything* about Iowa.'"

Christopher's Mom of Mendota Heights: "The other day, we were coming home from Christopher's physical—he's 6—and I said: 'How'd you like to be a doctor?'

"He immediately said: 'No. I wouldn't know what I was doing.'"

Joshua's Mom of Coon Rapids: "Yesterday, my son needed a blood test, and when I asked him which arm he was gonna use, he lifted up his left arm and said: 'This is my brave one.'"

Grandma June of Shoreview: "My son and his wife and I were going to go to Europe, and my son and his wife were concerned about leaving the kids for two weeks, and they wanted to make them real happy, so they took their extra change and put it under their little girls' pillows—so that when they woke up, they'd have a happy surprise.

"Heather woke up early, and she came running down the stairs with her hands full of money, and she said: 'Did I lose a tooth last night?'"

Neighbor Lady of Eagan: "I was talking to my neighbor in her driveway, and her 3-year-old boy comes up and says: 'Mom, Nick and me are gonna go over to Matthew's house to watch a video.'

"And she said: 'No. It's "Nick and I."'

"And he said: 'Mom, they didn't invite *you.*'"

John of Eagan: "Last night, while I was helping my 13-year-old daughter with a school project, *The Godfather* was on TV in the next room.

"In one scene, a baby is being baptized, and the priest is saying the Our Father in Latin. And as I reminisced about my days as an altar boy, I began to recite the Latin words from memory—at which time my daughter looked at me, somewhat astonished, and said: 'Geez, Dad, how many times have you *seen* this movie?'"

Penny of St. Paul: "When my daughter was about 2½, we were in Rainbow Foods one time, and it was really, really crowded, and I was frantically packing bags, trying to get out to the car. My daughter was sitting in the cart and suddenly screamed, very loudly—and she has a loud voice, anyway: 'My father's not crazy! He's a *genius!*'

"Everybody looked at her, and the lady who was checking out the groceries gave us a funny look. It took me the longest time to figure out where that came from—and I finally did! It came from *Beauty and the Beast.*

"I guess she watches too many movies, huh?"

The Woman in the Shoe of Andover: "Today I was at my 3-year-old niece's birthday party. Her name is Allison.

"Simba came to the party. When he left, Allison was crying and crying—and following him out. Allison's mom ran out to get her, and they stood in front of the house, watching Simba walk down the sidewalk.

"About four houses down, he started to get into a station wagon, and Allison all of a sudden stopped sobbing and exclaimed: *'Mom!* Simba *drives!'"* (The Woman in the Shoe, later: "My 6-year-old daughter was also at the party. She said Simba had bad breath.")

Grandma of Lake Elmo: "As we turned off Highway 8 and headed north for the final 15 miles of a trip to the cabin with our 3-year-old granddaughters, Grandpa said: 'I'm gonna look for deer.'

"Grandma said: 'I'm gonna look for bears.'

"A little voice came from the back seat: 'I'm gonna look for *giraffes.'"*

Dusty of Spring Lake Park: "My 8-year-old nephew was riding in the car with me. He was telling me all kinds of jokes.

"I asked him if he knew why the chicken crossed the road—and then told him: 'To show the deer and raccoon it could be done.'

"Not five miles later, there was a dead deer on the side of the road. My nephew said: 'The chicken *made it.'"*

A-May of Eagan: "A good friend of our family is getting married this Saturday. My 5-year-old daughter is her flower girl, and my 3-year-old son is the ring-bearer.

"We had talked with my daughter about what sort of dress she'd be wearing. We'd told my son he'd be wearing a suit.

"Michelle came over one day and picked my daughter up, and they went out and bought the flower-girl dress and brought it home.

"My son was quite upset, and he said: 'Where's my bear suit? I want my bear suit!'

"We said: 'What do you mean—a *bear* suit?'

"He said: 'Well, I'm the ring bear. I need a *bear* suit!'

"We think that he will be quite disappointed when he finally goes to pick up his little tux."

Andy Sue of Owatonna: "We were at my cousin's wedding, and she was standing up front with all of her bridesmaids. My 5-year-old daughter, Amy, turned to us and said: 'I hope the one in white wins.'"

Kat Woman: "My almost-3-year-old, Madeline, is going to be a bride for Halloween. (We recently went to a wedding.) She spent Sunday in her bridal attire and had a great time pretending to walk down the aisle, etc.

"When I asked her where she and her groom were going for their honeymoon, she said: 'Trick-or-treating.'"

Newport Angel: "I told my 2-year-old son, Scottie, that I wanted to have him be a cowboy for Halloween. And he said, just as cute as can be: 'Then I can say "Moooooo!"'"

Grumpy Old Grandpa of White Bear: "I just called my daughter and asked her what her little darling did cute today. She said: 'Well, nothing. . . . Well, just a minute,' she said. 'I asked him again what he wants to be for Halloween. He thought a minute, and then he said: "Well, Mom, how 'bout if I make a big penis costume?'"

"She didn't think it was too funny—but she knew that I would.

"She said: 'What makes little boys like that?'

"I said: 'Whether they're 3 or 63, it don't make much difference.'"

Grandma Barb of Roseville: "My two grandchildren go to day care after school. The other day, when their dad arrived to pick them up, he saw Andrew, the 6-year-old, with some other boys out on the playground. They were huddled around something.

"When Andrew got in the car, his dad asked him what they had been doing, and Andrew said they were looking at a magazine. (When I heard that, I thought: 'Uh-oh!'—just sure what was coming.) He asked what they were looking at in it, and Andrew said: 'Naked pictures.'

"His dad asked him what he saw, and Andrew said, rather disgustedly: 'Nothing. You got here too soon.'"

Steamed Crab of Inver Grove Heights: "My 7-year-old was downstairs, playing, quietly, and all of a sudden I heard this terrible banging.

"In my best Calm Parent voice, I called down: 'Josh? What are you doing?'

"There's a pause. He says: 'Playing.'

"'With what?'

"Another pause. 'My cars.'

"'And . . . ?'

"Another pause. 'The dryer.'"

Sherb of Exeland, Wis.: "I was in the post office the other day, and this little boy came in with a little girl behind him.

"I said: 'Is that your little sister?'

"He turned around and looked at her, studied her for a minute, and said: 'No. She looks different than that.'"

Gramma Judie of Woodbury: "My 4½-year-old granddaughter, Sara, happens to look very much like her mom. The other day, Sara was looking at pictures taken of her mother when she was a little girl. After a while of pondering the pictures, Sara said: 'Hey, Mom! You're wearing my face!'"

Judy of the East Side: "I told my son to get out of bed this morning, and he wouldn't. He was real pokey. So then they went and climbed in my bed, and I said: 'C'mon! C'mon! Get up! We've gotta go to school!'

"He said: 'Mom, this isn't me. This is just a big stain on your bed.'"

Mary of Maplewood: "A few years ago, my father gave us a small sculpture of the Last Supper. I showed it to my daughter, who was 3 at the time. She looked at the round, flat loaves of bread in front of each figure and said, 'They had pizza?'"

Sheri of Maplewood: "About a year ago, my friend Roxi felt it was time that her son Michael, who was 5 at the time, knew a little bit more about the Easter story—not just the Easter Bunny and goodies and stuff like that. So she told him the Easter story.

"A few days later, she was driving in the car, and he was in the back seat with his friend, and Michael was telling his friend how Jesus was hung on the cross and died, and how they took Jesus down from the cross and put him in a cave . . . and three days later, he rolled that stone away, and there was the Easter Bunny."

Daddy Squid of Frogtown: "On Easter Sunday morning, we decided to play Easter Bunny with our little bundle of joy, Brianna, so I put socks on my hands in order to disguise them as ears. Went outside, rang the doorbell, wiggled my 'ears,' and went back in the house.

"I said: 'Brianna, did you see the Easter Bunny?'

"And she said: 'Yeah—and he had socks on his ears!'"

Carol of Eagan: "My nephew was playing outside and talking to his neighbor. My nephew is 3 years old.

"His neighbor said: 'Say, Aaron, how old *are* you?'

"And Aaron said: 'I can't tell you.'

"And his neighbor said: 'Why not?'

"And Aaron said: 'Because I have my mittens on.'"

P. & P.'s Mom of Eagan: "This morning, my almost-3-year-old daughter and I passed a house near ours that had a SOLD sign on the realty-company sign.

"I said: 'Oh, somebody *bought* that house.'

"And my daughter said: 'How will they carry it?'"

Mom Jodi of St. Paul, who found a jam-packed parking lot at the grocery store on a shopping trip with her 8-year-old son: "I said: 'Wow, Joe, where'd all these people come from?'

"He looks out, and he says: 'Minnesota . . . Minnesota . . . Minnesota . . . .'"

The Dinosaur of Oakdale: "We were at a car show today, and there was a boy about my daughter's age (18 months) sitting in a stroller. My daughter runs up to him and starts crying 'Baby baby baby'—as she says to any young child, regardless of their real age.

"After we walked away, this little boy's older sister (who was around 4 or 5) comes up and pulls on my shirt and says: 'Excuse me, lady, but that little boy who is with me is a *toddler,* not a *baby!*'"

Jack's Aunt of Highland Park: "My nephew Jack was very precocious verbally, but still a toddler at heart. Right when he was about to turn 2, his mother walked into the bathroom and saw him sitting amid reams and reams of unfolded toilet paper.

"She said: 'Jack, what are you *doing?*'

"And he said—with conviction, and a little glee: 'I'm being wasteful.'"

Julie of Cottage Grove: "Last night, my 3-year-old daughter, Maddie, was getting ready for dinner.

"I said: 'What do you want for dinner?'

"And she said: 'I want a Pop Tart.'

"I said: 'No, you can't have a Pop Tart for dinner.'

"She said: 'Well, then I want breakfast.'

"These kids are gettin' smarter and smarter each day."

The Reading Doc of Rochester: "My 3-year-old granddaughter, Beaner, is a very intelligent little tyke. . . .

"I keep a very large jar of bubble gum in my office (courtesy of **Bob** of Rochester), and Beaner invariably cons me out of a piece whenever she comes over.

"On this particular occasion, she asked for some gum, and I said she couldn't have any right now because we were going to eat right away—but she could have some after supper. She promised it wouldn't spoil her dinner and said she needed to have some gum now.

"I firmly reiterated: 'No! No gum until after supper!'

"She persisted, so I knelt down in front of her and held her face-to-face and said: 'Papa just said "No," and around here that means NO! Now what part of "No" don't you understand?'

"She kind of squinched up her face in thought and then said: 'The N!'"

Dan of St. Paul: "My two daughters have their little cousin over for the afternoon. They were out playing in the back yard, and I was putting a few additional layers of duct tape on a refrigerator that we're sending to NSP. They asked me what I was doing, and I told them.

"My older daughter said: 'That's duct tape'—to which her little cousin said: 'Quack, quack.'

"The older one explained that it's not duck tape; it's *duct* tape.

"At which point, my younger daughter pipes up: 'Yeah, that means it *used* to go "Quack, quack."'"

Scandinavian Mama of Shoreview: "When my cousin was about 5 years old, he announced to his mom one day that he was running away. She said: 'We'll miss you—but you've gotta do what you've gotta do.' So he packed his little suitcase and trudged off down a long driveway, dragging his suitcase behind him.

"Some time later, his white-blond hair and clear blue eyes were seen boppin' back down the driveway. 'Hey, Mom!' he called. 'Could you give me a ride?'"

Jeanie of Woodbury: "When my two granddaughters, who are cousins, were younger—maybe 7 and 9, or thereabouts—the older girl, Julie, had begun to doubt the Tooth Fairy story. In fact, one day she told Sarah that she had discovered who the Tooth Fairy was. She said: 'It's my mom.'

"The next day, Sarah said to her mother: 'I know who the Tooth Fairy is.'

"And Kathy thought: 'Oh, no. She's already figured it out.'

"And then Sarah continued: 'It's Aunt Roxanne!'

"Aren't kids fun?"

Cindy of South St. Paul: "I attended a First Communion this past Saturday for my 8-year-old niece, Jessica. I had my almost-3-year-old niece, Ashley, sitting on my lap, and the kids making their First Communion were helping the priest set the altar up for Communion. They had put a white tablecloth on the altar, along with a container of Communion wafers and a clear glass wine decanter with wine in it that was almost the color of cherry Kool-Aid—a very bright red.

"Ashley turned around and looked at me and asked: 'Are we having Kiddie Cocktails?'"

Packer Backer of Somerset, Wis.: "While visiting Como Park Zoo, my 3½-year-old nephew, Jacob, asked my sister: 'Mom, what do polar bears drink?'

"Her reply: 'Oh . . . water, I guess.'

"To which he added: 'And Coke, too—right?'"

Young **Molly** of St. Paul: "I was with my 6-year-old cousin, Andrew, at Wal-Mart the other day, and we stopped in the cafeteria to get a pop. We decided to get the large, 32-ounce pop. It was one of those pop dispensers that offers you about eight different kinds, and all you do is press the square that indicates that kind of pop.

"He insisted on pressing the square himself, and once the cup was filled and he saw how much pop we got, his eyes couldn't believe it and he said: 'Wow! How can that little square hold so much pop?'"

Grandma Margaret of Hastings: "I was down by the Mississippi River with my little granddaughter, Sarah, who is 6. She looked at the water, and she saw all the foam, and she said: 'Oh, Grandma! Look at all the people that have spit in the river!'"

Bev of White Bear Lake: "My 6-year-old grandson was over, and we took a walk to the park. And while we're there, he's playing on the monkey bars, and he spits.

"So I said to him: 'Oh, Josh. That's a *terrible* habit!'

"'Oh, Grandma,' he said, 'this is just a phase I'm going through.'"

BULLETIN BOARD SAYS: Bev—and the rest of us—can only hope.

Jeanne of St. Paul: "The parents just dropped the kids off for their weekly visit to Grandma and Grandpa. Katie—the 4-year-old—waved goodbye to her mother and father, and she said: 'I love you both—no matter what.'"

Gramma Barb of St. Paul: "Last week, my grandson Matthew was eagerly waiting for the school bus for his first day of school. His mom, Nancy, asked Matthew if he would like her to follow the school bus in the car—to make sure he got to school OK.

"'Whatever makes you comfortable, Mom' was the reply.

"Guess he's ready for school."

Cathy of River Falls, Wis.: "I was serving breakfast to my 4½-year-old. Asked her what she wanted for breakfast. She said she wanted waffles—and then she went into the refrigerator, while I was fixing the waffles, and got out two slices of bologna.

"She turned to me, and she said: 'You know, this is part of a complete breakfast.'

"I think she might have been watching too many commercials lately."

Alex's Mom of St. Paul: "My son Alex, who turned 5 yesterday, loves ham sandwiches. On a recent Sunday night, not wanting to cook much of anything, I decided to use a canned ham we had received as part of a gift pack. I showed Alex the key on the side of the can and unwound the side strip and popped open the top to reveal the ham.

"Never having seen this before, Alex exclaimed: 'Canned *ham?* I have *so* much to learn.'"

Jeannie of White Bear Lake: "My 5-year-old is very into losing his teeth—although he hasn't, yet. He has repeatedly bothered me to check to see if his teeth are falling out yet. One day, he came to me and said: 'Mom, will you see if I have any loose teeth?' So I checked his teeth, and my husband said: 'Taylor, why do you want your teeth to be out so bad?'

"He said: 'Well, Dad, I need a new look.'"

Paul W. of St. Paul, speaking of his 4-year-old son: "After a very busy day of going to the park and runnin' around and goin' shopping—and all the busywork— one Sunday afternoon, he was very tired. Lay down on the couch.

"Just kinda kicked back, and Ma—my wife—walks around the corner and says: 'Hello, bud. What's up?'

"And he looks at her for a moment, pauses and, with a heavy sigh, rolls his head around and says: 'I think I just need more leisure time.'"

Annette of New Brighton: "Napping is serious business at my sister's house, and my sister does not tolerate any funny business.

"My 3-year-old niece, Caitlin, decided to take a nap with her doll one afternoon. My sister went to check in on Caitlin several minutes later, to see if she had settled down. Caitlin was awake, but her doll had been moved to her toy crib.

"'Why'd you move your doll?' my sister asked.

"Caitlin responded: 'She kept foolin' around.'"

Thompsons of Maplewood: "Our grandson arrived from Missouri to spend a week. Hardly with us two hours when he said: 'Am I driving you crazy yet?'"

Grandma Bev of Roseville: "A couple of weeks ago, I watched three of our grandchildren and two of their friends for the afternoon. They were great—but I did have to lower the boom once.

"A little later, 8-year-old Becky said: 'Grandma, you're kinda *cute* when you're mad.'"

The Bikini-impaired Mom of 4 of Apple Valley: "Last Sunday, we were drivin' up to Osseo for a swim in my sister's pool, and the kids were excited, and my oldest son—almost 11—says, out of the blue: 'Mom, I'm sure glad you're not one of those sexy moms who wears a bikini.'

"How's that for a compliment?

"I said: 'Even if I had a sexy body, you wouldn't want me to wear one?'

" 'No way!' he says. 'That's gross when it's your mom.'

"P.S. This is the same son who said, not long ago: 'Mom, do all the kids think their mom is the prettiest mom?' I love that kid."

Laurie of Frederic, Wis.: "Last night, my 3-year-old, Daniel, asked if he could go to the pool. I said no, and he replied: 'But other kids are!'

"I said: 'Yes—but *they* have nice mothers!'

"He said: 'I have nice mother!'

"I said: 'Well, how come she won't let you go to the pool?'

"He got the strangest look on his face. Then his eyes got big, and he said: 'Don't know!'

"He really wanted to believe he has a nice mother, but the facts weren't adding up."

The Domestic Goddess of Lakeville: "My 3-year-old was swimming in the pool, and she was playing with a beach ball. I told her to hold the beach ball and try floating.

"She says: 'Why?'

"And I said: ' 'Cause it'll keep your head above water.'

"And she says: 'Why?'

"I said: 'Because it's filled with air.'

"And she said: 'What is? My head?'"

Linda W. of Eagan: "My dearest friend and her husband have been doing a lot of landscaping in their back yard. Their neighbors came over, and they have a 6-year-old boy, and they asked: 'What have you been doing here lately?' And Kim said: 'Oh, we just got the big landscaping bug.' And she explained everything they were doing—with putting up little walls and flowers and trees and bushes and all of this stuff; went on and on for, like, 10 minutes or so.

"So this little boy looks up at her and says—when she was finished; very politely: 'Can I see it?' And Kim said: 'See what?' And he said: 'The big bug.'"

Flange Man of Minneapolis: "After the space shuttle *Challenger* exploded—around the time the presidential commission made its report—the thing was in the news a lot again, and my daughter asked me one day why it had blown up. She was about 6 at the time. I went into a long, detailed history of Morton Thiokol, and solid rocket boosters versus liquid rockets; went on for about 20 minutes and finally said: 'They think it blew up because of bad seals.'

"And she looked at me with the saddest look on her face and said: 'Ohhhhh, Daddy, did the seals die, too?'"

Star of White Bear Lake: "My 8-year-old son, Brandon, went to see *Apollo 13* with his dad the other day. We were discussing the movie and how much he liked it, and I said: 'Did you know that was a true story?'

"And he said: 'I didn't know Tom Hanks was an astronaut.'"

B.A. of Apple Valley: "The other day, my husband was leaving for work when he turned to my 2½-year-old son and said: 'Well, Taylor, you have a good day today.'

"Taylor looked up at his daddy and said: 'Daddy, you have a good day, too. And don't make a B.M. in your pants!'"

Cheri of Cottage Grove: "I'm in the process of potty-training my son, who's 3 years old. One day, he came walking out of the bathroom and I noticed that his pants were wet.

"I asked him: 'Carl, did you have an accident in your pants?'

"He said: 'No.'

"So I asked him: 'Then how did your pants get wet?'

"And he said: 'My penis did it.'"

Gloria of St. Paul: "My 5-year-old grandson, Bobby, was stranded in the bathroom—out of toilet paper. He kept calling and calling to his mom for a roll of paper, but she was in another part of the house and couldn't hear him for several minutes.

"When she finally arrived, he gave a sigh of relief: 'Phew! It's about time! Two more seconds, and I would have gotten hemorrhoids!'"

Just a Mom of St. Paul: "Yesterday, my son was in the bathroom, and he had the door closed, and he was in there forever. I needed to go to the grocery store, and I'm hollerin' at him: 'C'mon, Joey! Hurry up! Let's get goin'!' And he's takin' forever, and I said: 'Joey, what is taking you so long? Why are you still in there?'

"And he looks at me and says: 'Mom, I think I've got fiber.'"

Carrie of Fridley: "My daughter Veronica—she's 7—was in the bathtub, and I said: 'Veronica, get out of the tub. You've been in there for an hour.'

"She said: 'Well, how long is that?'

"And I said: 'As long as two "Full House"s.'

"And she said: 'Oh, really? Which *ones?*'"

Auntie Debbie of Plymouth: "My sister Lori was in her kitchen doing dishes while her 4-year-old son, Alex, watched TV in the living room. Lori thought Alex was watching cartoons, but she discovered he had changed the channel when he walked into the kitchen with a very concerned look on his face and said: 'Mom, are you going to be on "Jenny Jones" when someone steals your man?'"

Bob of Rochester: "My friend Dale was baby-sitting for his 3-year-old niece. They were doing different things—playing Barbies, and then they had a little tea party. They sat at her little table, and they were gonna have cookies made of Play-Doh.

"She brought her little pot around, and she said: 'I'm sorry. I'm all out of tea. Would you like some cappuccino?'"

Kathy of Litchfield: "I've been divorced for about two years. My 5-year-old daughter comes up to me the other day and says: 'Mommy, I think it's time to get a new dad.' I was busy doing some work, so I said: 'Sure, whatever. Go out and play.'

"She comes back about five minutes later going, 'Mommy, Mommy, I found him. I found my new daddy. She holds up the J.C. Penney catalog in the underwear section for men and says: 'I want this one.' She'd picked him out.

"I said: 'Jessie, we can't order guys out of the magazine.'

"And she said: 'Sure you can, Mommy. You can charge him.'"

Grandma Lean of Center City: "My cousin's husband had just come in from chores. Both of his children were sitting up to the table, and his wife, Marlene, was putting dinner on the table.

"She had burned the potatoes a bit, so Bob couldn't resist teasing her a little: 'Gee, kids, Mom burned the potatoes. Maybe we should get a new Mom!'

"Bob was grinning pretty big when both little heads nodded in agreement—until his son piped up and asked: 'Can we get a new Dad, too?'"

Sally of St. Paul: "My parents baby-sit my daughter, Alison, while I'm at work.

They had a cat named Charlie who had one of his eyes removed and sewn shut, due to an infection.

"When Alison was 3 years old, Charlie died, and her grandparents bought a new cat. I called from work to see if the new cat had arrived, and Alison was so excited to tell me: 'Grandma and Grandpa got a new cat today! And guess what! He has two eyes!'"

Anonymous woman of Roseville: "Last Saturday, with the extended family over, it was noted by all that our old—14-year-old—cat was failing. Some thought was given to her demise. Our 7-year-old granddaughter made the comment: 'I know why you don't want to put her to sleep, Grandma.'

"I said: 'Why?'

"And, wise beyond her years, she said: 'Because then our kitty would probably die—and we'd miss her.'

"How true."

R.F.K. of the East Side: "The other day, I was driving around Como Lake with my granddaughter—on a rainy, rainy day—and I said: 'Boy, the only thing that likes a rainy day like this is ducks. They can be out in the middle of the lake, and the rain just falls on 'em and runs off their backs. No problem.'

"And she said: 'Yeah—and even on a nice day!'

"I said: 'Yeah, on a nice day, the ducks are out in the nice cool lake, and when they come out, people feed 'em corn and bread. They've really got it made.'

"And she just looked straight ahead and said: 'Life is good.'"

The Love Child of Eagan: "Today, my 3-year-old was looking at a picture of my husband and me before he was born, and he said: 'Well, where was I?'

"I said: 'You were up in heaven with God still.'

"And he said: 'Who's that baby?' He pointed to a picture of himself.

"'Well, that's you!' I said. 'That was after God sent me a beautiful baby boy named David.'

"And he said: 'Boy, that God's a good thing.'"

J.J. of North St. Paul: "I teach first-grade Sunday school, and I asked a question for which the answer was 'Jesus.' The little girl who always answers first—and she's *always* right—blurted out: 'God!'

"I was giving that look that says 'Well, that answer wasn't *quite* right,' and my daughter, who's often too shy to answer, says: 'Jesus!'

"And the first little girl didn't want to be outdone, so she says: 'Yeah. That's what I meant—but I call him "God" for short.'"

Sande of Woodbury: "My father-in-law passed away a year ago. Our 4-year-old grandson, Michael, was very close to him and misses him very much.

"Last spring, as Michael was preparing for the year-end program at preschool, he said he wished God would let Papa come down from heaven to be there. I explained that that couldn't happen, but that the rest of our family would be there—and if he sang clearly and loudly, we would hear him, and Papa would, too.

"He thought about that for a moment, and then he said: 'But Grandma, I don't think I can sing that loud.'

"To Papa: We know you can hear us even when we whisper—and we miss you."

A.J.'s Mom of Little Canada: "My son A.J. was having a discussion with his father this evening when I heard him say: 'Dad, when I get big like you, I'm going to marry Mom, and we will have one boy.' He paused only for a brief second, then looked at my husband and said: 'Dad, what are *you* going to do?' I peeked in the room, laughing.

"My husband said: 'I suppose you heard that.'

"I smiled and said: 'Yeah. What *are* you going to do?'

"He has yet to answer the question, so my son and I are *both* wondering what his answer will be.

"There's no love like a son has for his mother—especially when he's 3 years old."

Judy of St. Paul Park: "When our son was in preschool, he would look up at me with his big brown eyes and say: 'Mom, when I grow up, I'm gonna marry you.' And I would hug him and say: 'Victor, the day will come when you won't want to marry me.'

"When Victor was in the first grade, he looked up at me and said: 'Mom, remember how you said the day would come when I wouldn't want to marry you? Well, this is the day.'

"He made me smile with tears in my eyes."

CHAPTER TEN

'TIL DEATH DO US PART

It began with **Lulu** of St. Paul: "I am proposing a new category, which is: things that go on your permanent record as a spouse. An example would be:

"When we were first married and we were lying in bed and I got an uncontrollable case of the hiccoughs, my husband—Starbuck, also of St. Paul—decided to scare the hiccoughs out of me, and screamed . . . and scared me so much that I burst into tears and was just unconsolably frightened. Cried and cried. Finally got over it, and we went to sleep.

"This was Mark No. 1 on the Permanent Record, and it still comes up: how he still feels bad about the time he made me cry, trying to scare away the hiccoughs— although the story always ends with: 'Well, I did get rid of those hiccoughs, didn't I?'"

Melissa of Lakeland: "Last night, my dog crawled into bed between my husband and me and put her head on my pillow.

"As I was falling asleep, I said: 'I love you.'

"Hearing no response, I said: 'Oh, don't you love me, too?'

"My husband laughed and said: 'I thought you were talkin' to the dog.'"

Jill of Roseville: "My husband and I celebrated our 12th anniversary on October 8th. I was just thinking about how much we've changed in the last 12 years—and how much more comfortable we are with each other now.

"One example: One night right after we had gone to bed, we were both lying on our sides, with my husband behind me. After a couple of minutes, he gently patted my hip. A couple of minutes later, he gently patted my hip again. I was thinking it was a pretty sweet gesture at the end of a long day.

"After the third time he patted my hip, I began to wonder why he was doing this. When I turned around, I realized he was *measuring our butts*—to see whose butt was bigger.

"I yelled: 'You jerk!'—and we both got a pretty good laugh out of it.

"Now, see, he wouldn't have dreamed of doing that when we were first married—but, then again, 12 years and three babies ago, it wouldn't have been near as close a call."

Andrea of Woodbury: "My husband and I were watching 'Entertainment Tonight,' and they had a segment on La Toya Jackson posing for *Playboy.* I said: 'Boy, if I had a body like that, I'd pose for *Playboy* in a minute.'

"He said: 'Well, I think you *could* pose.'

"I said: 'I couldn't pose for *Playboy!*'

"And then he comes back with: 'Well, I didn't mean *Playboy*. I meant one of those cheaper magazines.'"

Betsy the Bean Counter of St. Paul: "I was sitting in front of the television with my beloved, just kind of scanning the Sunday-evening selections. He had the clicker in hand, as normal.

"I said to him: 'Oh, did you hear they're interviewing all of the *Playboy* Bunnies from the past 20 years . . . on what they've done with their lives since they were posing in the nude?'

"And all of a sudden, the clicking gets a little faster—but he tries to look real nonchalant. He's clicking, looking, clicking, looking—and he finally goes: 'You know what channel it was on?'

"And I just started laughing."

Pam of St. Paul: "My son is 12½—and the testosterone is just starting to flow.

"Last week, I was standing in the kitchen when my son arrived home from gymnastics. He walked in with his dad and proceeded to sit at the kitchen table.

" 'Mom,' he said, 'I was talkin' to Dad on the way home, and I want to know if you'd let me have a *Playboy.*'

"Well, being a mother of the '90s, I started to tell him that if he wanted to look at a naked woman, there were any number of books he could look at, but I felt that *Playboy* only depicted women for sex and nothing else.

"I told him: 'When you're looking at a *Playboy,* you're not thinking that that woman is probably a good mom, or a good doctor, or a good lawyer. You're just thinking: "Boy, I'd like to have sex with her"—and there's so much *more* to women than that.' I said: 'And besides: You probably won't believe this right now, but sex is just a very small part of a relationship.'

"So after my whole speech, I look over at my husband—who's been sitting there awfully quiet—and I said: 'Well, do *you* have anything to say?'

"And he says—real sheepishly, with his head down, like a little kid: '*I* told him he could *have* one.'"

Beanie Burger of Westby, Wis.: "My daughter, Brooke, received an Aladdin paper-doll set and was playing happily with it until yesterday.

"The humidity had really affected the cardboard figures, and they wouldn't stand up straight for her. She handed me one in her frustration and said: 'Here, Mom. Make Aladdin stiff!'

"My husband glanced over his paper and said: 'Well, if anyone can, she can.'"

Charity of Eagan: "Today, my husband and I were playin' Monopoly, and I landed on the Community Chest spot and drew the card that says 'You have won second prize in a beauty contest. Collect $10.'

"And my husband said the sweetest thing; he said: 'Awww, you should've won $10,000, honey.'

"I just thought that was sweet."

BULLETIN BOARD WAGS: It is, indeed. But we can't help wondering: Did he think you should've gotten first prize—or just a lot more money for second?

Lady C. of South St. Paul: "The other day, I was out in the garden, right in the middle of it, wearing my bathing suit. I bent over, like one of those old-lady cutouts that people have in their yard, and my husband said: 'What's that *beautiful* thing bloomin' in the garden?'

"I went: 'Which? Which one?'

"And he said: '*You,* silly.'

"Wasn't that a nice thing to say?"

K.A.B. of Burnsville, awaiting the arrival of her first child: "I'm at the point where I'm no longer slim, but neither have I taken on that definite pregnant shape. I'm feeling rather unattractive. Believe me: I wouldn't mind looking definitely pregnant, but right now I think I just look out of shape and overweight.

"So one day, while I'm straightening up the house—waiting for my tummy to grow, and again feeling unattractive—my husband bursts into the house with a huge bouquet of gladiolus.

"'What a wonderful surprise,' I say. 'They're beautiful.'

"'No,' says my sweet husband. '*You're* beautiful.'"

Cajun Chris of Woodbury: "I went to college in New Orleans and have a love for spicy foods. However, I sometimes have problems processing cheese products. *[BULLETIN BOARD NOTES: This is not a good sign.]*

"I recently made the mistake of having, for lunch, two cheese burritos, with an extremely generous portion of refried beans. *[Uh-oh.]* Later that night, my wife, Karen, wanted to rent a movie, so we went up to the local video store. (I should mention now: My wife is pregnant with *twins—our first and second.)*

"Karen went to the Romance section, while I looked for an Action movie. My stomach had been uneasy all afternoon. The burritos and beans were giving it all it could handle. *[Oh, dear.]*

"All of a sudden *[Oh, no! Not all of a sudden!],* I was stricken by an enormous gastric episode. *[Isn't that just a beautiful way to put it?]* In a panic, I rushed to find Karen so we could leave.

"As I neared the Romance section, it happened! *[Not here! Not now!]* I experienced a tremendous, but blessedly silent, posterior breeze. *[Ahhhhhhhhh!]* It stopped me in my tracks—and, of course, one of the Immutable Laws of the Universe is: When this sort of an 'accident' occurs, some stranger always happens to round the corner and enter the area.

"The poor man understandably shot me an angry, sickened look. Seeing that Karen was out of earshot, I pointed to her and blurted out: 'Please forgive my wife. She's *pregnant.'*

"The man gave me an embarrassed look of apology and scampered off to another area of the store.

"I feel bad about my cowardly act, but what could I do? Sorry, Hon!"

The Merry Rose of St. Paul: "My daughter was born last year on Grand Old Days. We had gone there with the intent of walking the baby out, because I was tired of being pregnant.

"We had been talking to some friends of mine. When we said goodbye, I turned around and felt my water break. I turned to my honey and said: 'Honey, I think it's time.'

"He said: 'Are you sure?'

"And I said: 'Well, there's a bathroom down there. I could check.' So we went half a block back from where we'd come, and I went into one of the Satellites to check. He was standing at a little refreshment wagon—getting a glass of lemonade.

"I came out and said: 'Honey, my water's breaking.'

"And he said: 'Just a minute, then'—and he turned around and bought a corn dog."

Emma Rose's Dad: "Emma Rose was born here in St. Paul on February 21st, and during labor my wife put me in charge of music—basically to keep me out of the way, so I wouldn't pass out on her.

"I was playing a combination tape with a lot of different artists, and at one point—during a particularly stressful contraction, when she was crouched down on the floor—James Brown's voice came blaring through the speakers, screaming 'I feel *good!*'

"I got quite a chuckle out of it at the time. My wife was less than amused."

Noelle of Rosemount: "I gave birth on March 21st of this year, during the NCAA tournament. My husband and the doctor, in between contractions, kept watching the basketball game and discussing what was going on in the game.

"My mom was there, and she kept having total conniptions—because I had an epidural, and I couldn't feel my contractions, so I didn't know they were happening.

"The doctor and my husband were watching the game, and they kept missing my contractions. They were like: 'Oh, we'll catch her the next time.'"

Christina of Maplewood: "I was in the hospital, having just delivered our first child—a beautiful girl—when a John Wayne movie comes on. And my husband takes a picture of John Wayne on the television! Hard to understand."

New Mom of Minneapolis: "After trying to have a baby for a couple of years, my husband and I are really savoring every moment with our new son. He's a month old, and like a lot of first-time parents, we're documenting every first he has.

"My husband went to make copies of Max's birth certificate, with the footprints—and he brought it back home, and he was so proud, and he says: 'Look!' He'd enlarged the footprints so they'd be easier to see, so instead of these nice, tiny little footprints, they're these huge, monster feet that take up half the page—which kind of defeats the purpose.

"He's recopying the baby's footprints."

Katie of Maple Grove: "Last night, my husband and I realized that we had been zapped by parenthood. We finally got our 3-year-old to bed at 10 P.M., and instead of sharing a romantic few moments, we spent the next 15 minutes trying to find the rest of the hidden pictures in *Highlights* magazine.

"We looked at each other and laughed."

The Home Creator of St. Paul: "My husband hates the smell of Doritos, particularly on my breath, so I try to make a point of not eating them when I'm home.

"I had been out and had some left over, and happened to finish them up when I was home. A couple minutes later, he's holding our 2-month-old baby, and I'm standing next to him, talking—and all of a sudden, he looks at me and says: 'Is that your breath that smells so bad, or did the baby poop?'

"I looked at him, and I said: 'Well, thanks a *lot,* dear.'

"And the funny part is that it really didn't bother me—having been married for a while, and having kids.

"But I knew it was time to brush my teeth."

Herta of Mac-Groveland: "One night, my husband and I were sitting out on the front porch, and he looked up at me and said: 'Herta, your feet smell.'

"I said 'Hmmmm'—and leaned over and smelled my own foot and said: 'No, they don't.' Whereupon he leaned over and smelled his own foot and said: 'Never mind.'

"I just thought that was interesting—that he assumed it was me. Isn't that typical?"

BULLETIN BOARD REPLIES: We really couldn't say—but we'll take your word for it.

The Queen's Mum of Vermillion: "We've been married for well over 30 years, the man I love and I.

"When I was a very young bride, still groping my way through the mysteries of marriage, he said to me: 'Before you prepare sauerkraut, you should call my mom. Nobody does it like her, and if you're gonna do it, you might as well learn to do it right.'

" 'Well!' I thought. 'This must be some Luxembourg secret that the rest of us Germanic folks don't know about'—so I dutifully called my mother-in-law. I said: 'Ma, what's your secret to sauerkraut? The man says nobody makes it like you, and I have to learn to do it right.'

"I hung on the phone, waiting for the convulsive laughter to die down, and she finally gasped and said: 'Well, first I open the can.' "

Dan of the West Side: "One day, I was out in my front yard planting grass seed. I did that about 10 o'clock in the morning. After I'd worked hard all day, I came in the house, and I was looking at the grass-seed bag for instructions on how to take care of my grass. On the front of the bag, it said 'Fast-growing Seeds.' I proceeded to tell my wife: 'Oh, look, honey, this is fast-growing grass.'

"I got up and walked to the front window, and I said: 'Oh, look, Molly! There's grass growin' already!'

"She jumped up from the table and ran to the front. This was, like, six hours after I planted the grass seed. I thought that was the funniest thing. She didn't appreciate it that much."

Alpha November of Cottage Grove: "Last spring, my 12-year-old daughter complained of a 'tummy' ache, and shortly after that, my wife and daughter were resting on our bed having a tender mom/daughter talk. I assumed that these were signs that my daughter was having her first menstrual period.

"My suspicions were confirmed the following morning when my daughter called me into the bathroom. Sitting on the toilet, wearing a bathrobe, and holding one my wife's 'super plus' tampons, she said: 'Mom's at the store. How do I use this?'

"After a long pause and a deep breath, I told her I didn't have any experience with that sort of thing, but if she handed the tampon to me, I could see if there were any directions on it.

"While I was staring blankly at the tampon, wondering what to do next, my wife, who was standing in the bathtub hiding behind the shower curtain, burst out laughing.

"It was at that moment that I realized the whole thing was a setup, it was April 1st, and I was the fool. (Again.)"

Sherry of Woodbury: "A few years ago, we bought a futon for the guest room, and my husband decided that we could then get rid of the twin bed that was in there. Well, this was the twin bed I had when I was growing up, and I was kind of attached to it—but I reluctantly agreed, and we put an ad in the paper.

"After about a week, no one had shown any interest in this bed and I had had time to reconsider. So I told him I just really didn't want to sell the bed. Well, he reluctantly agreed. He did point out that we had wasted money on this newspaper ad.

"Of course, the very next day, an elderly gentleman calls—and he's *very* interested in the bed. Wants to know everything about it. I explained that it wasn't for sale, but he was very persistent—and finally he offered me a thousand dollars for the bed. I thought that was kind of odd, but I just kinda laughed and told him it wasn't for sale.

"At that point, his voice changed—and my husband's voice comes over the line, saying: 'You wouldn't take a thousand dollars for that bed?'

"We still have the bed. We now refer to it as The Thousand Dollar Bed.

"And I still have the husband."

BULLETIN BOARD NOTES: And he—perhaps more to the point—still has you.

Hoof Hearted of Rosemount: "My wife will never let me forget that I called her by my ex-wife's name . . . *[BULLETIN BOARD INTERRUPTS: Let us pause here to let you consider: What would be the single most embarrassing time and place to call your wife by your ex-wife's name? No; not then, and not there. But Hoof Hearted knows . . . and now he'll tell you]* . . . at the altar on our wedding day.

"My father gave me more crap for it that day than she did, but I haven't heard the end of it since."

Jeanne of St. Paul: "We are celebrating our 43rd wedding anniversary today, and I gave my husband an anniversary card. He read it, and he said: 'Thank you, Jane . . . I mean *Jeanne.*'

"I thought that was pretty funny."

Been There and Done That of Maplewood: "If you recall, back in the old days when you first got married, why, you had all these loving names: Sweetheart and Darling and Honey.

"Well, over the years—40-plus for my child bride and I—I've kind of gotten into the habit of not listening when she's speaking to me. The other day, to get my attention, she yelled out: 'Hey, Liver Spot!'

"Worked like a charm."

Barb of Mahtomedi: "First of all, I'll tell you that my husband and I have been married 39 years. Recently, during a very romantic interlude—at an *extremely* crucial moment—I moaned and cried out. My husband was *thrilled* over my response—until I told him I had a very painful muscle spasm in my leg.

"Needless to say, his ego was deflated, also.

"Then we laughed about the joys of middle age."

The Big Cheese of Maplewood called to describe a romantic interlude at the end of a very nice evening (dining out, after-dinner drinks—the whole nine yards) with his wife of more than 20 years: "After a while—a while for *me,* anyways— and a considerable effort, I started to get some beads of perspiration on me. One of the beads of sweat dropped down and hit my wife, and she looks up at me and says: 'Are you sweating—or are you drooling?'

"I was . . . stunned. I mean, you know, I completely lost the moment. I guess my manlihood or something was questioned.

"Later on, we were layin' there anyways, kinda reflecting on a nice evening, and I just looked over at her and I says: *'Drooling!* How could you say *drooling?'* "

M.J. of Apple Valley passed along his wife's response to the indecent proposal in *Indecent Proposal:* "She said: 'Honey, if Robert Redford asked me to have sex with him for a million dollars, don't worry. I'd do it—but I'd close my eyes and think of you.' "

Terri of Burnsville: "It's our 25th anniversary this week. I remember back, six weeks after our son was born, my husband had planned a romantic evening—the first in a very, very long time. We were all excited.

"He had candles everywhere, and romantic music on the stereo, with a blanket laid out before the fireplace. He told me to lie on the blanket while he got the champagne. We were trying to act really mature, which we still don't seem to be.

"The mood is set. Into the love nest walks Steve, my 6-foot husband, trailing a small child's wagon behind him with the champagne and glasses. He was all crouched down, so low to the ground. He was wearing this stupid old smoking jacket; I don't even know where he got it. I laughed and laughed and laughed until I cried.

"That's my Steve, and I love him the way he is and thank him for letting me be who I am, even if that's not a traditional wife."

Carl's Neighbor: "Our friend Mark will turn 40 on July 4. My husband decided it would be fun to send a pair of women's panties, anonymously, to Mark each day for about a week before his birthday.

"When Mark received the first pair, he assumed that his wife, Sonia, had something to do with it. That night, he went into their bedroom, slipped on the lacy yellow panties, and called his wife. When Sonia entered the room, Mark was leaning seductively against the door frame, asking 'How do you like my new panties, honey?'

"He realized immediately, by the look on Sonia's face, that she had nothing to do with the panties. Boy, was his face red!

"But, you know, Mark's kept himself in pretty good shape for a 40-year-old. I'll bet he looked *sweet* in those lacy yellow panties."

Mike of Mounds Park: "My wife and I were expecting some friends over to spend the evening with us.

"They arrived earlier than expected.

"My wife was upstairs getting dressed.

"Not knowing our friends had arrived, she yelled down: 'Honey, is there anything you want before I get dressed?'"

Susan of Bloomington, Ill.: "My husband and I were married in St. Paul, 17 years ago. We were pretty much both virgins on the day we wed. *[BULLETIN BOARD NOTES: Delicately put.]* While I had never been around the block, I guess I'd been out to the corner—but my husband had never even been on the front porch.

"After about the first six weeks of the gentlest and kindest sex I ever could have imagined, I suggested to him that I was probably capable of . . . I don't know . . . enduring a little more vigor? So the next time he came to me, I was laying back on the pillow, and he walks over and lifts me up by my shoulders and gives me a good shaking—then lays me back down and proceeds to make the gentlest and kindest love, as I'd had in the previous six weeks.

"I've been blissfully happily married for 17 years. And five children later, I guess it's safe to say he's developed a strong sense of vigor—and I, a very good sense of endurance.

"I think with all of the bad marriages in the world, that was probably the sweetest thing for our Permanent Spousal Record."

Pete's Wife: "For our honeymoon, Pete made reservations—and he asked for twin beds, 'cause he thought that was for two people. He's mad at me for telling. Bye. . . . It's kinda cute. . . . He's really not dumb. . . . It was a *cute* thing."

BULLETIN BOARD REPLIES: Better stop right about there, Pete's Wife—lest someone (Pete, perhaps—assuming that he's all he's cracked up to be) start to suspect that the lady doth protest too much.

Fay's Friend of western Wisconsin: "My husband and I both made some marks on our Permanent Spousal Records when we began farming together.

"He had grown up on a farm, but I hadn't. His dad had the unfortunate habit of yelling and yelling and yelling at the boys when they were helping him with the farm work, and my husband—even more unfortunately—had a tendency to use the same technique on this rookie when we got started.

"One memorable day occurred when we were going to move some newly purchased pigs from the barn to a lot back in the woods that he had made with an electric fence around it. There was a handle on the back side of the lot which, when connected to the perimeter fence, would make the electric wire around the pigs' lot hot, once the wire had been put up behind the pigs.

"The plan was to drive the pigs back there, put the wire up on the front side as quickly as they got in, and then make the fence hot.

"Well, my husband had been yelling at me all day long, and I was pretty well unglued by the time we got to moving the pigs. When we got back there, he said: 'Now as soon as they get in that lot and I yell "Go!," you run just as fast as you can to the back side of that lot and hook that wire up and make this fence hot.'

"He neglected to tell me that I would have to wait for him to finish hooking the bare wires together on the front side of the lot—and by this time, I was so frazzled that I probably would have jumped off the top of the barn without thinking if he had told me.

"So we got the pigs back there; he yelled 'Go!'; I ran as fast as I could, without looking back, quickly hooked up the wire, and made the fence hot around the pigs. I looked back to see if I had done it fast enough—just in time to see him finish hooking up the bare wires . . . and the current hit him! Ka-*pow!* He sprawled in the dirt, and the air turned really blue for a while.

"When I think of how ornery he was that day, I can still picture the look on his face—and it's still satisfying. He's gotten a lot better about the yelling, but he still has days when I think to myself that a little shock therapy might not be a bad thing for him.

"And I'll tell you: Yet today, when he gallantly holds down the electric wire with his hat or something for me to step over, I still make sure that I have one hand on him as I go over. After 16 years, I'm still dreading payback."

JB's Wife: "Last weekend, my daughter wanted to look through my jewelry box so I could tell her where each item came from.

"One of my favorite pieces is one given to me by JB years ago, when we were dating. It is undoubtedly one of the homeliest necklaces I've ever seen, and I told Rachel the story about the night her dad gave it to me:

"JB was a struggling farmer—and in order to support his farming habits, he sold life insurance part-time. He was quite a good salesman. It was exactly one year since the night we met, and I was going to take JB out for a nice dinner. We were all dressed up and ready to leave when he said he had a surprise for me; he told me it was something he'd had for a while and that his mother had told him he should save it for 'that someone special.'

"I was quite excited to open it, since he made kind of a big deal about it—and there, inside, was a gold necklace with a round pendant about 1½ inches in diameter. The pendant was adorned with a pearl and chips of a diamond and a few other stones—and was in the shape of . . . *AN INSURANCE BUILDING!*

"Rachel asked if I had to actually wear it, and I told her that I immediately asked her dad to put it around my neck so I could wear it that night.

"Rachel noticed that the gold chain was missing, and she astutely reasoned that I must have put the chain to better use. She suggested that maybe I could take the stones out and make something prettier out of them. I told her I'd never do that, since this pendant was very special to me.

"After all, how many women out there have a necklace in the shape of an insurance building?"

Sailboat Jo: "My husband has been taking a celestial-navigation course—the better to eventually steer our sailboat to new, interesting places in the world.

"The last two weeks, he's missed his class. He couldn't find their meeting place. This makes me nervous."

Sharon of Minneapolis: "I've been married for 11 years, and I've been taking a lot of little, minor criticisms from my husband lately.

"I thought: 'Well, I'd better see what I can do to negotiate on this point.' I said to him: 'Honey, look. Why don't you do this: When you're just about to say something like that to me, why don't you just not say it 50 percent of the time?'

"And without missing a beat, he said: 'I already do!'"

Annette of the Zoo Annex: "One year, my husband gave me one of those sweet, mushy anniversary cards, and he signed it: 'Thank you for seven of the most wonderful years of my life.'

"We had been married eight years. I said: 'Honey, this is a nice card, and I'm glad you remembered our anniversary—but we've been married for eight years, not seven.' And then I was trying to take the pressure off a little bit, and I said: 'Which one of the years was not wonderful?'

"His quick response was: 'Oh, it wasn't one full year. It was just a little of each of the eight.'"

Katie of Stillwater: "On Valentine's Day, I got my typical funny card for my husband. It said: 'Hubby, I wouldn't want anyone else on Valentine's Day.' Inside, it said: 'I've already got you all trained and everything.'

"I open up his card to me, and there's this beautiful black-and-white picture of a little boy with red roses in his arms. The roses are the only thing colored on the card. And on the inside, it's blank except for his writing, which is as follows: 'I still love you with the heart of a child, strong and deep. Though my body gets sore and weak, we continue on together. I love your style.'

"I wanted to crawl into a hole."

BULLETIN BOARD OBSERVES: It does appear, however, that Katie's card was accurate, if not all that funny.

Bernie Beermann of Inver Grove Heights: "Each year on Valentine's Day, my wife/companion/sweetheart writes me a little poem. I was lookin' forward to reading this year's version.

"I got home last night, and she said: 'Well, I was too busy at work today to write you a poem, honey—so I made you a copy of last year's.'

"Better than nothin', right?"

J.A.T. of Coon Rapids: "Tonight my other half, Eric, headed out for an all-nighter of snow plowing. Seeing his solo set of footprints in the snow, going away from me, really pulled at my heartstrings.

"Sometimes it's the little things that make you realize just how much you love someone—and how much a part of you they have become."

Fingers of Apple Valley, through her tears: "I just lost my best friend Saturday, in a car accident, and we buried him yesterday. And I didn't realize how much this was gonna hurt. I just wanted to share some things that he used to do, as kind of a tribute.

"When you'd always have Dumb Customer Jokes, I used to think about one he used to do—and it used to drive me crazy . . . but now I'll never hear it again. It seems . . . it seems a real shame.

"When we used to go to restaurants together, he would always . . . when the waitress or waiter would come over and ask if we'd like something to drink, he would *always* say 'Yeah, I'd like a margarita!' . . . or a daiquiri, or some alcoholic drink—when we were sitting in a Perkins or a Country Kitchen or some little family restaurant in the middle of nowhere. And probably the first hundred times, it didn't bother me so much, but after a while, I used to just shake my head and roll my eyes because I always knew what was coming. And now . . . now I think I'm really gonna miss it.

"He was my best friend, because we were married for 5½ years. We were divorced, too, but we didn't stop being friends.

"He used to love to go out to eat. It was just his favorite thing in the world. He always said I was a great cook—and a lot of people did, so I knew he wasn't just saying that—but he used to always take me out to eat, because he said when I cooked, he didn't get my company, and no matter how good my cooking was, sitting across the table from me and being able to talk to me during the whole meal was more important to him than getting home-cooked.

"He was a really kind, loving man, and I didn't . . . I have so many things that I still want to say to him.

"I just want to say to people out there: Be careful. He was killed in an auto accident. Be careful driving today. It's a wet, rainy, awful day, and I . . . I just hope everyone gets home safe tonight, because nobody should have to be in this much pain."

Shari of White Bear Lake: "My husband really loves to rattle my cage. You know, like when we're in the grocery store, he'll tell the cashier: 'My wife just *lives* to bag groceries.' Or he'll tell a clerk: 'I want a really special anniversary gift for my wife. Will you please show me your best toilet seats?' Another thing he likes to say to clerks is: 'Oh, I've found the way to make my wife really happy. She just *loves* a new mop head.'

"Well, the other night we were in Byerly's, and he's coming toward me down the aisle, doing this little jiggle-swing-and-sway dance—and he thinks no one's around.

"I nodded toward the woman in back of him and said: 'She saw you.' He had this look of shocked embarrassment.

"As the woman passed, she said: 'I found it rather *exciting*, if you ask me.'

"Well, he won that round—but we're still laughing."

Doctor Friendly of St. Paul: "At her request, I removed a tiny skin lesion from Mrs. Friendly. When I was done, I said—with perhaps just a touch of unneeded arrogance: 'You know, for a patient in the office, that would cost $75.'

"Without hesitating even a second, she said: 'You know that dinner you ate tonight? In a restaurant, that would cost $30. Are you sure you want to play this game?'"

The Frenchman of St. Paul: "I was razzin' my wife the other day here, and I told her—sarcastically: 'Yeah, that looks *real* good on you.'

"She said: 'You know what'd look real good on you? A blindfold.'

"I was laughin' too hard to answer her."

Cheryl of Exeland, Wis.: "One day last month, my husband, my daughters and I were eating supper. Jim was reading the paper as we ate—*Pioneer Press,* of course.

"We have this little cocker spaniel named Sammy, and I've been trying to convince Jim that we need to have her clipped. So, after a nice supper, I decided to broach the subject once again. I said: 'I have an appointment to get Sammy clipped on Wednesday.' Not leaving time for argument, I continued: 'It's so matted and dirty. I really think it needs to be done.'

"Jim looked up from the paper and said: 'That's a good idea. I haven't liked your hair since the *last* time you got it cut.' He then continued: 'It has a round, pouffy look to it.'

"Well, my mouth dropped open, and the girls started to giggle. Jim looked around the table with a puzzled look. I proceeded to tell him what I had said—about the *dog.* His mouth dropped open, his face turned red; he'd thought I'd said *I* was getting my hair cut—at Sandy's.

"I was afraid to ask him what he really thought about my hair being dirty and matted.

"Ah, well. So much for supper conversation. Love him, anyway."

Linda W. of Eagan, calling from her brand-new home: "The weeds in the front yard were up to my knees, so my husband went out there with the weed whacker to get these weeds mown down; we didn't want to use our new lawn mower, because there's rocks and nails and things under there.

"He'd been out there for going on two hours—just weed whacking, weed whacking—and then he came in the house, all sweaty and full of weeds, and he says: 'Come here. I have to show you something.' And I said: 'Right now? I just sat down. I've been cleaning for two hours.'

"He goes: 'I have to show you right now.' I say 'OK,' and he says: 'You have to come upstairs.'

"So we go up and look out the top-floor window, and I look down, and here he'd weed-whacked a big letter I and a heart and the letter U in the front lawn. I thought it was the sweetest thing. I had tears in my eyes and gave him a big hug."

Short Timer of Barron, Wis.: "It turned out to be a happy occasion for all concerned. The dance band quietly debated—and then chose to play the requested song. With grace and innocence, the happy couple danced, under the spotlight, to their music of choice. The gathered friends and family smiled broadly and applauded the couple.

"Later, however, the dancers were made fully aware, over and over, that they had chosen 'Please Release Me' to highlight their wedding anniversary."

Michele Lee of Rochester: "When I was at work today, these two older people came into the museum and were telling us that they'd been married for 60 years, and their daughters were with them, and we were saying what a lovely couple they were, and we said to the husband: 'You should take your wife on a second honeymoon.' The wife looked at us and told us that he had made her whole life a honeymoon.

"Every time I've told someone that story today, I've started to cry—because I think it's one of the sweetest things I've ever heard."

The S.O.G.G. (Stubborn, Ornery German Girl) of Eau Claire, Wis.: "My husband doesn't drink coffee, and he never has—but every morning, he gets up before he would have to and makes a nice fresh pot for me.

"More than that, he's stayed with me for seven years since I suffered a head injury and brain damage. I'm the luckiest, most blessed person walking the planet, but it hasn't been easy. Somehow this wonderful man has managed to keep his sanity through years of my speech and physical therapy; my unreasonable reactions and rage; and changes in our lives—physically, mentally, financially, socially.

"There are many, many times when I think: If I was married to me, I'd sure want a divorce. Matter of fact, I often wish I *could* divorce myself. And yet he's always here, and believes in me.

"How in the world do you begin to show and express your love and gratitude in a situation like this?

"We both do try to keep our sense of humor, believe it or not—because yes, laughter *is* the best medicine. So I'm looking for a John Prine–type singer/songwriter who will help me with my song 'There's No Way to Deal With a Brain-Damaged Woman With PMS.'

"I could go on forever, but I'll just say: Thank you, Bruce, for all your patience, love and understanding. I love you."

The Ice Man of Eau Claire, Wis.: "Thirteen years ago, I broke my back, and it's been a series of one operation after another. It's been very hard on my family, and it's been particularly hard on my wife.

"One day, I was layin' there, thinking, after having another surgery, and I asked her; I said: 'Does this get to the point where it's beyond you? Where you don't want to do it anymore?'

"And she said: 'I will never leave you. You had an accident; you didn't cause it to happen. And I made a contract with you, and God, on the day that I married you. I will always be here for you.'

"Any man could stand to hear that—any time."

CHAPTER ELEVEN

Where Have You Gone, Mrs. Malaprop?

She and her whole clan are still as talkative as banshees on a hot tin roof:

A.M.W. of St. Paul: "I work with Mr. Malaprop. On his way out to lunch, he told me to keep the fort burning."

John and Bernadette Friedell of Shell Lake, Wis.: "Reacting to his son's restlessness, our friend was heard to say: 'Be patient. Rome didn't burn in a day.'"

Ann Onymous of St. Paul: "Yesterday, Mrs. Malaprop attended a party, and she was overheard listing for someone all of the things she had done that day and all of the things she still had to do. When she finished, she sighed and said: 'I just guess I have too many onions in the fire.'"

The Music Man of Blaine: "At a recent church dinner, we had some of the men from the church dressed up with shirts and bow ties and black pants—as waiters. However, one of the gentlemen came in wearing his son's pink bow tie and cummerbund from a recent dance he had been to.

"One of the other men in our church turned to someone at our table and said: 'I wonder where he got that pink concubine.'"

Cheryl of Inver Grove Heights: "We were at dinner at Old Country Buffet, and the woman next to me was trying to reach something on the back of the counter. She said: 'You have to be an extortionist to reach anything in this restaurant.'"

Mel of Siren, Wis.: "Several family members were discussing various degrees of education. One person mentioned a bachelor of arts degree, and someone else had just acquired a doctorate in pharmacology. My sister-in-law, not one to be left out of any conversation, proudly announced: 'My husband is going back to school to get his IUD.'"

Sweet Cheeks of Portland, Oregon: "The university in the town I was living in was conducting a nicotine-patch study, where smokers wore a nicotine patch on their arm instead of smoking. A coworker of mine was telling me about another woman in the study who was having a hard time not smoking.

"My coworker went on to explain that this may have been because there were three types of patches given to the participants: two patches with different levels of nicotine—and then a third patch that was just a placenta."

Julie of the Midway: "We were at dinner last night; a group of colleagues got together because one of us retired. We were sitting around the table at Buca, and they were playing Italian opera music. Jerome, who is always kind of known for his malapropperyisms *[BULLETIN BOARD NOTES: That's what the lady said!]*, sits up and says: 'Oh, that's the opera singer I like—that Placenta Domingo.'"

Denise of Stillwater: "At the salon I work at, the other day, one of my clients was discussing the fact that she was a stay-at-home mom even though her children are junior-high and older. Her one daughter in high school had some friends over during Homecoming Week, and she had made some homemade dinner rolls, and they just thought they were fabulous.

"She said that she was a regular June Cleavage. And she said it twice. I couldn't believe it."

The Domestic Engineer of Inver Grove Heights: "My husband and I were looking at exercise equipment yesterday. As the salesman was describing a treadmill to us, he said it didn't have a lot of bells and whiskers."

The Beermeister of Woodbury: "After going to the eye doctor, my girlfriend said that her prescription had not changed—and that the doctor hoped her eyes would improve on their own. She said: 'Yeah, right. Won't be long, and I'll be wearing bottlecaps.'"

Judy of Bayport: "A person who recently called our office mentioned that she'd been in a sticker-tape parade. My mind's eye has been delighted with the vision of all of these people parading down a street in New York, trying to pull off thousands of stickers being tossed from skyscraper windows."

Puppy of West St. Paul: "At my work, there's this lady who said that everyone kept ignoring her—like she had the flag or something."

The Como Runner of St. Paul: "Mr. Malaprop is heading up one of our quality-improvement teams at work. He said that if we did our project right, we'd be killing two stones at once."

BULLETIN BOARD SAYS: We shall resist the temptation to compare the killing of stones with the actual accomplishments of most quality-improvement teams.

C.B. of Stillwater: "A friend of mine is Mrs. Malaprop. The other day, she was telling me that her husband uses the kitchen table to pile up papers and other stuff he doesn't put away. This really bugs her. She said sometimes there's hardly room for plates and serving dishes.

"She said she told him: 'Clean up this mess. You're already skating on thin eggs.'"

Carl of St. Paul: "After a hard day at work the other day, my wife came home and said: 'It was really a mess. They dumped the whole ball of fish in my lap.'"

Diane of Hudson, Wis.: "Yesterday we were having a serious conversation at work regarding employee contract negotiations, and someone said: 'That really opens a can of fish.'"

Sue of Fergus Falls: "My husband and I were discussing something that he wasn't too excited about doing. He said: 'That's just not my can of worms.'"

Darlene of Mahtomedi: "My dad and my brother-in-law were talking about a relative of ours that lost $200 gambling, and my dad says: 'Oh, well, that's nothing to them.' And my brother-in-law says: 'Yeah. To them, that's just a kick in the bucket.'"

The Wordsmith of St. Paul: "I did a Mrs. Malaprop myself the other day. Somebody asked me a question that I really didn't know the answer to, so I took a guess at it. I qualified my answer by saying, at the end: 'Of course, that's just a stab in the back.'"

Angela of St. Paul: "I was talking to my dad, and in response to something I said, he said that I'd hit the nose on the head."

Santa's Buns of Mendota Heights: "Reverend Malaprop was preaching at our church last Sunday—and he made his point at the pulpit by proclaiming that God had hit the nail on the thumb."

Sue of South St. Paul: "I'd like to report my husband, Mr. Malaprop. He asked our daughter last night: 'How does it feel to have the hand on the other foot?'"

Elizabeth of Eagan: "A very dear young friend called me recently to tell me about a wedding she was in. She said that some of the parishioners were at odds with the minister who performed the service—and they were trying to have him disrobed."

Torry's Mom of Apple Valley: "My father-in-law was telling us at the cabin one day that his son was a chip off the old hat."

Pat of White Bear: "I work with Mr. Malaprop. Last night, we were talking about the interviewing process that we're going through for some new jobs at our company, and he said: 'If I were one of those people being considered, I'd definitely put my ball in the hat.'"

D.A.D.: "I was talking with my in-laws, and conversation got around to gambling, one of their favorite pastimes. We were speculating about the casino at Turtle Lake and their thoughts of making it an overnight trip. In wondering what the rooms of the nearby motel would be like, my father-in-law said: 'It really doesn't matter what they are like. All we need is a place to hang our head.'"

BULLETIN BOARD NOTES: Sooner or later, that's the gambler's fate.

Lois of Maplewood: "I overheard a woman at work say the other day: 'You could have knocked me over with a brick.'"

Frank of Pine Springs: "I was at a meeting at work, and my boss wanted some action on some particular problem. He wanted us to get right on it—'but,' he said, 'be careful not to rattle any feathers.'"

Paul of St. Paul: "Yesterday, a woman I work with was discussing one of our customers. She didn't think they were a very reputable firm. She said: 'Yeah, I think they're kind of a slide-by-Mike operation.'"

P.J. of Marine on St. Croix: "I received a thank-you card in the mail today from my cousin and his wife. My sister and I had sent some new outfits for their second child to Phoenix, where they live. The thank-you card says it was awfully nice to get some new outfits for their second child, so that he didn't have to wear 'hammy downs' all the time."

Leslie of parts undisclosed: "I met a very nice, well-spoken (at first) sales rep who was complaining about the very competitive nature of the business she was in, proclaiming it to be a true doggy-dog world, lamenting that the doggy-dog practices employed by her competition were making it difficult for her to do her job success-fully, and that this doggy-dog attitude was causing their mutual clients concern be-cause in order for these clients to deal with the sales reps, they had to adopt the same doggy-dog manner.

"I just smiled."

The Ladies in Marketing: "Our co-worker Deb B. watches 'Days of Our Lives' faithfully and was telling us how Jack was trying to woo his ex-wife back—but his ex was not buying his change of heart and told him to get lost.

"Deb exclaimed: 'Jack walked away with his head between his legs. It was so sad I almost cried!'

"As we all giggled, she looked at us funny and added: 'You know, like a dog.'

"We all burst out laughing."

Tim's Mommy: "I talked to Mrs. Malaprop on the phone the other day. She said that I was talking to the wrong tree."

Cathy & Suzy of Champps St. Paul: "We work with Mr. Malaprop. He was telling us about his girlfriend. He said that her bark is worse than her punch."

Fran of parts nearby: "When my friend Connie—who is very, very articulate and very well educated—wants to portray what a really nice person she is, she al-ways says: 'You know, my bark is louder than my bite.'"

Patty of St. Paul: "In our last conversation, my boss said that she was in second heaven and that since the money didn't come through, we were all going to have to bite the dust."

Julie of Blaine: "I discovered this morning that Mrs. Malaprop is in my car pool. We were discussing some proposed policy changes in our school building—and whether or not we should speak out that we oppose this administrative decision—and she remarked: 'Well, that would be biting off the head that feeds you. Oh, no. I mean: It would be biting off our own heads. Oh, never mind. *You* know what I mean.'"

Mabel of St. Paul: "I was sitting with a friend, over lunch, and we were talking about one of our fellow neighbors. She was complaining about him, and she said: 'Well, he's really bit himself in the foot this time.'"

Chuckles of St. Paul: "Ms. Malaprop . . . asked me, two days before our wed-ding: 'You're not about to get wet feet, are ya?'"

Mortimer of Eagan: "I was in a meeting the other day when a committee mem-ber was updating us on a new project. He reported that he was just getting his teeth wet and had a long way to go. Drooling next?"

In Transition of St. Paul: "I do believe Mr. Malaprop was recently doing a busi-ness transaction with me. When it came to money matters, he said, you have to put your face where your teeth are."

Chas. of St. Paul: "I was riding in the car with my sister the other day. She was telling me about her new job, and how she had to settle for something she was overqualified for—but she figured it was a good company, and if she hung in there, the promotions would come. In the meantime, she said, she would just swallow her tongue."

Peppermint Patty of Cottage Grove: "I work with Mrs. Malaprop. The other day, she told me an irritating customer really got under her goat. Good place for him, I'd say."

Shy Di of Shoreview: "My brother is Mr. Malaprop. A couple days ago, he told us that he was a prince in sheep's clothing."

The Butterfly of Como: "Mrs. Malaprop traveled with me recently. She was telling of a man who was 'a lamb in sheep's clothing. . . . No, I mean a sheep in lamb's clothing.'"

BULLETIN BOARD SAYS: He was warm, at any rate.

Pokey of Austin: "I work at the police department here, and one of the officers just came in with a bump on his head. I said: 'Jeez, what happened to you?' And he goes: 'Oh, me and a kitchen cupboard disagreed.' And then he goes: 'Yeah, you wouldn't believe it. It bled like a stuffed pig.'"

A. of St. Paul: "My grandma was telling me that she was pricked badly by a thorn when working with her roses. She said her finger bled like a stuffed horse. Funny thing is: She talks like that a lot, and I've learned to understand her. I'm sort of bilingual now."

Laura of West St. Paul: "We were discussing a particularly unpleasant social situation, and my husband spoke up with a caution: 'Now we must be careful. This may be the dark horse with the silver lining.'"

Marjie of Eagan: "I am married to Mr. Malaprop. The other day, we were talking about him getting more clients from work, and I said: 'Did you talk to them about how slow they have been to give you clients?' And he says: 'Why would I kiss a gift horse in the mouth?'"

Lois of Maplewood: "A woman at work said: 'Now, that's really the horse calling the kettle black.'"

Stan of St. Paul: "Somebody said today she was tired of beating her head against a dead horse."

Howster of St. Paul: "In response to a sister who had created a situation that got her into some trouble, my friend told her that she'd cooked her goose—and now she's gotta sleep in it."

Joe of St. Paul: "My wife just told me: 'Don't hatchet your chickens before they're laid.'"

Jennifer of Minneapolis: "During a philosophical discussion about the meaning of it all, my Significant Other reflected: 'Well, life isn't all beer and skillets.'"

M.B. of St. Paul: "My father-in-law is full of malaprops. One of his favorites is: 'Walk softly, but carry a big stink.' I'm not sure what he thinks it means."

Jody of St. Paul: "I was talking to my sister about how my brother likes to babble. She said he babbles incandescently."

Someone who'd really prefer to remain anonymous: "Early in our relationship, my husband and I were having a big argument about something or other. He tends to get a little lecture-y and pompous when he's being defensive, and while we were going back and forth, both of us trying verbally to outsmart the other, he said something to me that I thought was particularly offensive and patronizing. So I replied, real huffy and indignant: 'You think you know everything, don't you, Mr. Condensation?'

"I tried really hard to stay angry, but he was laughing so hard I couldn't."

Mrs. Kravitz on Kenneth of St. Paul: "One time, I was feeling kinda amorous with a boyfriend, and he was turning me down at the moment. I turned to him, and I said: 'You know, most guys would *die* to have a necrophiliac for a girlfriend.'"

BULLETIN BOARD MUSES: Unfortunately, that's the prerequisite.

Ann of St. Paul: "My husband was talking about how his secretary is so moody at work all the time, and he said: 'I think she brings a lot of luggage from home.'"

Peter of St. Louis Park: "It just so happens that Miss Malaprop is employed in our building. She's in a retail travel agency here.

"We were outside on one of these glorious, sweltering days recently, having a smoke—since you can't smoke in a building in Minnesota anymore—and she stubbed out her cigarette and was heading back up to her desk, and she sighed and said: 'Well, back to the old bump and grind.'"

Bud of parts hereabouts: "My boss's wife was talking about a woman in her office who wasn't working out as well as expected. She said she had told the woman's supervisor that 'if she can't cut the cheese, you should just get rid of her.'"

Sir Loin of Stillwater: "I was giving my wife an excuse for something I'd done, and she looked at me and leveled her eyes and said that that excuse didn't cut water with her."

Lady Jane of Lindstrom: "Mrs. Malaprop used to work with me. If something was not to her liking, she'd say: 'That's not my cupcake.'"

Spook of St. Paul: "I am married to Mr. Malaprop. If something's very easy to do, he says it's a cup of cake. And if he wants you to get lost, you can take a slow boat off a short pier."

Sue of St. Paul: "A coworker of mine seems to be related to Mrs. Malaprop. The other day, he told me that I was making a mountain out of a manhole."

Rene of St. Paul: "I saw Mrs. Malaprop on Phil Donahue. She was talking about how she had dated a lot of rotten guys and finally found Mr. Right. The way she put it was: 'You have to kiss a lot of toads before you find the fruit.'"

BULLETIN BOARD SAYS: Sounds like one of those alternative lifestyles we've heard so much about.

Gene of Inver Grove Heights: "About 20, 25 years ago, my wife and a couple of her golf friends were talking about a pilot who survived when his plane started on fire. My wife told her friends: 'The pilot was lucky he was able to ejaculate out of the airplane.' And she couldn't understand why they were laughing."

The Snake Pit Veteran: "We have a rookie in our office now. I think his name is Malaprop. We were going to meet at a certain time, and he wanted to make sure that we had circumcised our watches."

Jarl of the East Side: "One day while we were talking about what would happen after we died, my friend Jay turned toward me and said: 'Well, all I know is: I just want to be castrated and thrown in a lake.'"

BULLETIN BOARD MUSES: What a way to go.

Misplaced of Maplewood: "I caught my boyfriend explaining to his mother that a friend of his had died and been cremated—and he had to go to the urination."

Wendy of the East Side: "A friend of mine made me swear that I wouldn't tell anyone, but . . . a mutual friend of ours told her that another friend's husband had died—and that she'd had him cremated and kept his urine on the mantel."

Housewife of Prescott: "Mr. Malaprop was commenting on my legs the other day and said: 'Nice yams.'"

California Girl of Roseville: "Last night, we were hangin' out, and my boyfriend said he was so hungry he was going to gouge himself."

Oscar of Roseville: "On a recent evening, when there was a clear sky and a nearly full moon, I mentioned to my wife that moonlight was shining in the window of our bedroom across the bed. Later on, she was reclining on the bed, feeling pretty relaxed, and she said to me: 'I just love basting in the moonlight.'"

K.P of Luck, Wis.: "I live with Mr. Malaprop. We were driving home, and he was talking about this guy he knows who makes beef jerky. He said that the guy takes scraps of meat and serenades it overnight."

Connie of Highland: "Mrs. Malaprop came to my book club on Saturday and told a long story—and then said that she and her friends were standing around chewing the breeze."

Liz of West St. Paul: "Someone at work the other day was talking about something being as cute as a bug's rear."

Stacy of Minneapolis: "I know a girl who said: 'Oh, it was just like something you experienced before. You know, like soup du jour!'"

Karl of St. Paul: "I was with my girlfriend at a play, and she was telling me about the people who were sitting up in front of us; they were some old neighbors of hers. She was telling me about how many animals they have.

"She said: 'They have quite a *ménage à trois.*'"

The Amazonian Temptress of Rosemount: "Last week, an elderly aunt called me to tell me she was going out of town for a few days and asked me if I'd keep an eye on her house for her while she was gone.

"I said that I'd be happy to and asked her where she was going.

"She told me: 'I'm headin' over to Voyeurist Village, to visit some friends.'

"I asked her: 'Don't you mean Voyageur Village?'

"She responded: 'Voyeurist, Voyageur—what's the difference? They're all Norwegians.'"

Carolyn of Mankato: "Our friend Deb was telling us how she was going to have new curtains made. The curtains were going to be a beautiful cotton material on the front, and she planned to put a little Muslim on the back. I thought we'd die laughing."

An Average Joe of St. Paul: "Recently, while reading Bulletin Board, I've been experiencing a strange juxtaposition between 'Mrs. Malaprop' and the 'Please release me!' chronicles. *[See Chapter 6.]* In fact, I've begun to confuse Mrs. Malaprop with another famous lady, Simon and Garfunkel's Mrs. Robinson. With a little work on the lyrics, away we go:
"We'd like to know
"A little bit about you for our files.
"We'd like to learn about
"Your prostate leg.
"Don't stop now, you're finally
"Breaking a second wind.
"Stroll around the town
"We can read you like a glove.
"And here's to you, Mrs. Malaprop,
"Never look a gift horse in the eye
"(Sigh sigh sigh).
"God bless you, please, Mrs. Malaprop,
"St. Paul holds a place for those who missay
"(Hey hey hey, hey hey hey).
"Misspeak in a public place
"Where everyone's sure to hear.
"You know that song like the back of your neck.
"It's your Purgatory,
"A woman can change her mind.
"This time you've really struck a psychotic nerve.
"Coo coo aah-choo, Mrs. Malaprop,
"Loyal readers love you more than you will know
"(Woe woe woe).
"What's that you say, Mrs. Malaprop?
"A coworker has intesticle flu
"(Boo hoo hoo, boo hoo hoo).
"Running at the mouth
"On a Sunday afternoon,
"Going cannibalistic on the kids.
"Laugh about it,
"Shout about it,
"When you've got to choose,
"Usually when you do, you misuse.
"Where have you gone, Pablo Que Pasa?
"Bulletin Board turns its homely eyes to you
"(Ooo ooo ooo).
"What's that you say, Mrs. Malaprop?

"Pablo's paid the pauper and gone away
"(Hey hey hey, hey hey hey)."

Kellen-Sierra of St. Paul: "We'd been having problems for days with a slow-draining bathtub. One morning after my hubby's bath, he said: 'Boy, I don't know what happened, but the tub's draining like a bandit.'"

Silly Sue: "Recently, all of the children and grandchildren were getting together to go through a grandparent's house—to divide up the estate—and my daughter said she made out like a banshee."

Donna of the Midway: "I took my car to get a tune-up, and I told them to check the power steering, because it seemed to be leaking. Went back to get my car, and everything was done.

"I said: 'Well, what about the power steering?'

"The mechanic said: 'Yep. It's leakin' like a banshee.'"

The Loon: "A coworker came into my office and said: 'Hi, boss. It took me a long time to get here today. It was raining like a banshee out there.'"

Sammy of The Saintly City: "I'm sitting here watching a rerun of 'Roseanne.' It's a Christmas episode. A woman just walked in the house and said: 'It's snowing like a banshee.'"

The French Whiz of Forest Lake: "When my brother first went into the Army Reserves, he was told that he snores like a banshee."

Max of Forest Lake: "I've got an employee who, over the weekend, was having some tooth problems—and explained to me today that she was takin' aspirin like a banshee."

Jim of Woodbury: "I was listening to NPR this morning, and there was a report by a woman complaining of the frustrations she's had trying to break through the glass ceiling. Her best efforts included 'networking like a banshee,' but she was still having trouble with that glass ceiling."

Toni of Blaine: "Last Saturday, the woman at the slot machine next to me commented that the darned thing was eating her nickels like a banshee."

Stupid of "good ol' A.V. (Apple Valley)": 'At choir the other day, a girl said: 'I was NordicTracking like a banshee.' Then a girl on my volleyball team said that her skin itched like a banshee.

"Someone needs to take control of these banshees."

John the Magnificent Wizard of western Wisconsin: "I don't think Bulletin Board should leave the subject without discussing what banshees *really* do.

"Lovers of literature know that the expression so often misquoted comes from Herman Melville's *Moby-Dick*.

"Old Captain Ahab was whaling like a banshee."

Twisted Sister of St. Paul: "I've gotta tell you what I just hate. What I really, really hate is reading a little excerpt from the Mrs. Malaprop section . . . and then rereading it . . . and then rereading it—and then not getting it.

"Makes me feel dumb as a banshee."

CHAPTER TWELVE

CAUTION! Words at Play!

Triangle Man of St. Paul: "I just saw an ad for a new movie called *Johnny Mnemonic*—and I'm wondering how on earth they expect me to be able to remember the name of that movie."

The Ornithodontist of Winona: "My brother and I went into an Italian restaurant, and they asked if we would like to eat outside, because it was a nice day. My brother said to the hostess: 'Yes. Then we could have fettuccine al fresco.'"

Mary Kay of Arden Hills: "The kids' [Happy Meal] cheeseburgers had the customary cheese, pickle, mustard and ketchup. Only a burger was missing.

"I asked Steve if he thought I should call Bulletin Board with our cheeseburger story, and he quickly replied: 'Sure—only you'd better beef it up a little.'"

Cuddles of St. Paul: "I spent last week in Omaha. Came back here New Year's Eve day. On the way back, the sun finally broke through the overcast, and a rainbow—or icebow, or snowbow; whatever it is called—came out, from one horizon to the other. It seemed to follow our bus, and had everyone on the bus just enthralled with the beauty; it probably lasted about four hours. Never seen anything like that before.

"There was a young lady—looked like a freshman in college, senior in high school—sitting across from a guy who was three sheets to the wind, and I heard her say to her companion: 'That must be the sot at the end of the rainbow.'"

Leslie of St. Paul: "A few weeks ago, I was painting our bedroom. The color was Faux Blue; it's kind of a gray-blue color. As usual, my big tabby cat, Buster, was hanging around to see what I was up to.

"I painted one wall under the windows, and I was working on another section of the wall. When I turned back to dip the brush in the paint can, I saw a faint paw mark on the wall just under the windowsill. It looked like Buster had rested his foot there for a second while looking out the window.

"Sure enough, a few inches away on the wood floor, there was this big blue paw print. I found Buster and washed off his paw and went back to painting—and a few minutes later, it occurred to me what Buster had done: He'd made a Faux paw."

Lulu of St. Paul: "I call my mom's sidekick of 20 years my *faux pa*."

Honey-Do of St. Paul: "I was listening to the news about the tornadoes up north of the Twin Cities, and a couple of small towns were mentioned: Long Siding and Pease. The people on the television didn't seem to know where they were—but I did. I remembered an old WCCO radio commentator asking, on the air, why it took the train so long to get from Princeton to Milaca.

"The answer was: 'It stops at Long Siding and Pease.'"

Stephanie of Rochester: "Last week, after having a physical prior to a tubal ligation, my sister-in-law said she was fit to be tied."

Susan of Columbia Heights: "About three weeks ago, I noticed buds on my very favorite plant in my yard—and I was very excited. But for the past three weeks, they haven't changed at all; they just sit there, the same way.

"Today I was driving around, and I noticed the same flower in other people's yards—and theirs are all blooming. I was getting more and more jealous.

"And I finally realized that what I was experiencing was a case of Peony Envy."

Shari of West St. Paul: "I work at a bakery. We have a large jar filled with stemmed cherries that we use to garnish cakes.

"One of the decorators took a cherry from the jar, but it didn't have a stem attached—so he reached back in the jar, pulled out just a stem, and inserted it in the cherry.

"I informed him that he had just artificially insteminated that cherry."

U.N.C.L.E. Agent: "I have a friend who does a lot of inservice workshops for teachers, and he refers to the goofy ivory-tower ideas he hears about as *academentia.* "I think the way he uses it, you can be part of the academentia community (as in 'In academentia, it is generally accepted that . . .') or you can have it (like a condition or a disease).

"Most of the teachers seem to get a kick out of it."

Steve of Minneapolis: "I used to carpool with Judy, a friend who worked in the same office. Every morning on our way to work, Judy would continually spray and fuss with her hair. I used to tease her that it had the look and feel of concrete.

"One cold morning as we walked from the parking ramp, Judy slipped on the icy sidewalk and nearly fell before grabbing my arm.

"I warned her: 'Judy, you better be careful now. You could fall and break that hair.'

"She responded: 'Yeah, I guess that's what you'd call a *hairline fracture.'*"

Jerry M. of Highland Park: "A buddy of mine worked at Calvary Cemetery during his summers in college. He said there wasn't much to do there during the winter, so the cemetery only employed a skeleton crew."

Happy Harley of Hastings: "I suppose that a young fellow who just had his millionaire father cremated would probably brag to his friends that he got his money the honest way: He urned it."

Jean of St. Paul: "A friend of our daughter's accompanied us to the Historic State Theater in Minneapolis. As we admired the restoration details, I wondered if the style was baroque.

"My daughter's friend stated that, indeed, baroque was the only style that *should* be restored.

"As my daughter and I exchanged wary looks (her friend has a reputation), he explained: 'If it ain't baroque, don't fix it.'"

CHAPTER THIRTEEN

Off the Tongue, Into the Ear

Ace of Wyoming: "I have a new category for you. It's: favorite words to say or to hear.

"Two of my favorites are *slick* and *pesto*. Both of them are fun to say, and *slick* is especially fun to hear on TV. You can hear it as an adjective or as a nickname; either way, it's great. The word *pesto* is just fun to hear—especially if you give it a long twist at the last syllable. Say it sort of like Ed Sullivan: *pes-toooooo*."

Doug the Janitor of Hugo: "My favorite word is *mellifluous.*"

BULLETIN BOARD NOTES: As in "My favorite word, mellifluous, is."

Nurse Steve of Winona: "One of my favorite big words is *borborygmus*. That's actually the technical term for growling of the stomach. I thought your readers would like to know."

Biz of Woodbury: "My favorite word happens to be *uvula* [pronounced with a very long, Scandinavian-type first "u"]. It always brings shocked surprise when you say 'Oooh, my uvula hurts' or 'My uvula is sore today.'"

Ruth of Eau Claire: "My favorite word is *epididymitis*. It's inflammation of the epididymis, which has something to do with the male anatomy.

"*Epididymitis*. It's a cool word."

Slick of Ashland Oil: "*Epididymitis* is also one of our favorite words down here at the weld shop—but it's not a unanimous choice. The lone dissenter, known as Slapper, has suffered not once but twice from this malady.

"So, Ruth, next time you say or hear *epididymitis,* think of poor Slapper and his 'something to do with the male anatomy' swollen to the size of two softballs as the nurse comes in with her six-inch needle to relieve the swelling—and you can really snicker, because *we* do."

Elsie of St. Paul: "I wanted to add a nomination from the central part of Europe. The word is *zmrzlina*, which is the Slovak word for ice cream. That's five consonants to start it off—so they're gonna make you *work* for it."

Fulana de Tal of St. Paul: "I see that you allow foreigners in your fun-words category, so I'm sending my favorite.

"I have to explain that Brazilians cannot let a word end in a consonant; they have to add a vowel every time. When they appropriate words from another language, this produces some strange and often mellifluous pronunciations. Also, to make the 'ing' of a verb, they add *'ando.'*

"So they take a simple English word like zigzag—matter of fact, it isn't English; it's French!—and when they want to say that they have been sewing in a particular pattern, or running in a particular pattern, or driving back and forth up a mountain, they say they have been *ziggi zaggiando. Ziggi zaggiando. Ziggi zaggiando.* "Say it several times, as fast as you can. Doesn't it sound great?"

Margy of Minneapolis: "*Susurrador*—Spanish for 'whispering'—is the most lovely word. Say it a few times, rolling the double R. It sounds exactly like whispering wind in the pines."

Balder of West St. Paul: "My favorite word is *Fingerspitzengefuehl*—a German word which means 'to sense in your fingertips.' It's usually used in anticipation, or premonition, of something that's about to happen."

Sig Mazero of St. Paul: "I have a favorite word. It's *humuhumunukunukua-puaa*. It purports to be, and I believe it is, the name of a Hawaiian saltwater fish—a fish smaller than its name. I also use it as an expletive."

Paul of Andover: "One of my favorite phrases is *Mele Kalikimaka*—meaning Merry Christmas in Hawaiian."

Ancil Payne of St. Paul: "In a linguistics book, decades ago, I saw mention of a French person's thinking something that no native speaker of English would ever think: that *cesspool* is the most beautiful word in the English language."

Super Seventh Grader of St. Paul: "I came across a list of words in my science book that really rolls off your tongue. It's: *oxygen, silicon, aluminum, iron, sodium, calcium, potassium, magnesium.* It's a list of the eight most common elements on Earth—but I think it's just kinda fun to say."

T.B. of Highland Park: "The favorite word of one of my teachers in high school was *strumpetocracy*. It had something to do with a government run by strumpets—if you could possibly imagine that."

BULLETIN BOARD MUSES: It's hard to imagine a government run any other way.

Mary Jo of White Bear Lake: "My words are names of places. My favorite is *Saskatoon, Saskatchewan.* Then: *Kokomo, Kankakee, Keokuk* and *Kalamazoo.*"

Tweet of Roseville: "My favorite word is the name of a lake in Massachusetts. It's Lake . . . uhhh . . . oh, boy, I forget the name of it! It's *Chargoggagogg-manchauggagoggchaubunagungamaugg.* It's referred to on the maps as Lake Webster. Good luck with the spelling!"

BULLETIN BOARD NOTES: We're informed by our Official Unreliable Source—and the Worcester Public Library unofficially confirms—that Chargoggagoggman-chauggagoggchaubunagungamaugg means: "You fish on your side, I'll fish on my side, and we'll both fish in the middle."]

Lady Jane of Lindstrom: "As any good train-watcher knows, there are a lot of fun words on boxcars. My very favorites are *Erie Lackawanna.*"

Butch of Mendota Heights: "If you want to have fun with a word, say *Chickamauga* five or six times. You'll sound just like a freight train barreling across the prairie."

The Estate Manager of Arden Hills: "Speaking of words that have an interesting or thought-provoking sound, I've always thought that our city to the northwest, *Wahpeton . . .* if you say it several times over and over, *Wahpeton-Wahpeton-Wahpeton-Wahpeton . . .* sounds rather like a flat tire on a car."

Jerry of Welch: "My two favorite words are *thank you.*"

BULLETIN BOARD SAYS: You're welcome.

Debbie of Inver Grove Heights: "My favorite word is *ubiquitous.* It's a word you don't see around much. Ha, ha."

Kim of Roseville: "I have a wide variety of favorite words—but my favorite word is *eclectic.*"

D.J.V. of the West Side: "One of my favorite words is *procrastination.* I would've called sooner, but . . . well . . . *you* know."

The Bread Maker of St. Paul: "Some of my favorite words are actually names. I love some of the classical-music names that kinda roll out—like *Esa-Pekka Salonen* and *Yo-Yo Ma.* "And some of them start out slow and roll around in your mouth and then explode—like *Zubin Mehta* and *Pinchas Zukerman.*

"But my very, very favorite is *von Dohnanyi* [von DOCCHH-non-yee, with the DOCCHH being exceedingly guttural—from Christoph von Dohnanyi.

"As I was kneading the bread tonight, I was doing it to the rhythm of *von Dohnanyi, von Dohnanyi, von Dohnanyi.* Just fantastic. I just love that—the sound of it; the rhythm."

R.J. of Hammond, Wis.: "I'm looking at a garden seed catalog, which is a simple pleasure in and of itself—especially in February—but the names of the flowers are so pretty to say and to hear: *alyssum, coreopsis, delphinium, heliotrope, lobelia, verbena, zinnia.*"

The Wordsmith of St. Paul: "English is such a wonderful language. Even for most unpleasant concepts, we have come up with words that have interesting and even delightful sounds. Mind you, I'm speaking of the sounds of the words themselves, not their connotations.

"Consider these: *confiscatory* (which occurred to me several times last night, when I was filling out the income-tax return); *asphyxiate; malodorous; phlegmatic; carcinoma; miscreant; annihilate; diabolical; acrid.*

"Aren't those just wonderful-sounding words, with horrible meanings behind them?"

Young Ratty of St. Paul: "My favorite word is *zyzomys.* It's the last word in the dictionary. It's a weevil, or something."

BULLETIN BOARD REPLIES: One of the vaunted Pioneer Press library's hernia-inducing tomes has one word after zyzomys: zyzzogeton. It's a South American leaf hopper, or something.

Young Chunks of St. Paul: "My favorite word is *hodgepodge.* I'm not exactly sure what it means, but I really like that word."

BULLETIN BOARD REPLIES: Our favorite word is dictionary. You could look it up.

The Mother of 2 of North St. Paul: "I'm calling in with a favorite word, which is *hara-kiri*—which is something I'm gonna commit if you don't stop with these favorite words."

CHAPTER FOURTEEN

Not Exactly What (If Anything) They Had in Mind

'Net Wit of St. Paul: "My brother just sent me an e-mail:

"'I'm reading a great book called *The Language Instinct.*

"'It lists some amusing headlines that have actually appeared in newspapers:

"'Child's Stool Great for Use in Garden'

"'Stud Tires Out'

"'Stiff Opposition Expected to Casketless Funeral Plan'

"'Drunk Gets Nine Months in Violin Case'

"'Iraqi Head Seeks Arms'

"And my personal favorite:

"'Queen Mary Having Bottom Scraped'"

Diana of Hutchinson: "I really loved the headline on the 14th: 'Latimer will not run for governor; HUD aide says he's happy being useful.'"

Jim Olson of Sarona, Wis.: "I'm a retired high-school English teacher; I taught high-school English for 33 years. I had a freshman student write, in a composition, one time: 'Edgar Allan Poe is one of my favorite authors. Edgar Allan Poe writes about women, and other terrifying experiences.'"

Danielle of St. Paul: "When I was in junior high or high school, I was sitting around with a girlfriend of mine, and we were talking about names of people and whether they looked like their name or not. My friend said: 'You know, I don't think your dad looks like a Bill. I think he looks more like a . . . a Dick!'

"We looked at each other, and she realized what she'd said, and we just started laughing and laughing and laughing. Umpteen years later, I still get a big kick out of it."

Traveling on Amtrak of Newport: "A funny thing happened while I was upon Amtrak, on my way to Minnesota: We were traveling through Montana. Had stopped at a station to pick up passengers. On the way to the next stop, the intercom came on, and the conductor said: 'At our next stop, we will have a service stop, and we need some extra time to service the train—so if any of you would like to stop and spread your legs, there will be ample time.' Well, the whole train just erupted."

Doctor Friendly of St. Paul: "A young man I had never met before was in the office today. As soon as I walked into the examining room, I noticed that he was standing—which is kind of unusual.

"I shook his hand and invited him to sit down—an invitation which he seemed to ignore, so I remained standing, also. I made a little small talk, since he was obviously nervous and very ill at ease. This didn't seem to calm him much, so I tried again: 'Please have a seat.'

"He looked around, almost as if he hadn't heard me, so I tried one more time: 'Won't you please sit down?'—and I sat down, to show him the way.

"He finally did, but didn't look very happy about it. Finally I got the chance to ask: 'So what is it that seems to be the problem today?'

"'Oh, doctor, I have the *most* painful hemorrhoid!'

"Oh, well. I had the best of intentions."

Anonymous woman: "I do data entry for a refund company. The other day, I was typing in names and addresses of people who wanted to get two six-packs of Tab free, and on the card it had a couple lines where it said: 'Is there anything we should know about Tab?'

"One guy had written: 'It tastes terrible, but what the heck? It's free!'"

Linda of Vadnais Heights was paying close attention as she assembled the documentation she needed—a cash-register receipt and a UPC symbol—to cash in on a free-soap offer: "While circling the price of the soap, I glanced through my other purchases to make sure I no longer needed the receipt. I think the Jergens company could be quite entertained if they look closely enough: Kodak film, Energizer batteries, underwire bras, Duraflame logs and K-Y Jelly. All the makings of a hot night in front of the fireplace!

"I had no idea I led such an exciting life."

Gary of St. Paul: "The most laughably foolish thing I've done is: In my first year of college, I asked a Bible major out to a movie. The movie I chose was *The Groove Tube*—which, in the first scene, featured full-frontal nudity. Needless to say, it was the last date with her."

BULLETIN BOARD REPLIES: Correct us if we're wrong, but if memory serves, the first scene of the Bible also has a little full-frontal nudity.

On the other hand: Bulletin Board's Dept. of Film History and Religious Studies notes that nowhere in the Bible are any major (or minor) figure's genitalia dressed up like a puppet.

Rose of Eagan: "My husband, who has a funny way of expressing himself, asked the kids over lunch the other day: 'Is it just me, or does the cat box need changing?'"

Stevie of Oakdale: "Me and my older brother were just constantly climbin' the trees and buildin' forts and crap like that. One time, my mom's like: 'If you fall out of that tree and break your leg, don't you dare come runnin' to me. . . .'"

Sunny of St. Paul: "I work as a waitress at an ice-cream parlor. Whenever we bring a sundae out, we bring along a side dish of mixed nuts, and at the table, we offer to sprinkle the nuts on the sundae for the customer.

"One time, a family of three persons—a dad and a mom and their 7-ish-year-old daughter—come into my restaurant, and the dad is like this totally happy-go-lucky, 'Leave It to Beaver' type of dad, and they order sundaes, and I bring the sundaes and the mixed nuts out, and I offer the nuts to the father.

"I said: 'Would you care for any nuts?'

"And he said: 'No, thanks. I already have two.'

"I realized he was talking about his wife and his daughter, but I had to clamp my mouth shut to keep from laughing."

Kiki of Oakdale: "I have a story about my friend Noodles' mother. They have a plethora of food at their house; I mean, they have more variety than my local corner convenience store! One night, we were over there, and her mother was offering us food and telling us about new recipes, and my friend says to her mom: 'Mom, all you ever talk about is food!'

"And her mother replies: 'Oh, baloney!' "

Dick of Woodbury: "I arrived early in a small town in North Dakota; I was supposed to have an appointment with a gentleman. It was a rainy day, and I went into a restaurant just to kill some time and have breakfast.

"The restaurant was anything but ideal. When I walked in, I saw several buckets around to catch the drippings through their roof. I sat down to order breakfast, and the waitress must have been a throwback to the '40s who liked to give cute names to things that people order—such as: Two poached eggs on toast would be 'Adam and Eve on a raft.'

"I ordered soft scrambled eggs, and she turned and yelled into the kitchen: 'Bring out a plate of snot.'

"At that point, I'm afraid, my hunger went away."

Bonnie of Apple Valley: "Tonight at a church meeting, one member said to the pastor: 'I think I feel a lunch coming up.'"

Sheila the Moundian: "The person who's responsible for changing the charming mini-homilies on the sign in front of our Westonka churches must have been inspired by the old saw 'Today is the tomorrow you worried about yesterday.' But, unclear on the concept, it read: 'Today is the day after yesterday.'"

The Rare Spotted Aaron of St. Paul: "I was in Town Square today, and I was sitting across from a 'Now Hiring' sign in front of McDonald's—and at the bottom, it said: 'People Are Our Most Important Ingredient.'

"And yes, folks, they are now hiring."

Bare Lar of Fridley: "A sign I've seen at the Burger King in our area: 'Free College Football Cup.' That just isn't the kind of collector's item that I would like."

Lonster of St. Paul: "I was just watching a Burger King commercial—not that I actually turned on the TV for the commercial itself—but the commercial's on, and they showed a horse running at the same time the narrator of the commercial said: 'Fast food.' I'm wondering if they were aware of what they were suggesting there."

Enid of "right near the Fairgrounds": "I wonder if I'm the only person who gets uncontrollable giggles when that 'Say yes to horse racing' commercial comes on the TV.

"While the announcer says 'Yes,' the horse answers: 'Nay! Nay!'

"When I worked at a racetrack, some 50 years ago, we used to say that horse sense was what horses had that prevented them from betting on people. I *still* think there's some wisdom to that."

J.C. of Maple Grove: "I was watching a Trident sugarless-gum commercial on TV when it struck me: Trident is Latin for 'three teeth.'"

The Happy Elf of North Oaks, a young orchestralist: "We were at our dress rehearsal at Orchestra Hall for our very last concert of the season. We had just performed the '1812 Overture' for the first time, with the full effect of the bass drums—about 10 of them. And it was just *fabulous;* it was so . . . *big!*

"We were all just sitting there, and our illustrious conductor—he was pumped, and it was so neat, and he went on about how great a concert it would be . . . and, of course, taking into consideration the emotional effect music can have on some people, he announced that there wouldn't be a dry seat in the house."

Pat O. of Apple Valley: "I overheard an amusing conversation last night in a restaurant: Man No. 1 walked up to Man No. 2 and said 'Hi, it's nice to see you'—and shook his hand. And then he said: 'Oh, you'll have to excuse me. My hands are a little bit damp. I just went to the bathroom.'

"Now, I think I know what he *meant,* but that's not really what he *said*—and you should've seen the look on the face of Man No. 2."

Anonymous: "Today I happened to notice, above a urinal at a Green Mill restaurant, an advertisement for Concordia College in St. Paul. The headline on the advertisement was: 'Are You Where You Want To Be Right Now?'"

Joe of Oakdale: "My new brother-in-law was havin' a party, and he was talkin' about their bathroom. They just had it remodeled, and he said he'd put more money into that than into remodeling the whole kitchen. I'd had my bathroom apart for two years, so I knew. I said: 'Yeah, it's unreal what you can dump in a bathroom.'"

Joanne W. of Oakdale: "Today I called a business, and they said that if I wanted to speak in Spanish, I should press 2.

"I thought: 'Gee, that would be a lot of *fun!*' So I pressed 2.

"And guess what! I *still* couldn't speak Spanish."

Elizabeth of Eagan: "I had to call the IRS today, to get some information, and I was on hold with their lovely Muzak—which was playing Joni Mitchell's 'Raised on Robbery.'"

Mark of Coon Rapids: "I'm calling to tell you about something that happened at work here last Friday. For an hour, at lunch, we had a guy talking to us about rewards and recognition and positive reinforcement and creating good feelings among team members—teaching us how important encouragement is, as if we didn't *know* that . . . but anyway, we were learning it again.

"We have kind of a Former Top 40s kind of Muzak here in the building, and as we were leaving this rewards-and-recognition seminar, Linda Ronstadt was singing 'You're no good, you're no good, you're no good. Baby, you're no good.'"

BULLETIN BOARD REPLIES: As if you didn't know that.

Barb of St. Paul: "My sister's baby was getting kinda tired and fussy, so she asked her husband, Joel, to put the baby down.

"His reply was: 'OK. She's bald, toothless and incontinent. How's that?'"

Also of Woodbury: "When my wife was a little girl, she often enjoyed visiting her elderly grandmother, where she spent much of her free time just curiously roaming through the many rooms of this mysterious old house that her grandmother lived in.

"In one of the rooms, she found a dresser with drawers containing perfumes, soaps and other fragrant items. This became a favorite stopping place for her, as she journeyed through the house many, many times.

"When sharing this precious childhood memory with me, years later, she stated that she used to enjoy smelling her grandmother's drawers."

Rowdette of Vadnais Heights: "We work on a social-services staff in a hospital, and we all carry beepers. My coworker Betty misplaced her beeper, and she ran around the hospital looking for it, and she couldn't find it.

"Our beepers have three settings: Off, Vibrate, and Beep—and because the Beep is so loud and potentially obnoxious, we're all told to put it on the Vibrate setting.

"So after about an hour of frantic looking, Betty ran up to the nursing station, where there were several people standing, and said: 'I've misplaced my vibrator!'

"There was *total* silence all around."

Matt of St. Peter: "My wife, who has a phobia of dentists, was at the dentist's office the other day when the dental assistant called her back in to have her cavity filled. As she peeked from the reception area down the hall to the dental chair, the dental assistant said: 'Come on. It won't hurt.'

"Well, my wife started walking down the hall—and she met an elderly, stoic-looking man, prim and proper, and she asked him: 'Did it hurt?'

"He stopped and looked at her with a strange look and said: 'Excuse me?'

"My wife repeated: 'Did it hurt?'

"And he said: 'Well . . . well, no'—in a flustered sort of way. And he continued out into the reception area.

"At this time, my wife realized that the two receptionists were holding their heads in their hands and just laughing to tears. She continued on in to the dental chair, and within a moment, one of the receptionists—still laughing so hard that she was crying—came in and said: 'He wasn't in for dental work. He just came in to use the bathroom.'"

Big Louie of St. Paul:"Three or four years ago, we were shopping with our grandsons. They were 6 and 8 years old, and they were fascinated by the lobsters and crabs in the live tank at the supermarket.

"A lady came by and had the butcher fish out six crabs and put them in a plastic-lined box. They were just fascinated to watch the butcher with his tongs take out these live crabs.

"Then, after we did our shopping and on our way out the door, the lady with the box was walking ahead of us, and my 8-year-old grandson piped up, in a loud voice: 'Look, Grandpa! There's the lady with the crabs!'

"Everybody looked. She turned around and held up the box for everybody to see."

Peggy of St. Paul: "I just asked my 2½-year-old son, Jake, if he wanted to come outside and help me repot some plants. He said: 'Sure!'

"And then he's yellin' to the neighbors across the street: 'Hi! We're planting pot!'

"And I thought: 'Oh, great. That's *all* I need.'"

Nick of Hudson, Wis.: "My wife was going out to do some mowing a week or two ago, and she wanted to know if I had some old clothes she could wear. I suggested that she wear some of my old military-type clothes.

"She looked at me and said: 'I just can't see myself in camouflage.'"

Darrell Pangborn of Inver Grove Heights: "I was a 19-year-old Air Corps private in World War II, and I was stationed for a short time in Salt Lake City. I'd made contact with a youth group at a local church, 'cause I enjoyed their choir singing and the fellowship such groups enjoy.

"On this particular occasion, I had invited to dinner an attractive young lady from the group, and we went to a Chinese/American restaurant. I was doing my best to make a good impression, as a 19-year-old would, and I thought I was doing OK.

"We both ordered chow mein—and when it came, I proceeded to pour what appeared to be soy sauce all over mine.

"With a somewhat horrified look, she said: 'You don't put *that* on chow mein, do you?'

"I replied: 'Of course! That's what makes it taste good!'

"With my first bite, I discovered that the bottle contained steak sauce, not soy sauce. But rather than admit that I had made a gross error in judgment, and trying to save face, I smiled with every bite and finished the whole dish.

"That was probably the worst meal I've ever eaten, and it was *years* before I trusted those soy sauce bottles in Chinese restaurants."

Jim Fitzsimons of St. Paul: "A few years back, I went out to Sheridan, Wyoming, to be in a wedding that a couple of friends were having. After the wedding was over, and the reception, those of us who went out from Minnesota and from other states to be part of the ceremony went up to the bride's family's cabin, which was up in the mountains just outside of Sheridan.

"I was sitting on the porch of one of the cabins talking with some of the locals who had cabins up there, and I noticed an animal standing by the trees just beyond the cabin. The sun was hitting this animal at an odd angle or something; it made it look bigger than I guess it was.

"I thought it was some kind of feline critter, but I wasn't sure what kind; I thought maybe it was a bobcat, or something like that.

"So I asked one of the local people. I asked: 'What kind of animal is that?' And I pointed over at it.

"The woman that I asked looked over at this creature and then looked back at me, and she says: 'That's a *cat!*'

"When she said that, I felt like such a bonehead that I turned and pointed to the dog that was lying at my feet on the porch, and I said: 'Oh ... well ... what kind of animal is *that?*'"

CHAPTER FIFTEEN

Our Pets, Ourselves

The Red Fire Hydrant of Cottage Grove: "We stopped over at our in-laws' today. They have a dog named Petey, who's gettin' kinda old.

"I was standin' barefoot on the grass, just talkin', and my daughter said: 'Mom, watch out!' I looked down—and there was Petey, liftin' up his leg and peein' on me!

"I knew my legs were sunburnt, but I didn't think they were *that* red.

"P.S.: My horoscope for the day said: 'Maintain a sense of humor.'"

BULLETIN BOARD REPLIES: That's all well and good, but where are these astrologers when you need 'em? Surely you'd have profited more from this advice: "Maintain a safe distance from confused, incontinent old dogs."

Good advice any day.

The EIEIO Ranger: "My simple pleasure is my little three-legged cat Eddie, who has never failed to make me smile or laugh at least once a day for the last five years.

"I've been working on a dummy for Halloween—and haven't made the head yet. The dummy was propped up on the couch, posed in a seated position. On Saturday, I came out of the shower, and there was Eddie, all curled up in a ball, asleep on the dummy's lap.

"A cat, missing a leg, asleep on the lap of a dummy, missing a head."

Kitty of St. Paul: "For all of those people who think that dogs are the only lovable pets and that cats don't do anything amusing or interesting, here's a story for you:

"About two weeks before she died, Muffin could hardly walk, let alone jump on the surfaces she loved—namely our couches or bed. My husband put her on the porch one day when it was really sunny; she loved to bask in the sun. And then he went down into the basement to work.

"After a little while, our other cat, Rupert, came down to visit him and started crying and yowling. My husband thought it was just for food, so he told him he'd be with him in a few minutes. Rupert went back upstairs, but he was anything but peaceful. He was pacing the floor, yowling, screaming and crying. My husband knew that something was wrong.

"He came upstairs. Rupert led him into the bedroom, where poor little Muffin was on the floor, looking up at the bed, wishing she could jump up there. After my husband picked her up and placed her on the bed, Rupert turned and walked away, his mission accomplished."

Puppy Owner of East Bethel: "Our family has a single-brain-celled, 8-month-old black Lab puppy who, when tied up outside, has decided Minnesota spring weather is not for him. Hence, he has spent the better part of the last two weeks digging his escape route to China in our back yard.

"My husband, who is thoroughly disgusted with him, spent the better part of Saturday morning with a big shovel, walking back and forth 50 yards to my garden to get black dirt to fill the holes in.

"The dog was chained to a tree so he could remorsefully observe his master working so hard to undo his dirty deed. He quizzically watched my husband packing and stomping the ground so grass would grow, filling in all of these holes.

"Finally, the dog got the idea. As my husband laid down yet another shovelful of dirt, he looked up to see the dog three feet away, digging yet another hole. My husband looked at me and said: 'You know, that dog's lookin' at me like I'm stupid because I'm walking all that way for dirt when there's perfectly good dirt right here!'

"And we thought the dog was stupid!"

BULLETIN BOARD REPLIES: Give us another call, Puppy Owner, when your pooch heads out to buy you a wheelbarrow.

Dennis of Austin: "Last spring, I was visiting my daughter and her family for a week. One evening, while we were enjoying an excellent spaghetti dinner, I was attempting to amuse my 2-year-old granddaughter.

"I was aping the meatball scene from the movie *Hot Shots, Part Deux,* which in turn was a parody of the meatball scene in the movie *Lady and the Tramp.*

"Anyway, I was pushing a meatball with my nose along the edge of the table towards my granddaughter when, suddenly, my pet cocker spaniel jumped up and snapped up the meatball—along with the tip of my nose.

"For a while there, everything was chaotic, with my nose bleeding profusely, my granddaughter squealing with delight, and my daughter in a panic.

"We got the bleeding stopped and discovered that the tip of my nose was hanging by a string of skin. So we got some tape, taped my nose back in place—and my nose, since then, has healed nicely, but it's left me a round, button-size scar on the tip of my nose that, every time I look in the mirror, is a reminder not to put my nose where it doesn't belong."

David Stever of St.Paul: "Our dog's name is Bear, and everybody in the neighborhood knows Bear, who is a Great Pyrenees—a big, white dog, and she likes to bark.

"Last summer, somebody had the audacity to walk his dog down the sidewalk on the other side of the street. Bear was looking out the third-floor window and decided that she was going to bark at this person and his dog. Bear pushed the screen out of the window and continued to bark. The dog continued to walk down the sidewalk. Bear decided to stick her head out the window. The dog continued to walk, and Bear continued to bark. So Bear pushed her way out the third-floor window.

"She hit the little roof underneath the third-floor window, then hit the porch roof, and then missed the sidewalk and hit the front lawn. The guy across the street saw this—and said that the dog landed with an audible 'Oooof.' He then came over and led Bear into our back yard, where we found her—and she walked like everything hurt, but there was no damage, other than to her pride.

"We never found out the details until the guy came around with his dog the following day, and Bear, who's quite aggressive when anybody walks by our fence, saw this person and—it's the only time my wife and I have ever seen this—walked to the far end of the yard and stayed there while the guy explained what had happened.

"So once again, I apologize to all of our neighbors for Bear's barking—but here, at least, is a good story."

The Original Newcomer of St. Paul: "When I attended a seminar a few months ago, I sat next to a young man who had a really beautiful brochure for his business. At one point, he mentioned to the class that he was the only employee, but I noticed that he had 'B— W—— and Associates' on the brochure.

"When I questioned him about it, he told me he thought it sounded more professional that way—so he had named his cat Associates."

BULLETIN BOARD MUSES: Truth in advertising!

Sharon of Roseville: "A new employee joined our department some time ago and learned that everyone in the department owned cats.

"Day after day and lunch after lunch, he was forced to listen to tedious stories about everyone's cat (or cats, as the case may be). Occasionally he would get a word in edgewise, usually about a snowmobile trip, but the conversations always returned to cats.

"I remember the day that he finally succumbed. It was Monday at 11:15 A.M. We were all standing by the elevators for our race to the lunchroom. All of a sudden, we heard this terrible coughing and hacking. We waited, and a young woman walked past. Her coughing continued as she disappeared down the hallway.

"'Hairball?' he said."

M.C. of St. Paul: "Recently, I rejoined the church of my childhood. I did so just as the parish was preparing its pictorial directory, and I was asked to sit for a photo. What rotten timing! Or, as the French say: *'Quelle fromage!'* I hate having my picture taken. My pictures always look as though they should have numbers on the bottom.

"Vanity? Well, yes—but not just because of graying hair (premature) nor double chin, which I prefer to think of as a foster chin. The real reason is: The cat stole my dentures.

"This feline, rejoicing in the name of Eartha Kitty, made off with my bottom teeth in the middle of the night. She was always fascinated by the bedtime ritual of placing the dentures in a glass of water and dropping in a tablet of Denture Rot Not, which fizzled and bubbled for several minutes. Folding herself into the cat-guarding-a-mousehole position, she watched until the water cleared and then, Jeeves-like, shimmered out of the room.

"One morning, I woke to find one-half of my smile missing. I knew immediately that E.K. was responsible. When I confronted her, she gave me an inscrutable smile, turned her back, sat down and began to wash her ears. This is catspeak for 'I neither confirm nor deny. Leave me alone.'

"I followed her for days, but never found the missing molars.

"Why did she want them? Was she bored with her toys? Did she wear them at night to terrorize my older, more sober cats, Bill W. and Dr. Bob? Did she use them to scoop out the litter box?

"I finally admitted defeat and decided to order a new set. In the meantime, I make do with the uppers. My friends tell me the gap is only noticeable when I smile or eat or talk.

"To guard the remaining dentures, I put them in the refrigerator at night. (Even this is not perfectly safe. I once had two Persian cats, Momerath and Borograve, who managed to extricate a roast duck from the fridge and close the door behind them. I found it sitting in the middle of the kitchen floor. I have tried to figure out how they coordinated this: 'Mo, you hold the door, and I'll get the duck.' 'OK, Bo.')

"To combat the force of gravity, I use a state-of-the-art adhesive—Stuck for Life. But I don't do lunch; nor do I sit for photographs. Thus I am the only member of the parish whose picture is not in its directory."

Country Cat Lady: "This is a tale of two kitties:

"Many years ago, a mama cat showed up in our barn with three wild kittens. At my first glimpse of them, the littler female made the meanest face a tiny kitten could and hissed with all her might. I lost my heart on the spot and resolved that someday I would tame that little spitfire.

"The male kitten disappeared, but the two girls stayed—and began to look to me for their daily meals.

"A year and a litter of kittens apiece later, the three mamas were tame enough to capture and take to be spayed. In the process, the wildest one escaped in my house, which was never the same again . . . and, despite my warnings, managed to repeat the feat at the vet clinic—an experience none of them ever forgot, either.

"The mama became my house cat for many, many years. Soon after she died, the wild one—by then 12 years old—got sick one brutally cold Christmas Eve, and we gambled and brought her inside.

"She hid in a closet for three weeks, only coming out after the house was quiet and dark, to eat and use the litter box. Her manners were always impeccable. Talking to her and reaching in to stroke her elicited the loudest of purrs.

"Finally she'd had enough of the closet and began making herself at home—and it was such a pleasure to see. After six months, she slept on the bed. After a year, she sat on laps. She went from running for cover at the sound of a strange voice to being head of the welcoming committee. She was always around me or under my chair, always with that incredible rumble-purr turned up full volume.

"She kept her fierceness and her independent ways, sometimes using them on my behalf. If a spider made me scream or the dog pestered me, she came running with her fur on end, fully ready to attack whatever my problem was. She was the only bona fide Attack Cat I ever knew.

"She had her rules, though—such as: Don't sit in her favorite chair after 7 P.M., and never, ever touch her feet.

"She became what was totally contrary to her nature, just out of her love for me, and always she made me be a better person. I had to earn her trust. I had to work to be her friend and, finally, just to keep her alive as her kidneys began to fail.

"Her sister, who was incredibly sweet and gentle, adamantly resisted all attempts to make her a house cat, and she, too, suffered rapidly declining health.

"Last week, after nearly 17 years of sharing our lives, I realized it was time to let them go. Thanks to the kindness of our vet, they both passed on from the comfort of our living room.

"But what a huge void in a household such a little cat leaves."

R.J. of Hammond, Wis.: "We very recently buried one of the world's great dogs—a big, happy, exuberant German shepherd who, at only 8, went unexpectedly into heart failure.

"She was as strong as an ox, but too gentle to kill even a mouse. She lived only to please and be near the people that she loved. Those who have loved and lost a pet will know the emptiness in our home and the ache in our hearts right now.

"I wanted to tell one story about her. Several years ago, the dog, my son, and I went outside. Our son uses a wheelchair, and he and the dog went one way around the house while I went to the garage. Shortly, I heard her barking her panic bark— a higher-pitched, rapid, breathless sort of bark that I knew meant: 'Help! Help! This is serious!'

"I found her trying to stay between our son and something in the tall grass at the edge of the yard. It turned out to be a young skunk. She had been sprayed two or three times and knew that skunks were bad news. It was obvious she wanted to run, but no matter who moved, she steadfastly stayed between them.

"Never mind that had it been an adult skunk, her barking probably would've gotten them both sprayed. She did the only thing she knew to do, which was to shield our little boy and call for help.

"That one incident showed me, as much as anything, that in that big heart of gold of hers, she was a true hero.

"I read a quote somewheres that seems appropriate: 'Our pets give everything. They give their all. And in return, they only ask what little bit we can spare.'

"That sure fits."

CHAPTER SIXTEEN

The Verbing of America

Nouns and adjectives doing double duty—sometimes for the better, and sometimes for the worse:

Kellen-Sierra of St. Paul: "We have several indoor cats, so I do a lot of litter-scooping. I just received a litter scoop I ordered from a catalog, and this is what it says on the label:

"'CHROME PLATED

"'SUITABLE FOR USE WITH "QUICK CLUMPING" LITTER

"'USE SCALLOPED EDGE TO SCULPTURE LITTER'

"Sculpture litter?! There's even a picture on the label showing 'sculpturing'! I don't spend *enough* time in the litter boxes? Now I'm supposed to make sand castles in it?"

A Retired Teacher of western Wisconsin: "I was following the Funeral Mass in the Joy and Praise Hymnal at a Catholic church, and I was really surprised to read, at the end of the service: 'The priest will sprinkle holy water on the casket and incense it.'"

BULLETIN BOARD NOTES: They expect you to lie around underground for all eternity, with some dead guy inside you—and then they're surprised that you've got a short fuse?

The State Employee: "Here I am, putting in volunteer time—that is: working without being paid, on Sunday morning . . . and it actually happens to be my birthday. (Cue the violins.) So I thought I'd take a break and call you about something I noticed.

"Several weeks ago, signs appeared on the front doors of our building: 'No exiting after 6 P.M. This door is alarmed.' I sure hope these doors calm down soon. Perhaps we should talk to them, in soothing tones."

The Hazel-eyed Girl of St. Paul, a waitress: "At work, we have nachos and artichoke dip. The other night, I laughed at myself after telling somebody to please 'chip this plate' so I could bring it out to the customers."

Tim of Inver Grove Heights: "I work at a popular family restaurant in the Twin Cities here, and oftentimes on Sunday, early mornings, we get quite a push from the churchgoers. They come in in *herds*. Maybe it's appropriate that oftentimes we ask the hosts and hostesses to water them for us if they have a minute or two."

Charo of St. Paul, another restaurant worker: "First of all, the hostess greets, seats and menus the customers. And then the waitress will come up and special them, napkin them and drink them. After they're served their drinks, they eat—and then we coffee them, and then we tab them.

"So, actually there's a lot of weird verbs."

BULLETIN BOARD REPLIES: And then, even if the servers have greeted, seated, menued, specialed, napkined, drinked, coffeed and tabbed to the customers' perfect satisfaction, they face the risk of getting stiffed.

Daughter o' Bobcat of Woodbury: "My mom and I were in a candy store. They had a sign on the cash register saying: 'Please aware cashier if you have a gift certificate.' Ruined my appetite for candy."

Angel of Mercy of Mendota Heights: "A parent of a child with a cold called the clinic I work at to ask for some advice. He said that he had been vaporizing the child all night."

The High Priestess of Ravenna Township: "I had a doctor's appointment today. They had me fill out a sheet of paper on which was listed a variety of embarrassing and invasive prophylactic procedures, and we had to indicate whether we had or had not had them within a certain period of time.

"I tried to hand it back to the woman at the desk. She handed it, instead, back to me and said: 'Oh, no. Give that to the nurse when she rooms you.'

"The verbing of America is insaning me."

P.J. of Hastings: "I work at a nursing home, and the other day, this older lady was yelling for help. I stopped and said: 'Do you have to go to the bathroom?' And she said: 'Well, no. I've already stooled in my pants.'

"And my immediate reaction was: I cracked up, and I thought of you guys immediately. I just had to call and tell ya."

BULLETIN BOARD REPLIES: Well, we're terribly flattered—but could someone please go help that poor woman!

Pat the Middle-Aged College Student of Wells: "I was at the River Hills mall in Mankato last weekend, and I was walking past a security guard who was talking to a friend—and I heard him say, very matter-of-factly: 'I'm surprised they don't urinate us more often.'

"Well, I was sure that I had misunderstood him, and as I was walking, I kept trying to figure out what I had really heard—and finally it dawned on me that what he was talking about was being tested for drugs."

Puddle Duck of West St. Paul: "Talking to a fellow I work with, I told him that he was ornery. He said: 'Some of these people around here *deserve* to be orneried at.'"

Susan of Maplewood: "My son is not being the most gentle creature these days. He and I were playing with his teddy bear—and in the process of manhandling it away from me, my son poked me in the eye. My husband looked over and asked what had happened, and I found myself telling him that our son had just *three-stooged* me in the eye."

Julie of the Midway: "I was at choir practice last night, and we came to this part in this piece that we're singing where our choir director, Steve, wanted the chorus to swell and get all . . . big. He said: 'I really want it big. I want it Cecil B. De-Milled.'"

J.P. of Mendota Heights: "We have three little kids. When they don't like something they're eating, they just spit it right back out, no matter where they are—just like Tom Hanks in *Big,* so we say they are Tom Hanksing it.

"Speaking of action verbs, I just heard 'WIPE!'—so I better go."

Charles of Eagan: "We're going to a resort up north for a week in July. Our two cats are staying home. We could ask the neighbors to feed them for us, but it occurred to me that one of the kids' day-care teachers might enjoy getting out of her apartment and spending a week in our house—so I think we should ask if she can Kato the place while we're away."

Betsy of Robbinsdale: "What's really weird is to have your *name* verbed.

"I'm an editor and a writer, and a coworker of mine came to me with a piece of writing he wanted me to help him with. He showed it to me, and he told me what he was trying to say. I made a couple of suggestions, and he said: 'Yeah, that's right. Just Betsy it.' And he wrote on the side of the page: 'To be Betsied.'

"I was just speechless. I'd been verbed. This verbing thing has gone too far."

Pat of Maplewood: "Recently my boss put a document on my desk with this note: 'Please English this up for me, and I'll give it to someone to computer.'"

BULLETIN BOARD NOTES: At least your boss said "Please." That's the important thing—isn't it? Well, OK. One of the important things.

Georgeanna of St. Paul: "I'm taking a course in Renaissance Literature over at the venerable U of M, and while reading various 17th-century rhetoric books written before the word 'translate' came into vogue, I've been coming across the word 'Englished.' Instead of saying that a text was translated, they say that it was Englished. "So: Before the verbing of America, you can bet that Europe was being well-verbed."

BULLETIN BOARD NOTES: In France, even at the dawn of the 21st century, they're perpetually in a fearsome snit over the Englishing of Europe. Sacre bleu!

Brett of Milwaukee: "There was a teacher at school who needed to get the attention of some students down the hall, and she yelled down to another teacher: 'Tell them to *tout de suite* it on down here!'"

Heidi of Chippewa Falls, Wis.: "I was picking on my best friend, Poopie, because she has these terrible grammar skills. She got really defensive and shouted: 'Oh, shut up! I can grammar.' I thought: 'Yes. Exactly.'"

MDW of St. Cloud: "The English department at SCSU is proposing a new emphasis in its master's program: an emphasis in college teaching.

"The proposal, written by three members of the department, states: 'With an emphasis in College Teaching appearing on MA transcripts, our graduates would be more clearly credentialed as having professional expertise in an area that would support all their pursuits as college teachers.' *[BULLETIN BOARD ATTEMPTS TO TRANSLATE: If it looked as though our graduates knew how to teach college students, they'd have better luck getting jobs as college teachers.]*

"Later in the proposal, it states: 'It will regularize into an emphasis a series of courses that already exist.' *[TRANSLATION: Really, nothing will change. It will only seem to.]*

"I guess we shouldn't look to the future college teachers of English to fight the verbing of America."

Maureen of the Midway: "I was sitting in a class—continuing ed for teachers—today at Hamline. The professor's from out of town; Iowa, in fact. And we were talking about how people tend to see the negative in things. And she said: 'Yes, we definitely have a tendency in our society to awfulize things.'

"Auuuugggghhhh! I could just scream!"

BULLETIN BOARD NOTES: Thanks, but that Auuuugggghhhh was perfectly adequate.

August Rubrecht of the University of Wisconsin–Eau Claire: "Loitering in the vicinity of the *Oxford English Dictionary* today, I recalled that **The Trivia Queen** had recently charged Jane Austen with reckless verbing because she used *image* as a verb. I ambled over and looked the word up.

"Turns out the earliest citation of such a use means 'to form a mental image; to conceive.' It is way older than Ms. Austen, or even her great-great-grandparents: about 1440. The sentence cited in the *OED* comes from something titled *Jacob's Well:* 'He ymagyth and castyth beforn in his herte, how he wyll makyn it.' In the line The Trivia Queen quoted, the meaning could be different—'to describe (esp. vividly or graphically)'—but even that one goes back to 1628, 147 years before the defendant was born. By the time she arrived on the scene, the victim was already verbed. Considering the strength of her alibi, I declare Jane Austen not guilty of this act of verbing.

"She may not be entirely innocent, though. Look at what she wrote: 'Oh how can I her person try to image and portray . . . ?' If *image* means 'describe' instead of 'conceive,' she committed redundancy.

"P.S. I refrained from saying she redundified. I expect some credit for that."

BULLETIN BOARD REPLIES: You've gotta love an academic with a sense of humor. That credit enough?

The Wordsmith of St. Paul: "This is an excerpt from a novel that I'm reading: A woman has just confided in her friend that she and her husband, who is a marriage counselor, are not getting along very well. Her friend replies: 'It is ironic, isn't it? Helping other people cope with their stresses puts him under so much stress that he's not getting along with his own wife. Who theraps the therapists?'"

BULLETIN BOARD REPLIES: Therapists, therap thyselves.

Pope Tom of Mankato: "I have a verbing of America for you folks. It comes to us from page 256 of the paperback version of *The Client* by John Grisham. I will begin reading: 'What sort of person would watch a video of a tacky souvenir shop in the French Quarter? Americans no longer experience vacations. They simply Sony them, so they can ignore them for the rest of the year.'

"Americans Sony our vacations.

"It's a trademark. It's a verb. Who could not love this country?"

P.J. of St. Anthony Park faxed us a copy of an advertisement with the headline "Unisys LifeLine CAD makes other emergency response solutions look a little out of date." In the ad's body copy, we read: "Our clients know we do more than supply information technology. We apply it. We work with them to help CUSTOMERIZE[SM] their operations, maximizing service to the public—their customers."

At the bottom, in the legally required teeny-tiny type, it says: "CUSTOMERIZE[SM] is a service mark of Unisys Corporation."

Wrote P.J.: "I guess we are now registering our verbings. Saints preserve us."

Kathy H. of Eagan: "Last night, I was teaching my 8-year-old how to use WordPerfect on our computer. I showed her the function keys and how the F7 key was to exit the program when she was done. This morning, as she was leaving for the bus stop, she said: 'Bye, Mom! I'm F7ing out of here.'"

Skrubby of Shoreview: "Me and my two friends were sitting here eating Gummi Bears, and my friend said: 'Look! If you saliva it, it turns clear!'"

BULLETIN BOARD SAYS: And in the background, we could hear someone— the friend, we're guessing—say: "You're a dork."

Kit of Rice Lake, Wis.: "I have a friend in New York who . . . ummmmm . . . he's a really nice guy, but he has a hard time finding women who want to be with him. Last time I talked to him, I asked him how he was and he said: Oh, he wasn't doing too well, because he had been just-friendsed by another woman."

Sheila the Moundian: "Part of my job is to listen to taped telephone conversations of people that I supervise—as a quality check. I heard one last week tell somebody: 'Let me rest-assured you.'"

King-Z of Inver Grove Heights: "I'm was lookin' at the paper, and I saw an ad for a Buick dealer that says 'GET $895ed.' So I went in to my boss and told him that I need to get 6-percented—or at least cost-of-livinged—so I could afford to get 895ed.

"You can guess what he told *me* to get."

Scott of St. Paul: "I saw a commercial on TV the other night that asked if I wanted to be two-doored, four-doored, vanned, minivanned or convertibled.

"Where will it stop?"

BULLETIN BOARD REPLIES: It won't. So let's enjoy the ride.

CHAPTER SEVENTEEN

On the Air

Hot enough for ya? From **Bob Woolley** of St. Paul: "This happened in Illinois, when I was living there during the scorchingly hot summer of 1988:

"*K., the stupid weatherman:* 'So temperatures will remain well above average for at least several days. Back to you, J.'

"*J., the even stupider anchorman:* 'K., aren't the temperatures always above average this time of year?'

"*K., obviously a bit flustered, perhaps for the first time realizing that he was sitting next to the one person on Earth who understood less about the weather than he did:* 'Well, I mean above the seasonally adjusted average.'

"*J., blissfully unaware of his own deepening stupidity:* 'That's what I mean. The season makes it warmer than average.'

"*K. with growing consternation:* 'Uh, well. You see, the temperature is going to be even higher than it usually is for this time of year.'

"*J., with a really embarrassing air of superiority, obviously convinced he has caught the weatherman in a major blunder:* 'But K., this is always the hottest time of the year.'

"*K., wishing he had taken that job with Channel 6 after all:* 'Don't worry about it, J. Just take my word for it: It's going to be hot.'

"*J., with a confident chuckle:* 'That's just what I have been saying.'

"Now, I may not have gotten the words exactly right, but I swear that exchange took place in almost those exact words. And I just couldn't believe it."

Forecast: ZZZZZZZs! Here's **Ms. Anonymous** of "The Ice Palace Capital of the World" (echoed by many, many others, and most notably by **Sunny Daze** of St. Paul, who proposed a support group called FOG—Forecast Outsider Geeks—whose 12-step program would include "1) I am powerless to stay awake during weather forecasts" and "12) I will enjoy the uncertainty and adventure of every day"): "OK, so I'm getting older, and my mind seems to drift off more than it used to. I blame it on eating out of aluminum pans in my formative years—and/or perhaps the mercury from my fillings has seeped into my brain.

"Anyway, I always have the best intentions of knowing what the weather will be like tomorrow, so I watch the evening news. But by the time they get through the highs, the lows, the hots and the colds throughout the country, the barometer readings and the dewpoints, and the average temperature of the entire world over the last four centuries, I am in a hypnotic fog—and all of a sudden I'm aware of men in helmets crashing into each other and falling into piles; sports are upon me, the weather slipped by me, and I don't know whether to wear my thermals or not.

"It would be a great help if the weather folks would blast forth a trumpet fanfare just before they do tomorrow's forecast. This, of course, would be helpful only if I made it through 20 minutes of the news—the lead stories of which are repeated about a million times. Why do they keep doing that? At 2 minutes to 10 P.M., you get the headlines; at 10 P.M., you get the headlines again; then they break for the first commercial and come back with the headlines again; and then they say 'But first . . .' and then lead in to the main story. By the time the second commercial comes, we have weeded out a few of the topics, but they still preview what's to come. On Channel 4, we must hear the Dimension topic 50 times before it is actually done. And by the time the broadcast is over, we may have heard the same story headlined five times. "Why do they do this?"

Ideas whose time has come (alas): Says **Jim Fitzsimons** of St. Paul: "I'm watching KARE-11 news, and weatherman Paul Douglas is out in the back yard talking weather while he's . . . *in* the weather.

"I'm thinking: This makes sense! I mean, if he's talking about snow, I *see snow!*

"I've lived here all my life, and I still don't know what that white, flakelike stuff is—that stuff that comes down from those gray, puffy things during the cold months of the year. Whenever *those* are.

"It makes sense that Paul is outside in the weather, 'cause I *need* those visual clues that his being outside provides.

"Weather is so complex: wet stuff, that blowing-air thing, and whatever that yellow circle in the sky is.

"A weatherman who's outside, so I don't have to be. Heck, I don't even have to look out the window!

"It makes sense."

Trick or treat! From **Roger** of Roseville: "One of the all-time-great bloopers on TV, to my way of thinking, occurred last Saturday on Channel 5's early-evening newscast. They had a report about underwater pumpkin carving over at Lake Harriet in Minneapolis, and the anchor came back with this observation—and the great humor of this was that it was said in all innocence to his coanchor . . . : 'My wife and I have a hard enough time doing it on the kitchen table—let alone underwater!'

"Well, nobody cracked a smile—but they went very, very quickly to a commercial, I noticed."

Cue the cat: From **Sheilah** of Maplewood: "Years ago, my best friend's younger sister coined a wonderfully descriptive term, *puffguffing,* for that unique coughing/wheezing/heaving act of a cat who is preparing to deposit a hairball on your favorite rug or chair. Example: 'Stand clear! Fluffy is puffguffing!'

"Anyone watching CNN on the morning before Thanksgiving might have caught their live puffguffing coverage. It was a truly amusing segment destined to turn up on a TV blooper show someday:

"It must have been a slow news day, and they were doing a feature on show cats.

One owner and her cat were at the studio desk with the anchorman, and another woman and her cat were in some remote location. The second woman was on camera answering a question when the off-camera cat in the studio began puffguffing. The sound is unmistakable.

"Sure enough, they cut back to the studio just in time for all to see this picture-perfect show cat spitting up all over the desk, the cat owner and the very impressive show ribbon the cat had just won.

"The poor anchorman's expression was priceless, but he retained his composure and finished the interview. Still, I think it will be a long time before he agrees to share a camera shot with another cat."

BULLETIN BOARD REPLIES: A couple of our colleagues, upon hearing the word (but before having the definition thrust upon them), thought puffguffing sounded like what a politician does—as, for example, when the president horks up a State of the Union address.

The more we all thought about, the more perfect the parallel seemed.

Lights! Camera! Aimless wandering! Confirming one of our long-held suspicions is **The Blue Ribbon** of St. Paul: "My old boyfriend used to work at WCCO-TV, and what we used to arrange, occasionally, was this: I would ask him to walk across the set behind the anchors, during the evening newscast, so I could have him look up at me. He'd pretend like he was shuffling papers. Then, he would call and say: 'Did you see me?' And I would say: 'Yeah!'

"It was great; he worked nights and I worked days, and it was just this fun little thing that we used to do."

57 channels, and nothin' on: From **Ms. Linda** of Eagan: "I came up with a cable channel: the All-Half-Hour Commercial Program Channel.

"You could have the lady with the Flowbee hair-mowing thing that you put on your vacuum cleaner that makes everybody look like David Cassidy. And then you could have the lady that puts the sandwiches in the sandwich-smasher/waffle-iron hybrid weird thing. And then you could have this head-to-head contest between the guy that has the food dehydrator that takes out all the water and just leaves the dry parts of food and the guy that does the juicer that takes out all the dry parts and just leaves the juice there. Oh, God, it would be great!"

Ms. Linda of Eagan, some time later: "In reviewing my plans for the Infomercial Channel, I realized that I had inadvertently neglected the most important infomercials of all: the ones with celebrities.

"The classic of the genre, of course, is Cher and the frumpy old beautician sitting around talking about how the frump's hair-care products made Cher so beautiful and confident that she wised up and left Sonny Bono. And at the end of this infomercial, in walks—oh, my gosh!—Ted Danson, who apparently came over thinking, on a whim, that he'd play Nintendo with the frump, but walked in on—to his endless embarrassment—the filming of a television commercial.

"I'll tell you what: I'm gonna start the Dignity Fund, and we can all contribute—and that way, when a celebrity gets that desperate for money, we can just pay them off and avoid this entire syndrome. Maybe then Ted can stop kissing up to schlumpy beauticians; Ali MacGraw—who made her career looking pallid and sick, I might add—can stop fawning over expensive makeup; Cathy Lee Crosby can get off the 'Let's Talk About Cellulite' talk show; Ricardo Montalban can stop hawking the Grillerie, which I'm sure is capable of making a perfectly good steak turn out like a piece of Corinthian leather; and Michael Landon can stop telling us, in a chipper voice from beyond the grave, that 'Where there's a will, there's an A'—also known as Buy Your Child a Bigger Brain. What's next on the education frontier, anyway? Bribe Your 3rd-Grader's Geography Teacher The John Davidson Way?"

No-goodniks: From **Lisa** of St. Paul: "My son and I were watching 'Bullwinkle', and Boris Badenov was explaining his plot to drive the Americans crazy: They would intercept our television signals, and instead of watching 'The Lone Ranger,' we would watch half-hour commercials for hair oil.

"It took 'em 30 years, almost, but . . ."

BULLETIN BOARD NOTES: Come to think of it, that Commie vixen Natasha Fatale does bear more than a passing resemblance to Cher. Just a coincidence?

Days of their lives: Reports **Merlyn** of St. Paul: "I've been sick for several days. Headache. Eyes watering. Ears ringing. In order to sleep in the daytime, I've had to cover the ringing in my ears with white noise—so the TV's been on constantly.

"Everything on daytime TV is a talk show. To talk on these programs, you have to be qualified. A family may come as a group, but at least one family member must have (a) a pronounced twang; (b) at least one tooth missing; (c) had sex with a close relative; (d) a trailer home; (e) a dead relative, killed by a celebrity; (f) a hatred for the human race; or (g) an opinion that's 180 degrees from normal.

"I hope this subliminal dose of venom doesn't keep me from getting well. I'd hate to be stuck in Talk Show Hell forever.

"Back to bed. Goodbye."

Wh-, where do, uhh, uhh, you, umm, bank? A whole series of "Ba-ba-b-bad ads" nominated by **Jim Fitzsimons** of St. Paul:

"Thi-, this, uhh, thi-, uhh, this ad is, is, is, is the, umm, umm, Nor-, Norwest, uhh, uhh, Banks ads where they have, uhh, uhh, Bob, Bob, Bob New-, New-, Newhart, uhh, answering, answering ph-phones, uhh, umm, like he's a, uhh, a, uhh, a, 24-hour, uhh, ba-, uhh, uhh, banker, or whatever.

"And, well, I, I realize that, uhh, Bob Newhart is, is, is, umm, is, umm, umm, known for his, his, uhh, sta-, sta-, stammering, umm, umm, but the, uhh, both the, uhh, uhh, tel-, uhh, tel-, uhh, TV and, and ra-, uhh, radio, uhh, ads are, are quite, uhh, well, umm, uhh-umm, umm, umm, uhh-umm, annoying and, and, and, and, and difficult to, uhh, to, umm, umm, umm, umm, umm . . ."

Zinnnnnnnggggggg! From **The Woodbury Wildcat:** "Today's nominations (buzzer) for Bad Ads (crowd 'ooh-ing') are the US West (thump) series that are continually punctuated (explosion) with buzzers (buzzer), cheers (crowd cheering), thumps (thump), and other annoying (head-shaking, whogga-whogga-whogga sound) sound effects (cars beeping, pingpong game, jet taking off). One (single cowbell) or two (hit cowbell twice) noises (kazoo on New Year's) can make your point (sound of arrow hitting target), but talk (crowd talking) about overuse (man grunting) of a medium (radio tuner alternating static and running across channels)! To say (crowd talking) they are annoying (annoying, high-pitched Woody Woodpecker–type comic laugh: ha-hahahaha!) and grate (sound of carrots on a grater) on my nerves (sound of a single guitar string being plucked) is an understatement (thump)."

How low can they go: A few more bad-ad nominations:

Tara D. and Lou M. of Center City: "It only *seemed* that TV advertising could plummet no lower than messy leaks from disposable diapers.

"It has truly ascended to a pinnacle of tastelessness and unbelievable dumbness. Would someone please explain to us what a semi-respected actress like Michael Learned (of long-ago Walton's Mountain fame) is doing, shilling membership in some sick group that calls itself The Sine-Aid Society???

"Is this like the Shriners? The Elks? Do they have conventions in Las Vegas? Do they elect a Grand Poobah? And what in the name of God do they do when they *do* convene? Sit around discussing the relative volume of mucus they each produce per annum? Hawk gobs of phlegm, competing for size-of-gob and hawking distance? Produce and compare greenish clots of bodily excretions for entry into the Sine-Aid Chronicles?

"We demand an explanation from the makers of Sine-Aid, or more appropriately, from the twisted ad agency that dreamed up this post-nasal-drip nightmare."

Floyd of the East Side: "It's the dinner hour, and I just saw a commercial about an itch so private you only talk to your doctor about it. Don't talk about *your* private itch during *my* dinner. These people gotta clean it up."

Andrew of St. Paul: "It's that radio ad for the Hoover vacuum cleaner—in which that woman is singing 'Nobody does it like you. . . . Nobody's got the power to please me.'

"Every time I hear that commercial, I just wonder: What kind of attachment does this thing *have?*"

CHAPTER EIGHTEEN

To Market, To Market

Close encounters of the commercial kind:

Sweet deal: Here's **Sailboat Jo** of Inver Grove Heights: "Is there a more perfect symbol of hope than a kid with a Kool-Aid stand? There he is, with his heart on his sleeve, vulnerable, hoping against all hope that some harried adult who's late for work—and in the wrong lane, anyway—will drive around the block, dig for quarters, pay an exorbitant price for a thimbleful of lukewarm Kool-Aid which he doesn't like anyway, and balance the sticky stuff while driving off again, usually spilling at least half on something white.

"No marketing expert would give this product a chance. The proprietor is usually too young to be practical, or he wouldn't attempt such a project. A heart that's been stomped on would not expose itself to such rejection. He still believes he has something worth giving, something that other people want.

"His eyes are expectant, pleading, hopeful as a car approaches, disappointed as it passes, and so full of joy when it stops that it's well worth a quarter to see.

"My advice is: Always stop at Kool-Aid stands. Get off freeways, go around blocks, invent reasons to drive by—and always tip the owner. You don't even have to drink it! Some kids in my neighborhood had Kool-Aid that was so bad I paid them extra not to have to drink it. Far from being insulted, they loved my business. Each time I drove by, we had to negotiate whether I was not going to drink a small or not going to drink a large—and I paid accordingly.

"When they got to trying it without a stand or a pitcher of Kool-Aid, they were working on a whole different premise, and our business relationship ended.

"Remember the three basic rules of mental health: Everyone needs something to do, something to hope for, and someone to love. A kid with a Kool-Aid stand fulfills two of these, and if you stop for some Kool-Aid, you might be the temporary fulfillment of the third."

The bean counters: From **Edith** of Marine on St. Croix: "I stopped at a roadside stand recently where a teenage boy was selling home-grown produce. I asked him how much the green beans were, and he says—holding up a plastic bag: 'Twenty-five cents for whatever fits into this bag.'

"I said: 'OK, I'll take some.'

"Well, he proceeds to cram these beans in this bag—and he keeps putting them in and putting them in, and I finally said: 'Stop! I don't *want* this many.'

"And he looks at me and says: 'Please, lady, take them. Then I don't have to eat 'em.'

"Well, I was eating green beans for three days, because my husband doesn't like them, either."

If you don't have anything nice to say: From **Ann's Little Sister:** "My sister Ann was shopping for a picture frame in a fancy department store in the Mall of America, and she had this picture from the '70s of her with her kids that she really likes.

"So she found this frame that she liked, and she put the picture in it to see how it would look. And then this saleslady comes up and says: 'May I help you?'

"My sister says: 'I'm trying to decide if I like this frame. I think it's kind of boring.'

"And the saleslady says: 'Well, you can't tell with that *awful* picture in it'—and she starts going off about how *horrible* the picture is, and how do they expect to sell the frame with that awful picture?

"And my sister, being the nice person that she is, couldn't bring herself to tell the clerk what a dope she was."

The nose knows: From **Lady K.T.** of Rice Lake, Wis.: "A few years ago, I bought a pair of green shorts at our local department store, convinced that they were going to match a green print blouse that I had at home.

"When I brought them home, as I was walking through the kitchen, I stopped and grabbed the scissors, clipped the tags off—and once I got into my bedroom, where the blouse was, I realized that the green print on the blouse did not match the green shorts. So I took the tags back out of the garbage, and a few days later, I went back to the store to return the green shorts.

"The clerk at the store was really questioning me about whether I had worn the shorts or not—even after I told her the story about why the tags were off. She still didn't seem quite convinced that they had never been worn. So there, in the busy store, in front of all of the other customers, she put 'em up to her face and *sniffed* 'em.

"Well, I must've passed the sniff test, because she did let me return the shorts—but boy, was I embarrassed."

Everything you never wanted to know (and would never have cared to ask): From **ABBA** of St. Paul, after eating (or, at least, planning to) at the Rainforest Cafe: "While we were waiting, the parrots and a 'keeper' were entertaining us by educating us on the life of a parrot. All the while, the keeper was exchanging kisses with one of the birds.

"The keeper said: 'I have to be careful when I kiss him. Parrots open their mouths when they kiss and use their tongues.' She continued: 'I have to remember to keep my lips closed, because when they kiss, they have a tendency to share their regurgitated food.'"

BULLETIN BOARD MUSES: "ABBA. Table for ABBA. ABBA?"

You could eat a . . . *what?* Reports **Jim Bob** of Merriam Park: "I have a friend named Don whose wife occasionally calls him Donner. We recently went to eat at a Red Lobster, and Don, just on impulse, gave his name at the reception desk as Donner.

"Of course we had to wait for a table—and while we were sitting in the bar, we had the pleasure of hearing someone announce over the PA system: 'Donner party, your table is ready.'

"Needless to say, by that time we were famished."

Dumb Customer Jokes: Some of which, of course, aren't the least bit dumb:

The Rag Peddler: "Went to the local garden store to show my wife up again on my green-thumb skills (luck).

"After I explained to the lady assisting me that I needed a plant for a shady area next to the house, she guided me through two or three plants and then came to a plant called impatiens.

"Before she could tell me one feature, I said: 'Perfect match! Now throw it in a bag. I want to get out of here.'

"After chuckling at my wit—which she's already heard too many times or didn't get—I bought six impatiens, explained my rudeness as a joke, said thank you and left quickly."

Lofty Lady of Lowertown: "Yesterday, I was unavoidably late for my mammogram. (Five years cancer-free! *Yeah!*) I knew how it threw everybody off, so when I left, I thanked them for squeezing me in.

"Do you think they've heard that one before?

"Also: Whenever I ask someone to validate me—as in parking—I keep waiting for them to tell me I'm smart and beautiful.

"They never do."

Doctor Friendly of St. Paul: "A patient today was telling me about his back pain.

"He'd found that the pain occurred only in certain positions. He said: 'It doesn't hurt when I'm standing. It doesn't hurt when I'm sitting. It only hurts when I'm lying.'

"I said: 'Well, that's better than having your nose grow.'

"He just looked at me, blankly. I don't know if he didn't get it—or if he just didn't think it was funny."

Victor of Hugo: "I went to a driving range and told the girl I wanted a bucket of balls.

"She said: 'What size?'

"I held up my thumb and forefinger in a circle and said: 'Oh, the usual size.'

"I was immediately ashamed of myself."

BULLETIN BOARD OBSERVES: Self-knowledge is the greatest.

Dumb Customer Jokes (payback time): From **Edith** of the East Side: "About three years ago, my daughter and her twin girls were at the zoo. We watched the little monkeys a while, then saw the ape, so we went over there to watch him. He was sitting upright, watching people.

"A big man next to us was making faces at him. Finally, he stuck his tongue out at the ape. I think he'd took as much as he could; when the guy stuck his tongue out at him, that was too much for the ape. The man turned his head and just leaned way back and opened up his mouth and just haw-hawed out loud and made the loudest noise—and before you knew it, the ape had peed right into the guy's mouth. The guy called him an S.O.B. and walked away.

"And the people—they laughed so hard, and they clapped their hands. The ape sat there, and he clapped his hands, too. Everybody was laughing so hard. It was the biggest kick watching the ape clap his hands when the man went away."

T.K. of Blaine: "My friends and I go to restaurants where the waitress or waiter will take our order and then say: 'If you need anything, my name is . . . so-and-so.' And as they walk away, we always look at each other and say: 'And if we don't need anything, what is your name?'

"Well, one time we decided to call the bluff. We were in Denny's one morning, and the waiter said: 'If you need anything, my name is Jeff.'

"And we said: 'And if we don't need anything, what's your name?'

"He said: 'Brian.'"

Hey, pal! Speak up! From **C.M.** of "that other city": "One time I went into the drugstore looking for something for laryngitis, and I *whispered* to the pharmacist: 'Do you have something for laryngitis?'

"And he said: 'Is it for you?'"

Open mouth, insert foot: That's the title bestowed on this story by **Annie** of Stillwater: "A few weeks ago, my sister and I were shopping at the Woodbury Outlet Mall. We went in one of the clothing stores and were just looking around when I spotted him . . . .

"He was one of the best-looking guys I have ever seen. He was an employee at the store. He approached us and said: 'What can I show you ladies today?'

"I very calmly replied: 'Just fine, thanks. How about yourself?'

"Before we could walk away, my sister couldn't hold it in any longer and burst out laughing. Boy, did I feel stupid."

Sitting down on the job: From **S.D.** of Woodbury: "Last spring, I was running behind schedule as I prepared for my daughter's birthday party.

"I ran in to a local ice-cream shop to get her favorite flavor. No one was around. Rock music was blaring, but not a soul in sight. After several minutes of impatient waiting, I decided to peek in the back room for help.

"I pushed open the swinging door and yelled: 'Anybody here?' I looked directly into the surprised face of a young male attendant sitting on the toilet with his pants around his ankles.

"At this point in the story, my husband can't believe I didn't leave—but I needed that ice cream, so I waited.

"Shortly, the young man emerged from the back room. We acted as though nothing had happened.

"I placed my order—and he froze the moment forever in my mind by asking: 'Prepackaged or hand-packed?' No trouble making *that* decision."

Life in the Service Economy: From **Dimples** of Cottage Grove: "I've worked in customer service over 20 years—and, of course, customers are wonderful, but over the phone, sometimes it's difficult to understand them, and it can be really frustrating both for the caller and for the one taking the call. If you have a bad connection, you know, s's can sound like f's, and b's like d's, and on and on it goes.

"I worked with a gal one time, and we don't know if she had a bad connection or it was the fact that the caller was from one of the Southern states, but she was having quite a time understanding him, and she could tell he was becoming very aggravated, and finally she asked him to please spell his last name.

"With his voice dripping with sarcasm, he began to spell: 'S . . . as in *stupid.* E . . . like in *ignorant.'*

"Of course, I'm very respectful of the e-as-in-ignorant callers, to this day."

Dave of Cottage Grove: "For most of the '70s, I worked at the Cottage Grove Coast-to-Coast hardware store. A lot of people might wonder why someone would work for eight years as a clerk in a hardware store, and it doesn't have anything to do with all the women who'd come in and say 'Where are your nuts?' or 'I need a screw' or 'Do you have caulk'—although for everybody there, that was kind of an expected thing.

"It had more to do with customers like this one guy who came in; he was looking through our brass hardware assortment, and he found some washers he wanted, and he said: 'How much are these?' And I told him: 'They're 10 for a dime'—which means, of course, a penny apiece.

"He said: 'Oh, geez! These things are *expensive* now!' And I thought: 'This guy's gotta be a contractor or something; he wants *huge* bulk amounts.'

"I said: 'Well, how many did you need?'

"And he said: 'One.'"

Sorry, wrong number! Here's **Fay's Friend:** "Last spring, a guy called—trying to sell me windows. I told him: 'No, thanks. We just bought new windows.'

" 'Well, how 'bout doors? We sell storm doors, too.'

"I said: 'No, thanks. We also replaced the door.'

"He proceeded to tell me about their wonderful patio furniture; I told him I don't have a patio.

" 'Well, how would you like to build a deck? We have deck kits on special right now!' Blah, blah, blah, blah, blah.

"I told him we couldn't afford a deck, and we were not interested in buying anything—period.

"Then he started this spiel on kitchen cabinets! I broke in: 'No, thanks—but say! This is your lucky day! We are breeders of purebred Limousin cattle, and right now, we have a fine selection of yearling bulls for sale. There are red ones or black ones, purebred or percentage bulls to choose from.' And I began reciting the pedigrees and vital statistics in agonizing detail, without stopping for breath or paying any attention to his protests.

"He said: 'But I don't have any cows! Why would I want a bull?'

"I said: 'You have called the right place! We also have yearling heifers, bred heifers or bred cows that we could offer for sale. We can set you right up in the beef business!'

"He said: 'Well, I don't have anywheres to put them.'

"I said: 'Buddy, you call on the right day, and this place might go pretty cheap.'

"By that time, he was laughing so hard he hung up on *me!*"

Just looking: From **Dee** of St. Paul: "I was watching an elderly gentleman—a very sweet-looking gentleman—in a convenience store. He was eating a Dove Bar and looking at the magazine covers of Cindy Crawford. And you *know* what he was thinking: 'Gee, life just doesn't get any better than this.' And I thought that was very sweet."

Hello, baby! Reports **Tracy** of White Bear Lake: "I work at a grocery store. The other night, a guy came through my lane with one pink rose. He said: 'I just found out I'm a dad.'

"I said: 'Well, congratulations!'

"And he said: 'Thanks. My wife doesn't know that she's pregnant yet.'

"I must have had this puzzled look on my face, because he proceeded to tell me: 'My wife did a pregnancy test, but she threw the box out, so she doesn't know if she's reading a positive or a negative. So she sent me to the store to read the box. Now I get to tell her that she *is* pregnant.' He was *so* excited.

"We talked about how great it is that the dad finds out before the mom, for once, and then he picked up the rose and said: 'This will be our third under 4.' Very proud look on his face. He said: 'I wonder if this will be a boy or a girl.' And then he said: 'You know, it really doesn't matter'—and he left the store, smiling."

CHAPTER NINETEEN

What Is *Right* With People?

A few of the thousands of Bulletin Board stories about the brighter side of human nature:

Peachy of Cottage Grove: "The past month has been the darkest, bleakest time of my life. You see, my precious daughter Kristina was killed, on my birthday, in a car accident while we were vacationing in Florida.

"My heart is breaking, and the pain I am feeling is unbearable. She was not only my daughter, but my cherished friend. The only thing that has kept me going is the incredible love and support of my family and friends, even strangers.

"But I must mention the officer in Florida, Corporal Gordon Jennings of the Highway Patrol, who did something out of the ordinary.

"The camera that I had been using that day was lost during the accident. We kept inquiring about it because I had taken many pictures during that day that, of course, were precious to me. We were continually told that there was no way the camera would be found.

"I especially wanted it because the last picture taken was one of Kristina and me on the beach. She gave the camera to my son Dan and told him: 'Take a picture of Mommie and me.'

"The last time my husband talked to Corporal Jennings, he said he was sure there was no way that the camera survived the accident, but he would walk that stretch of highway just to be sure.

"Just a few days ago, a package came in the mail from Corporal Jennings. He enclosed a note saying that he found the camera (which was one of the disposable kind) submerged in water and run over by a lawnmower!

"It is nothing short of a miracle that seven of those 24 pictures turned out—and, unbelievably, the one of my Kristina (Nina was her nickname) and me together for the last time was among them!

"I will cherish that picture forever, along with the many, many people, including Corporal Jennings, who have gone out of their way to help us in any way that they can.

"My wonderful Nina. I loved being her mother. I miss her and love her with all of my heart."

Mike of Lake Elmo: "My son Nick died last Christmas. June 27 would have been his birthday. On that day, we had a simple 'memory' time at home—just the immediate family. We had received a surprising number of cards that week from people who remembered that it was his birthday, and it touched us.

"As we were having supper, my daughter saw a van that she recognized drive slowly past our driveway. Then a familiar car. Then another. Then another! All in all, seven vehicles showed up, and they all parked in front of our house.

"Members of our church got out and came up to our back deck. They gave us a flowering shrub to plant in memory of our son, along with a card signed by all. Then one couple sang us a comforting and inspirational song. This was followed by everyone gathering around us while our pastor prayed for us, topped off with a hug from each and every one of them.

"We were moved beyond words and felt very blessed.

"We invited everyone to come in, but they all declined, saying they didn't want to intrude or interrupt; they just wanted to let us know that they remembered and they cared.

"Thank you, everyone, for showing us your love and for passing on the love of God."

Karen of Falcon Heights: "I want to report a really neat thing that happened in church last Sunday.

"Two-year-old Natalie went up to the front of the congregation for the children's sermon, and when she returned to her seat, she left her beloved blankie behind. All went well until, in the middle of Pastor Kathi's sermon, Natalie noticed that her blankie was missing and began to fret audibly. The entire congregation's eyes became riveted on Natalie's abandoned blankie, and their ears on Natalie's distressed whimpering as we wondered how this drama would be resolved.

"Finally, one of the teenage boys in the front row scooped up Natalie's blankie and passed it over his shoulder to the row behind him. The people in that row passed the blankie on to the row behind them—and the blankie traveled hand-to-hand down that row, across the aisle, and on down that row until it reached Natalie, who collapsed on her blankie with a sigh and a thumb in her mouth.

"Pastor Kathi interrupted her prepared sermon to exclaim that we had all just witnessed a perfect example of community caring. And so we had.

"Amen."

St. Pauli Girl of Maplewood: "At Battle Creek Park today, I lost track of my 3-year-old, Annie. Countless people helped me search for her. I don't think there was one person who heard my cries and did not stop.

"It's amazing how quickly a group of good Samaritans can gather.

"During the search, and then later when she was found, everyone was so kind. People asked me if I was OK—not 'How could you lose a kid?'

"Thanks for that, too."

The Pigman: "I was up north the week of May 29. Near Longville.

"One day, my traveling companion, The Most Beautiful Woman in the Front Range (MBWFR) and me were in Longville killin' time. We passed a parked truck and heard the wails of a crying child coming from the truck.

"We looked at one another, knowing one of us would go to the child. The MBWFR did, comforting the baby, who looked to be about 2 years old. She picked him from his car seat, held him, wiped his tears, stroked his head, walked with him and got him calmed down.

"Turns out the baby's mom was in the Laundromat and the child had misbehaved, and so she was, in her words, disciplining the child by abandoning him in that hot, stifling truck. To her credit, she did leave the windows down.

"The mom saw the MBWFR holding her child, came out, snatched the baby and shot the MBWFR one of those 'if looks could kill' looks. As the mom went back into the Laundromat, we got back in the car, looked at one another, shook our heads, drove away.

"It probably wasn't the smartest thing we could have done, and maybe in Longville it's OK to keep a kid in a car to teach him a lesson. But how could a person ignore something like that?

"To the woman in Longville: Please, if you choose to discipline this child again, don't abandon him again, alone in an open car. The next person who happens by may not have the heart, love and compassion of the MBWFR.

"Blondie, ya did the right thing."

Maggie of the Mountains: "Something disturbing happened to me today.

"I stopped on the way home to buy ice because my refrigerator is currently on strike. As I was getting out of my car at the convenience store, two young girls approached me. The youngest was maybe 13; the oldest looked like she might be 16.

"The oldest asked for a favor. I was expecting her to ask for a ride home or a quarter for the phone, or something like that. She asked me to buy her cigarettes. And, of course, I said no and I walked away. I didn't even think about it.

"She walked over to a young man, and as I walked past, I heard him say: 'If only I had my ID, I'd buy them.'

"Then I went into the store, and I picked up the ice, and I grabbed a carton of milk, and I didn't even really think about it—and the next thing I know, I'm standing at the counter looking at the clerk, and I'm telling him about those kids out in the parking lot soliciting strangers to buy them cigarettes.

"And the clerk calls somebody over. He goes outside. My purchases get rung up, I pay for them, and I go outside. The man meets me. He says: 'Those kids—it wasn't those three around the corner, was it?'

"We walked around the corner, and I said: 'Yes, these are the kids.' The boy said: 'No, I didn't ask.' And I said: 'No you didn't; she did'—and I pointed at the girl.

"She looked at me, but I know she wasn't seeing *me*. She was seeing an old fart, somebody who wasn't any fun, who wouldn't do something for her that she really wanted. For all I know, she was seeing her mom.

"And the next thing I know, the clerk has ordered them off the property, and I'm in my car and on the way home—and I realize I have something I want to tell that girl.

"I want to tell that girl: I didn't do the things I did to get them in trouble. I didn't tell the clerk to be mean, or because what they asked me to do was illegal. I did it because one day my aunt came home from work and found my uncle outside in his bathrobe, dragging his oxygen tank behind him, looking for cigarette butts along-side the road. And I did it because I watched my grandma's heart break the day they put her eldest son in the ground.

"And I know I didn't make any difference. And I know they found somebody else to buy them cigarettes. And I know that person thought they were being really helpful, and really nice, and doing nice kids a favor.

"I wish they had asked for a favor. I would have given them a ride home. I'd have given them a quarter for the phone.

"But they didn't ask for a favor."

Terry of Cottage Grove, a cashier at Target: "I had this little boy come through my lane today. He must have been about 13 years old, and he was buying an ac-cessory for his bike.

"Well, it came to $8.55. He stood in front in me with this wad of $1 bills and says: 'I only have $8.' I looked at him, thinking: 'Oh, great. Now what do I do? I'm gonna hurt the kid's feelings!'

"Well, there's a man standing behind him—about 20 years old. He hands the boy a $1 bill. The look of surprise on this boy's face, you wouldn't have believed. The kid looked at him, said: 'Oh, *thank* you!' And the guy says: 'Oh, no big deal.'

"Well, I turned and looked at him and said: 'That was awful nice of ya.' He says: 'Oh, no big deal.'

"The kid gives him back his 45 cents change, and then the guy says to me: 'Hey, you never know when I might need 50 cents. Comes back to you one way or an-other.'

"I thought that was a simple pleasure. Sent chills down my spine. . . ."

Angie of Lakeland: "This afternoon, my husband, son and I went to a movie in Stillwater. My husband's in a wheelchair and has very limited use of his hands, and tried to hold a small bag of popcorn and eat it by himself, but he was unable to, and dropped the popcorn in the aisle.

"A few minutes later, a young lady tapped my shoulder and handed me a re-placement bag of popcorn for him. She was with a young man sitting a few rows be-hind us, and she just decided to do this really nice thing. My husband said it was the best popcorn he'd had in a very long time.

"She even put butter on it."

G.G. of Maplewood, a woman of a certain age: "My daughter, my son-in-law and I went out to Wisconsin, to the Crystal Cave out there. When we were all gath-ered together and ready to go on the tour, I realized that everybody was wearing a jacket or a sweatshirt; I was wearing a short-sleeved cotton blouse. (I didn't realize that it was really cold when you got down there in the cave.)

"So we were standing there waiting to go, and this young boy—all I know about him is that his name was Matthew, and I'm sure he was about 12 years old—he came over to me, and he was taking off his jacket at the same time, and he had a sweatshirt underneath it. He came up to me, and he said: 'Would you like to wear my jacket? It's pretty cold down there.'

"I couldn't believe it. I was just overcome. You hear so many things about bad kids—but there are a *lot* of good kids out there, too.

"Believe me: I congratulated his mother on this wonderful young man. It's something that I will never forget."

Becky U. of St. Paul: "My faith in humanity has been restored—the other day, Wednesday, catchin' the bus in downtown St. Paul:

"It's rainin'. Cold. Obvious homeless man was roaming in and out of the bus shelter. He was cold.

"A young man, about 22 years old, walks up, takes off his leather baseball jacket, and hands it to the man.

"Man puts on the coat and walks away.

"People call 'em Generation X. X is for excellent."

Yo, J.D. of St. Paul: "A couple of weeks ago, I was riding the bus from Group Health on Como Avenue—the bus that goes into Minneapolis—and we were just about ready to get onto Highway 280 when I saw a man and a woman outside; I thought they were just kinda pushing each other, shoving each other—you know, playing-around sort of thing.

"And all of a sudden, the bus driver stopped and opened his door. He yelled out to the guy: 'Hey, buddy, let her go!' And when he opened the door, I could hear her screaming: 'Let go of me! Get away from me!' She called out to the bus driver: 'Please don't leave me!'

"So he called the police on the bus phone, and then he went to the door and he said: 'Ma'am, I've just called the police. They're gonna be here in a couple of minutes.' Then he came back in, and there were cars backed up behind the bus, wanting to get onto 280.

"He said to me: 'I wish I could stay here and wait.'

"And I said: 'You can't leave her!' So we didn't. There were five or six cars backed up behind the bus.

"Finally the guy let her go, and she ran onto the bus. She had mud all over her face and all up and down her clothes. She was just crying.

"The bus driver said: 'Do you want to stay here and wait for the police, or do you want to go?'

"She said: 'Just go. Just get me out of here. Just go.'

"So we pulled out, and the bus driver asked her if she was OK, and he gave her some Kleenex to wipe off the mud. And she said that the guy drives by her house every night, but she never thought he'd do anything like this.

"We drove a couple of blocks, and she asked the bus driver where he was going. He said: 'To downtown Minneapolis.'

"And she said: 'Well, I'd better get off here, because I need to go over to the West Side.'

"And he said: 'Well, I'd just be more comfortable if you stayed on the bus. I'll take you into downtown Minneapolis, and you can catch an express bus over to St. Paul. But I'd just feel more comfortable if I knew you were safe.'

"I got off at the University of Minnesota; I don't know what happened at the end. But I just wanted to say that because of the actions of that one bus driver, this woman was safe—and may be still alive. I just wanted to say that I think he's great. *[BULLETIN BOARD SAYS: You did good yourself, Yo J.D.]*

"And to that woman: I think you really need to report that guy, because you deserve so much better than that."

Door County of St. Paul: "I would like to thank the wonderful person who saved my 15-year-old cousin's life.

"My cousin was diagnosed at the beginning of December with a terminal heart condition and put on a waiting list for a heart transplant. The past few months have been an emotional roller-coaster for our entire family.

"On this past Monday, he went into cardiac arrest, and we knew that he was getting down to his last bit of strength. He was put on an external heart pump, but that wouldn't be able to hold him very long. A heart had to show up within the next week-and-a-half to two weeks, or we knew that would be the end.

"The very next day, on Tuesday, our family was informed that a good match was found and that the transplant would be performed that evening when the heart arrived at the hospital.

"This is *your* heart in my little cousin's body, and I want to thank you and your family for knowing that when your time was up, your organs could be used to save others' lives—including my cousin's. Because of you and your family's generosity, he will now be given an opportunity to play varsity football, graduate from college, get married and raise a family.

"He is one of the most wonderful people I know: sensitive, funny, generous and kind—someone who touches the hearts of everyone he meets. I credit you with saving his life, and I grieve for your family's loss—but I rejoice for the second chance at life you gave my cousin.

"Thank you, and may God be with you."

Glenn of Blaine: "We took our little family to the Twins' home opener Tuesday night. My son really wanted to catch a baseball—and, of course, one never came close. So after witnessing the first of many Twins losses this year, we were exiting the Metrodome and walked by the area where they'd been giving away baseballs if you filled out a credit application. We saw the empty boxes laying there, and we thought we'd poke around; maybe they'd left a ball. Well, they hadn't.

"And then just as we're leaving, I hear this voice from behind us say 'Here, honey.' I turn around, and this young woman is giving my son a baseball. It's an official baseball; it has the Twins' logo on it. It was the greatest thing.

"I just want that woman to know that Tuesday was his fifth birthday, and he really wanted a ball. He clutched that ball all the way home."

Beverly of White Bear Lake: "Yesterday, July 3rd, my daughter had to work, and I took my grandson, age 8, over to Silver Lake for a little fishing. Picked up some worms, got out on the dock, and accidentally he dropped his pole—his rod—into the lake.

"He lay on his stomach, on that dock, and looked down into the water with a broken heart. He was just so sad.

"A couple of gentlemen were there with their young sons, and they came over and tried to help—but we couldn't reach it, even with a stick I found in the trunk of the car.

"Close to 5, I took him home—and told him maybe his mother could find something long enough to get the rod.

"Shortly after 5, they went back to Silver Lake and were walking over toward the fishing dock—and there, on the grass by the walkway going out to the dock, was his beloved fishing rod.

"One of those gentlemen, I figure, must have gone home and gotten something long enough and retrieved it for him—and that made Christmas and his birthday and the Fourth of July all in one for that young boy. He was so happy.

"I want to thank whoever did that—and I'm very proud that there are people like that. Thank you."

BULLETIN BOARD MUSES: In that last paragraph there, Beverly has given us (at any rate) a new way of thinking.

It has never occurred to us to be proud to be human because there are very, very fine human beings.

We shall do so henceforth, when circumstances warrant—and shall resist the temptation to feel ashamed of being human because there are very, very rotten human beings.

Call us Pollyanna. You could call us worse.

Spunky Buns of Roseville: "We just had this beautiful snowfall, and my boyfriend—the doll that he is—he snowplows the sidewalks at the house where he lives in St. Paul, and he goes three houses down to snowplow the back driveway and the sidewalks of this little old lady on his block . . . just because he's such a nice soul.

"I asked him: 'Why do you go all the way down there?' And he said: 'Well, my grandmas are dead, so I adopted her as my grandma.' That's *so* nice.

"The lady came out to thank him. She's just standing there; she's, like: 'Oh, let me give you some money, honey. You're so nice.'

"And he said: 'No. Put it in the collection plate. All you've gotta do is smile. That's enough for me.'

"I thought that was just so sweet.

"And then I come home to my house, after church, and somebody had plowed my driveway for me. I mean, I'm young enough to do it myself, but one of my neighbors plowed my driveway for me, and that was just such a simple pleasure to come home to.

"It gives you faith."

CHAPTER TWENTY

The Simple Pleasures

Great-Grandma of the East Side: "I have to share my simple pleasure with somebody. I just *have* to tell you:

"As a senior citizen, many days I don't feel good and things don't seem right—but this morning, I was eating my breakfast, sitting here drinking my coffee, looking out the window, and the leaves from my red maple tree came floating down just like . . . oh, just so gracefully, like a ballet dancer. And they were just coming down, and the sun was shining—and all of a sudden, I just got so happy!

"It just made my day—and I thought of all the blessings that I have . . . and I sometimes don't appreciate 'em, but today I just am so thankful that I can enjoy nature and that I have a wonderful family and friends. I just feel all happy and blessed."

Curly Top of Le Sueur: "Years ago, I planted the old-fashioned red Rugosa roses at the south end of my porch. I planted them thinking how nice they'd smell when I sat on the porch—but I just never seemed to get a lot of time.

"This year, I've been getting up about 10 minutes earlier than I need to to leave for work, so that I can sit out on the porch and read a little, sip my coffee, and smell the roses.

"An added bonus to that simple pleasure is that sometimes I look out across the driveway into the pasture, and I see my husband patiently coaxing an arthritic old cow toward the barn for the morning milking, because she was so stiff she just didn't get up and come in with the rest of them.

"It's kind of a serene, pastoral beauty that you just don't get to see once the hectic day begins."

The GoGo Girl of White Bear Lake: "A simple pleasure: when a fall day is cool and dark, kind of dismal and moody, and the sun breaks out bright from behind the clouds and turns the colors of autumn brilliant in a split second.

"All at once the world blazes up, and the trees and bushes look like they are jewels set against the black velvet of the clouds. Just as suddenly, the sun slips away again, and everything looks like just another dark and gloomy fall day. It's beautiful!"

Kendra of St. Paul: "My daughter, who's 8 years old, has an unusual simple pleasure. She likes to go out in the garden in the mornings and warm up the bumblebees that have spent the night cold and wet on the flowers.

"She holds out her hand to them, and I think they must be attracted to the warmth; they climb right on her hand. Then she carries them out to a sunny spot, where they warm up, very quickly, and then they fly off to continue their frenzied bumblebee lifestyle.

"Now that she's back in school, I suppose I'll have to take over for her."

R.J. of Hammond, Wis.: "One of my simple pleasures, on warmer-than-normal late-fall days, is hearing the crickets start chirping again. It's such a cheerful, heart-warming little sound—a song about summer and warmth and nature, and a reminder of all the little forms of life out there.

"When it gets cold, the silence seems so empty—or else it's replaced by the harsh whisper of the wind in the dead grasses, or the calls of crows and blue jays; such lonely sounds, compared to the crickets'.

"When it warms back up, I can't wait to walk The Beast in the woods and fields and stand near the fence rows and ditches and listen to the last of the crickets, bravely chirping—just because they still can.

"Each time, we never know if it will be the last we'll hear 'em for the season—but we know they will be back. It'll be a long time, but the song will go on."

G.F. of parts hereabouts: "Call me impolitic. Call me a heretic. Call me a lunatic—but I've just been walkin' on air for the last couple days, because, dang it, I . . . love . . . snow.

"It's just amazing how six inches of snow can turn a dirty old city into a cozy little ski town overnight."

Calico of Cottage Grove: "It's a quarter to midnight, and the fresh snowfall looks like a bazillion little diamonds all over the ground. I thought it looked so cool; I had to tell you."

Hey Jo of Minneapolis: "A winter pleasure: waking up to a fresh snowfall and seeing the lacy pattern—unmarred by human footprints—made by the tracks of the many birds (and a few squirrels and neighborhood cats) that congregate in my back yard."

Debi of White Bear Lake: "When it's really, really cold out and you spray your windshield with windshield-washer fluid, it forms really, really pretty crystals all across your windshield. Even though it makes it virtually impossible to see out, it's still really neat."

Laura of West St. Paul: "A seasonal simple pleasure—ever so brief: It's the moment when you bring in your Christmas tree, put it in the tree stand, get it all set up. Immediately, lie down underneath it, and you'll feel this cold, scented air just flow down over your face. It only lasts for just a few minutes—and then it's gone. It's just wonderful."

Becky the Senior of Woodbury: "When I get up in the morning, I plug in my curling iron and my hair dryer before I wash my hair. I go wash my hair, and by the time I get back in my room, my feet are ice-cold.

"So what you do: You take your hair dryer, and you turn it on high, and you blow-dry your feet. It feels so good. Warms everything up."

The Original Newcomer of St. Paul: "This winter, I've been putting the baby's wipes box in a wipes warmer—a little heating-pad gizmo just for wipes boxes. My simple pleasure is putting my bra in there at night when I take it off, so that in the morning it's nice and toasty when it's time to get dressed."

Grandma Up North, on Valentine's Day: "The most highfalutin simple pleasure in my life happened today. See, when I was a little girl, during the Depression, I would wander around in the drugstore eyeing those beautiful heart-shaped boxes of chocolates, and inside the box . . . well, it didn't matter to me; it was the *box* that was so gorgeous—you know? With lace and curls and gold . . . and *everything* was so beautiful. I was attracted, you know, to . . . tacky?

"Anyway, today, it's so beautiful. My son . . . well, let's see now; I've had eight kids and 19 grandchildren, and today my son and my grandson bought me a most beautiful box of chocolates. The box was . . . *is* the most beautifully trimmed thing; it's got lace all around the sides, and gold braid, and satin ribbons, and big bows and flowers. I've never seen anything so beautiful. It is a dream come true.

"How can such a garish thing hold such joy? I don't know—but it does. It's wonderful, and I'm going to save it forever."

Doctor Friendly of St. Paul: "A simple pleasure is when you've had a cold, and your nose is all stuffed up, so you've been breathing through your mouth for two or three days—and then you *finally* hit that point when you blow your nose and all of the gunk comes pouring out in thick, green rivers, and it just keeps coming and coming, and you keep blowing, and there's more and more, and finally it's all cleaned out into one or two or three soaking-wet hankies, and . . . *voila!* The breath of life!"

Soupy of the North End: "When it was so cold, I saw the little birds outside, freezing, and I thought I'd feed 'em, so I broke up some room-temperature bread and put it out in the bird feeder—and I watched the birds, and the bread was steaming! It was like I gave them a hot meal."

G.F. (remember? the heretic?) of parts hereabouts—months and months later, apparently having had enough of winter: "Simple pleasure of simple pleasures: I took a walk around the lake today, since it's right there out front, and I was treated to seeing all of that lake ice being broken up and mounded high on the beaches—all honeycombed, the way it was, so the light shone through it in a kind of pale-green way.

"And then I got home this evening just in time for this lightning storm that hit. Lightning: What better sign is there that spring is on its way? Lovely, lovely stuff. Great boomers. Great flashes.

"Looks like springtime to me."

The Eco-Vigilante of Lake Elmo: "I opened up the door tonight, and I smelled spring. It's in the air. It's pungent. It's damp. It's fragrant.

"I've watched the skies the last few days, and I've seen at least nine or 10 hawks between Lake Elmo and White Bear Lake. I've seen red-tailed hawks, and I've seen red-shouldered hawks—and I've seen all of these *marvelous* migratory birds.

"And the ground's soft, and it's mushy, and it's muddy. I watched a drain hole open up in our lake tonight. It was just . . . fun: The crack opened up, and you

could see the water whirlpooling and sucking down into the lake. And it was just
. . . fun.

"And the birds! Six-thirty in the morning, and they're singing! The cardinals are singing. The blue jays are singing. The woodpeckers are singing. The pileated woodpecker is coming to the suet feeder and having breakfast. Haven't seen his wife yet, but she'll be around the corner. The geese are back! We've had geese coming back! We've had ducks! This is *marvelous.* Spring is a wonderful time of the year. You can see the birds in the trees, because there aren't any leaves.

"It's just . . . oooooooohhhh, like a renewal."

The Mother of Three K's of Somerset, Wis.: "This is the first night this year that I can go to sleep listening to the whippoorwills singing outside our bedroom window. There's nothing like hearing that repetitive *whippoorwill, whippoorwill, whippoorwill*—he never misses a beat—echoing through our quiet country neighborhood."

Hillary and The Weed Queen: "Our simple pleasure is pulling weeds. It's so great when you just pull 'em and they *rrrrripppp* and you get the whole huge chunk of roots and everything. Man, it's just great."

Chinny Chin Chin of St. Paul: "I have a nasty recurrent whisker that tends to grow in rather than out. Every few weeks, I notice that spot getting red and inflamed.

"I take a needle and dig through the top layers of skin, and soon I expose the delinquent hair shaft. A little probing teases it out, and I clip off this long, unwanted intruder.

"Seeing that perpetrator wind its way out with the prodding of the needle is more than a simple pleasure; it's a tremendous relief."

Eaf of the East Side: "I have braces, and I just got rubber bands on. I love taking my rubber bands off and *yaaaaaawwwwwwning*—dropping my lower jaw real, real far down, and moving my mouth up and down, freely, without rubber bands pushing my jaws together."

Gar of South St. Paul: "I just got my braces off a few weeks ago, after having them on for 2½ years, so my new simple pleasure is being able to run my tongue around my mouth and feel nice, new, wonderful teeth."

Kay of Apple Valley: "After I wash my bath towels, I like to hang them outside to dry. That way, they are nice and scratchy—so when you shower, you can give yourself an all-over body scratch. Rub all that dead skin off."

The Enthiomaniac of Stillwater: "Whenever you wear your hair up in a bun, you always get an itch right underneath it, just where you can't reach it. This is really annoying all day long, but it leads to a big simple pleasure, which is lettin' your hair down at the end of the day and just rubbin' your fingers around your head."

Bubble Gum of South St. Paul: "My simple pleasure is putting my hand into a box of raw macaroni and picking up macaroni and dropping it and picking it up and dropping it—to get a hand massage."

The Hat Box Girl of St. Paul: "Some time ago, I was riding home on a city bus and was just exhausted.

"These three or four guys at the back of the bus started singing—a cappella, you know. They were *so* good. They sang until they had to get off the bus, and when they stopped, everyone applauded.

"The bus driver—this older lady—told 'em she so was so impressed to hear young people sing like that . . . and without even swearing once. Just made my day—and, I'm sure, many others'. So if you guys are out there: Thank you for blessing us with your music."

Steady Tempo of St. Croix Falls, Wis.: "I had such an unusual experience today when I was driving home. I was listening to 99.5, my favorite radio station, and the wipers and the music matched—not just for one measure or two measures or three, but for the entire 16th-century-type song, from beginning to end.

"Now, that's *never* happened before to *anybody* in the whole wide world."

The Hazel-eyed Girl of St. Paul: "A simple pleasure: being home alone in the morning after everyone else has gone to school. I put on my radio station, just walk around in a sports bra and boxers, and sing really loud."

The Luckiest Lady in St. Paul: "This past spring, my husband collapsed while playing a gig, and he was diagnosed with cancer. There was a time there when I didn't think I'd ever hear him play again, or that he would be alive for another wedding anniversary, or any of all those other things.

"He's downstairs right now, playing the same damn notes over and over and over and over and over again—and it's music to my ears."

Mr. Chestnut of St. Paul: "You know, ice-cream cones are such a simple pleasure. I just love 'em. But too often, I'll get one and Mrs. C. will decline to—but later insist on having a lick of mine.

"I actually *lick* mine, and maintain a fairly rounded dome, and try to keep off the drips from the cone. But somehow I always forget that she doesn't do anything resembling a lick; instead, she does this kind of thing where she blobs her whole mouth down on top of the cone, and partly bites, partly sucks, partly pulls it off with her lips—and it becomes this mutilated, sloppy mess where each lip has sorta scooped out a little depression, and they come together at kind of a ridged peak.

"I mean, it's a horrible, mooshy thing! It looks like a little bare-[bottomed] elf sat down on it and made a little ice-cream wedgie or something. I just can't take it anymore. Bring on winter!"

BULLETIN BOARD REPLIES: Let's not get carried away here.

Sergeant Bilko of St. Paul: "We keep some of our linens in a cedar chest, and my simple pleasure is still smelling the pungent cedar *days* after putting clean sheets on the bed. Mmmmmm!"

Molly of Mac-Grove: "My simple pleasure is beating the heck out of my feather pillow until it is almost an orb, so fluffy and soft. Then I place it carefully at the head of my bed, sit down, and *FLOP!* back into it. Ahhhh!"

Georgia of the West Side, in a breathy monotone that sounded a bit like Jackie O. attempting to hypnotize someone: "One of life's very simplest pleasures, to me, is to be bone-tired, undress and slip into bed, snuggle your head into a cool, soft, cushiony pillow, close your eyes and let your mind review the events of the day, dismissing them one by one. Eventually you'll feel a peaceful sensation, like drifting and floating, drifting and floating, drifting and floa . . ."

Shoney of White Bear Lake: "I just have to tell someone of the delicious three bites I just ate—the most delicious three bites I've ever eaten in my whole life.

"I just made raspberry jam. I poured all of the raspberry syrup in the jars, and the syrup that's left in the pot. . . . I scraped it all off into a little puddle in the bottom of the pan, and I put chocolate chips—about 10 chocolate chips—in the puddle, which was still a little bit warm, and they melted, and then I *ate* it, and it was so good. I've never had anything more delicious."

Drowning in Domesticity of Birchwood: "For the first time in my life, I have a garbage disposal. I realize that these aren't new inventions, but I've never lived in a house or apartment that had one before, so my simple pleasure is grinding up lemon and grapefruit rinds in my garbage disposal. I just love that little cloud of citrus freshness that rises up out of the sink. In fact, I've actually found myself buying fresh lemons on a semi-regular basis expressly for this purpose.

"Guess I'd better start serving more fish."

Niccole of St. Paul: "My simple pleasure is going out on my dock and sticking my toes in the water—and just letting the fish nibble at them. Feels so good."

Dave of Backus, back home after a vacation even farther north: "I took my 4-year-old son, Bobby, out fishin', and he caught his very first fish. The look on his face and the excitement he felt is something I'll always remember. Forever.

"The last night we were there, we decided to go out fishin' one more time, before sundown. We hadn't been out there 20 minutes when he caught two sunfish right in a row. As I was puttin' the second sunfish on the stringer, the little guy looked at me and he said: 'You know, best buddy, do you think we could go back to the cabin? All this fishin's really tiring me out.'

"I turned and said: 'Sure, Bobby. We can go back to the cabin.'

"He says: 'Thanks, Dad.'

"Those moments, I think he'll remember for a long, long time—and I know I'll remember them forever. It's . . . it's just somethin' great. I wish everybody could experience that: fishin' with a kid, and watchin' the excitement when they catch their first fish."

W.W.J. of Minneapolis: "Recently, my wife and I had a chance to house-sit my brother's North Long Lake home, which produced a litany of simple pleasures:

"We saw a blue heron land on the dock and strut around. A gold bullfinch in the bird feeder. And then one evening, on a mosquitoless night, we sat on the dock, talking and sipping a little wine, and watched the dragonflies play on the water—and a fish jump up and grab one of 'em. Listened to the loons say good night. And then as the sun went down, we went in and sat in the front porch, looking out the picture window at the moonlit lake and listening to the quiet. You forget how dark and how quiet it gets out there in the country. To top it off, I saw fireflies. I don't remember when I'd last seen fireflies.

"There's something about a moonlit lake that brings out your atavistic feelings. Well, as the commercial says: It doesn't get any better than this."

Sam I Am of Apple Valley: "It was bad planning on my part:

"I had to get up early on Sunday morning to iron a shirt to wear to church. Standing at the ironing board, I glanced out the window and saw an exceptionally greedy squirrel carrying a whole ear of dry corn in its mouth.

"The prize was so heavy that the squirrel had to hold it in the middle to stay on kilter. It could take no more than four steps before it had to set the corn down and get a better grip, and it had to stop three times just to cross the street.

"I watched as the squirrel made its way home and disappeared into a grove of trees by the pond. Since my wife was already off at work and the rest of the family was still asleep, it seemed like a simple pleasure that God had arranged just for me.

"What a great way to start a day."

Young Maria of River Falls, Wis.: "My simple pleasure is that little grunting sound that puppies make when they're really close to your ear. It's the sweetest sound that I've ever heard in my entire life—and I get to hear it a lot, 'cause I work at the Humane Society.

"Somebody should make a little tape recording of it and . . . ummm . . . what's the word I'm looking for? . . . *sell* it! *That's* the word I'm looking for! Somebody should *sell* it, because it's the sweetest sound I've ever heard, in the entire world."

Stephanie of Andover: "Simple pleasure: walking out to my barn in the morning and hearing my horse nicker a greeting to me."

Skittles of White Bear Lake: "My simple pleasure is having my Siamese cat—Felix the cat, the wonderful, wonderful cat—sit on top of my chest and sleep at nighttime, knowing that she doesn't have too many purrs left in her. Every morning when I wake up, she's still there with me—but there's not gonna be too many more mornings."

Margaret of St. Paul: "I have a simple pleasure that I just discovered. I take a math class, so I'm sitting on my couch with my math book and paper and stuff, gettin' all frustrated and mad—'cause I hate math—and then my cat comes up and plops down smack-dab right in the middle of my math book so I can't do anything . . . and I can't help but pet him and kiss him all over. He just makes me feel so much better.

"But, back to work."

Grandma Cricket of Mahtomedi: "I had a special simple pleasure today: my granddaughter Shannon, who's 6 years old, reading to me the Dr. Seuss books that, not too long ago, I was reading to her. It sure was fun."

Free Spirit of Eagan: "I had a simple pleasure when I was a little kid: I used to always sit in front of the TV and watch Gumby and Pokey, which was my favorite program, and eat Apple Jacks.

"I recently got cable, and on Nickelodeon from 7:30 'til 8 o'clock is Gumby and Pokey—so again, this morning, I experienced a simple pleasure by sitting and watching Gumby and Pokey and eating my Apple Jacks. But even better than before is: Now I'm sharing it with my own little girl.

"It's a great way to start out the morning."

Quad P. of Eagan: "We haven't had a TV in our home for the past 15 years. The simple pleasures of not having a TV include seeing my children reading and playing together in the evenings, instead of sittin' in front of the tube. Sometimes when I take a bicycle ride at night through the neighborhood, it seems like every house has that blue haze coming through the windows, with people sittin' around watching the TV, and I know that in my house, no one's sittin' around the TV.

"Another simple pleasure of not having a TV is living through another election year and not being subjected to political commercials.

"And finally, maybe a simple pleasure of not having a TV around all the time is when you get to sneak over to a friend's house and watch a good movie or a football or a hockey game."

Linda of Columbia Heights: "Listen! *[BULLETIN BOARD NOTES: We listened— and heard nothing.]* That's my simple pleasure: I got all three of my preschoolers to nap at the same time. It's a little piece of heaven."

Monkey of St. Anthony: "When I'm sitting at the table eating breakfast or lunch or whatever, I'm reading a lot—and if it's funny, I start laughin', and my son starts laughin'. My 3-year-old son just *belts out* laughter, just like I do, and he has no idea why he's laughing—and that is a simple pleasure for me."

John of Anoka: "My little girl was born last Wednesday. She came out early, and she had a lot of problems. I got to hold her today, and she's eating, and it's what you would call a simple pleasure: To hold your little baby in your arms and listen to her cry. I never thought I'd ever love to hear a baby cry."

Peggy of St. Paul: "I have a simple pleasure: taking your 2½-year-old to see the ocean for the first time, and listening to him squeal and laugh and go 'Whoooaaaaa!' every time the water comes up and hits his little feet."

Daddy the Omnipotent of West St. Paul: "At night when I give Hannah a bath, she is washed up in about three minutes and plays for about 20. Since she can't be left in the tub alone, it is my brief chance to sit, drink a cup of coffee and relax while being excused from the diapers, Nuks, feedings, and swing cranking that our 11-week-old twins demand.

"Now if I could just figure out how to get the toilet to recline."

Cindy E. of Lent Township: "A simple pleasure of mine: Today I finished filling out my tax forms, and I took what was left of my tax tables and lined my birdcage with it."

Bill of Woodbury: "Just had one of life's little pleasures: It's being in the line at the grocery store, with the person in front of you having a full cart and you standing there with one or two items, and that person looking at you and saying: 'Go on ahead of me.'"

Jolly Rancher of St. Paul: "Simple pleasure: when some bad driver pulls out in front of the bad driver who just pulled out in front of you."

Kimm of Stillwater: "I've noticed this simple pleasure in the past week: those big, random, cheery sunflowers growing out of the medians and cracks along the highway. It makes me smile to see those bright pieces of summer popping out in the most unlikely places."

Myrtle the Turtle of St. Paul: "I got laid off yesterday. This was the third time in as many years. So I did what I've done the other times: I went to the office-supply store for a new, clean calendar—'cause that cheers me up every time. There's something really comforting about all of those uncluttered days, with nothing on there and no reminders of the old job."

Snufkin of St. Paul: "I'm pregnant . . . or I *was* pregnant. I just found out I'm losing the baby. And I was driving around, trying to figure out what I wanted to do to cheer myself up—and the same old thing: I went to Target and bought a whole bunch of underwear. There's something really comforting about buying new underwear. Who knows why, but that always seems to make me feel a little better."

"And for those of you who have children: Please don't ever give up on 'em."

Sir Charles of Chisago City: "I'm a divorced father, and nothing's more special than when my littlest one is spending the night and I wake up in the middle of the night with the arms and legs all over my face."

The Exiled King of the Cheeseheads: "A simple pleasure: eating my breakfast in my kitchen at 6:30 A.M., listening to the baby monitor as my daughter, the Dairy Princess Rosemary, wakes up. First the deep breathing gives way to babbling, then mattress-spring creaking, then a shriek of unmitigated joy as she discovers that her Tigger and her panda are, in fact, *still in the crib with her!*

"By far, the best radio station in the Twin Cities."

R.J. of Hammond, Wis.: "I hate hot weather, but one of the simple pleasures that it brings is watching my son swim in our little back-yard pool. He spends most of his time in a wheelchair, and mobility outside the wheelchair is extremely cumbersome—and increasingly uncomfortable for him, due to back problems.

"But water is The Great Equalizer, and it sets his body free. Watching him twist and spin and float and shoot across the pool with the utmost grace and an ease of movement—pain-free movement that he never has anywhere else—is a *huge* simple pleasure."

2J of South Minneapolis: "I'm sitting on the couch, reading the paper, watching the football game. The lights go out. Nearly all of South Minneapolis is in the dark, and it's spooky.

"So, after scrambling for a flashlight and lighting some candles, I sat there, not knowing what to do. I couldn't work on the computer, couldn't watch TV, couldn't play any music. So I ended up reading Bulletin Board by the light of the flashlight. (It's kind of tough, if you don't want to read the paper one-handed; you've gotta kinda wedge the flashlight between your head and shoulder or hold it between your chin and chest and then kind of wiggle it around so that the bright spot of the light lands where you're reading.)

"Anyway, the power was eventually restored. (It wasn't the terrorist act my hyper imagination thought it could be, and things were back to normal.)

"But for a while there, the dog was at my feet, I had a fresh soda, the world was pitch black, the house was quiet (the family was at the library). And you know what? It was awful.

"I like electricity. I like watching football. I like looking at the clock to see what time it is. I like turning on the lamp so I can read the paper. I don't like it all dark outside.

"So if you thought this was going to be one of those simple-pleasure stories about how nice and quiet it was and how refreshing it was not to have the TV and radio on, forget about it. If I wanted that, I'd go live in a cabin.

"P.S. Thanks to the guys and gals who worked to restore the power. Is this a great country, or what?"

A tag-team call, at 4 in the morning, from **Missy, The Gooch & Widget** of Eagan, St. Paul and West St. Paul—with Missy speaking, and The Gooch and Widget shouting nominations from the background:

"We've just got, like, a ton of simple pleasures. We thought, like:

"Jazz. And ice-cream cones. And harmony. And moonlight on the water. And mowing the grass in the summer. And smelling gas. The sound of dried leaves crunching under your feet. Canada. Sleep. Rainy days. Sunrises over the ocean. The smell of lilacs; that's the *best.* The dust particles dancing and swirling in the sunlight streaming through your window. Slippers. The sound of wind through the trees. Books. Big, mooshy leather chairs. The smell made when someone smokes a tobacco pipe. Grandmas. Laughing. Dairy Queen. Waterfalls. Watching meteor showers. Walks at dusk. Watching squirrels. Getting letters.

"The sound of a cork popping off a bottle of champagne. Duluth. Skipping rocks. Northern Lights. Bonfires. The sound of Scooby and Shaggy running on *Scooby Doo.* Dancing in the rain. Cabins. *Sesame Street.* Sleeping in the sun. Twilight. Eating snow.

"Cleaning your ears with Q-Tips. Big knit sweaters. The smell of grass clippings. Janis Joplin. Reading shampoo bottles in the shower. Rollin' down hills. Lightning storms. Singing. *Winnie the Pooh.* [In the background, Widget yells—with heartfelt enthusiasm: "Graduating!"] Graduating! Grandpas. Willow trees.

"Listening to the soundtrack from *Les Miz.* Grilling on pontoons. Skinny-dippin'. Cryin'. Family reunions. Walking barefoot in the sand. Camping. The smell of fall. Falling asleep listening to 'The Wall' by Pink Floyd. The rumble of an inboard engine. And the tonic at the end of a song; you know, it's, like, the ending chord of a song; it brings it all together; that's pretty sweet. Dreaming.'

"That's, like, a lot of our simple pleasures—so if you could get some of those in, we'd be really happy."

CHAPTER TWENTY-ONE

Parting Thoughts

Dennis of New Brighton: "One night recently, somebody was asked to leave a bar where I was. I guess they were upset, so they came out and kicked the side of my brand-new vehicle and put a large dent in it. I was really upset; I went to bed thinking: 'What a lousy thing to do.'

"The next morning, I got up, right after a storm, and went outside and looked at the dent, just cussing and swearing. And I was looking in the grass, and I saw a robin's egg lying on the grass. It hadn't cracked. The storm apparently had blown it out of the nest. So I picked it up—and all of a sudden, I could feel there was life inside there. Something was moving in that egg. Looked around, found a nest, put it in the nest; there was another egg in there.

"I thought: 'All the troubles I've got, somebody else has got worse troubles than I do.' I felt pretty good; forgot about the dent. It'll get fixed—and that's life.

"Sometimes, even a simple robin's egg can teach you a lesson."

Hannah's Dad: "A few years ago, I was out on my driveway, enjoying the fresh air, after having changed a nasty, all-over-the-bed diaper of my 5-year-old daughter, who was terminally ill and pretty much homebound, when a guy who typically would pass as a concerned neighbor approached me and commenced his pissing and moaning about having to take his 6-year-old son to a Twins game instead of going out with his drinking buddies.

"I would have given my right arm to be able to take my daughter out anywhere and enjoy the world with her, but at that moment I had to settle for standing on my driveway and listening to someone complain about being forced to have a good time with his kids.

"I just stared back at him, afraid that if I started ripping into him, I wouldn't be able to stop.

"He walked away with a miffed look on his face, probably wondering why he didn't get a supportive response.

"Just to really make your kids wonder what's up, go home and hug them again tonight.

"God, how I miss my Hannah."

Janet of Burnsville: "I was lugging my two *kinder* around, and we were on our way home for supper after a good round of errands, and karate, and all that other junk, and I was sitting at a light, and I just happened to notice in my rear-view mirror that there was a young dad in the car behind me. He must have had just a very,

very little baby in the baby bucket in the front seat, because I could see the handle of the baby bucket, but not the baby.

"Dad was talking to the baby really animatedly, and I could see him say, just as clear as day: 'I missed you so much today.' And that just made me feel kinda . . . neat. Kinda warm.

"I'm with my kids all day, and I wouldn't have it any other way, but moms and dads who can't do that—they love their little people just as much."

Peggy of St. Paul: "I always wanted to get married and have babies. So I got married, and we waited a couple years, and traveled, and then we decided it was time to start our family.

"We tried and tried and tried, and nothin' happened. And I started to get really angry and really depressed. I'd get mad at all of my pregnant friends and my pregnant family members, and I cursed God for picking me to be infertile.

"Finally, one day, I just went to my husband and said: 'Honey, I just can't do this anymore.' And he said: 'Good. Let's adopt.' And I thought: All right. I didn't think he was ready for that, but he was just waiting for *me* to be ready for that.

"So we did; we adopted a little Korean boy, and we've had him for a couple years now, and now I look back and I feel so bad for getting so depressed and angry and cursing God. And I think now: If I'd only known that God didn't pick me to be infertile; he picked us, special, to be adoptive parents—and it's a wonderful group to be in."

Plugger of Chippewa Falls, Wis.: "The neatest thing happened last night, and I just have to tell someone about it.

"I had a night class at the university, my husband was on a business trip, and the kids had to stay home alone. Yesterday afternoon, I started getting kind of worried about them killing each other while I was gone. I thought about renting a movie (the '90s version of TV baby-sitting), but I knew there wouldn't be enough time for them to watch it, do homework and get to bed at a decent time.

"I was feeling really guilty about leaving them home. To make me feel better, I bought them each a new book.

"I got home about 9 last night and found my daughter curled up in the recliner in the den with her book; her stuffed bunny, Velvet; and her real cat, Rodent. Her brother was upstairs in bed, reading. It was incredible: no grumping or tattling from either of them!

"We parents complain about our children not reading as much as we feel they should, but how many times do we rent a stack of movies or video games compared to how many times we bring home a book we've picked out especially for them?"

The Teacher of Lauderdale: "I have a son who's turning 11 on Wednesday, and I've just been sitting here marveling about the fact that I'm the father of an 11-year-old—which is even more amazing because I'm also the father of a 13-year-old. And their entering these teen years has me reminiscing and so forth.

"I remember back when I was all of 25, and just starting out with the family—and a good friend of mine who was the ripened old age of 37 told me to enjoy 'em at that age, because once you hit the teenage years, you just kinda . . . hang on. I never really understood that. I guess I liken it to this analogy: It's kinda like when you teach your children how to walk across the street.

"When they're infants and toddlers, we're pushin' 'em. We have the stroller; we come to the street; we look both ways—but we're in control. We tell 'em what we're doin', but we're in control.

"And as they get older: We get to the street; we're holdin' their hands—but we're still in control.

"And then there comes that day, when they're 8 or 9 years old, and they're standing next to you, and you're not holding their hands anymore, and you're hopin' and prayin' that they're gonna look both ways, and you walk across the street.

"And then there's that day when you're not there, and they're gonna cross that street by themselves, and you really hope that you did it right.

"And I guess that's what the teenage years are like: They're at that street corner, and they've gotta look both ways, and there are gonna be times when they're gonna look both ways and they're gonna make it safely across the street, and there are times when they're not gonna look both ways, and they're gonna step out in the street, and a car's gonna come whizzin' by, and there's gonna be a close call.

"I guess we, as parents, just have to hope and pray that we taught 'em to use the crosswalks in life and know when to go and when to stop."

Debaloo of St. Paul: 'My wonderful grandfather, who was a Polish Jew, died almost two years ago, at the age of 92. He had cancer—and though he didn't want to leave any of us, he was looking forward to the relief from his prolonged misery that death would bring.

"About six weeks before he died, his brother-in-law, who was in his 80s, died suddenly from a stroke—unexpected, out of the blue. One minute, he was taking a shower; the next minute, gone.

"My grandfather, feeling the unfairness of the matter, shook his head and said, very profoundly: 'Whoever invented life should be shot—or given a banquet.' He sure had a great way of stating the basics.

"We love you, Joe, and miss you as big as the sky."

Judy of Woodbury: "A couple months ago, I went out with my son to visit my ex-husband's father, who's in a nursing home. He's been there about four years—a prisoner, really, of his body. He's paralyzed, and he can't speak; he has some movement in one hand, but that's about it. His mind is good; you know, he knows what's going on. But I'm sure his days are just very long and painful.

"We went out to see him, and he was sitting in a wheelchair out in the hall, and I was kind of bending over him and hugging him and holding him—just talking gently to him. And all of a sudden, I became aware of this head on my back, and there were arms over my arms. It was this older woman, and, you know, she saw me giving affection—and she wanted some, too. She was so insistent that I come with her. Finally, a nurse came and got her and took her away. She wanted me to come, though.

"And then I looked up, and there was another lady sitting in a wheelchair just a little ways down, and she waved at me, and then she pointed for me to come and sit down and see her, too.

"It reminded me of having gone out to the dog pound and seeing all of the animals just wanting some . . . *attention* from somebody. You know, babies don't thrive when they don't get care, and I think old people are the same way. I think there's a lot of forgotten people who need some affection from other people—and if it's not a relative, then at least somebody who could volunteer some time to come and just talk.

"So what I'd like to do is just urge people to take whatever time they can and visit a nursing home—maybe see a relative, or just some stranger that they could be friends with."

Erin of Uptown: "Two weeks ago, I drove 6½ hours to Missouri, to visit my grandparents, and spent the weekend with them—just hanging out and eating ham sandwiches that my grandmother made and talking to my 81-year-old grandfather while I got my tire fixed.

"I got a nail in it that he noticed, and we hung out at the auto store for two hours and talked—and I don't think I'd ever talked to him as an adult about such intimate and personal things.

"On Sunday morning, before I left, my grandpa hadn't gotten out of bed to go to church with me, and my grandma said to go in and talk to him. So I did, and I lay down on the bed with him; I'd never seen him in bed before, and we just lay on the bed, and I stroked his hair and we talked about really intimate and personal things, and feelings that I'd never heard this man talk about before, to anyone.

"He sat up, and I scratched his back and rubbed his shoulders—and told him I loved him, and said goodbye.

"And the next day, he died.

"I just wanted to say: I love you, Grandpa. And: Don't wait to go visit people and tell 'em that you love 'em."

Lucky Mama of St. Paul: "When our two wonderful police officers got killed in the line of duty last year, my daughter was only 2—but, nonetheless, I took her to the Cathedral for one of the funerals. And it must have had a profound effect on her, because still, every time she sees the Cathedral, she says: 'Look, Mama. That's where the policemen got killed.'

"Well, that's not altogether true—but that's how she sees it in her own little mind, remembering the funeral.

"Just yesterday, we were driving by the Cathedral, and she goes: 'Look, Mama. That's where the policemen got killed.' And she goes: 'Mama, why did the policemen die?'

"I told her that a man who was very bad shot them both.

"She says: 'Why did he do that?'

"And I said: 'Well, because he wanted to do bad things.'

" 'Well, why does he want to do bad things?'

"And I says: 'Well, he just *decided* to do bad things—just like you decide to do good things.' I said: 'Why do you decide to be good?'

"And she looked at me so earnestly and said: 'I just want to be like you, Mama.'

"Oh, that's a big responsibility.

"So watch, parents. Your kids are watching you."

LaVonne of Coon Rapids: "My war story took place in the winter of 1990. I was in a miserable marriage to an out-of-work alcoholic who kept me isolated and practically imprisoned in our apartment. I finally got up the gumption to stand up to him one morning. I walked into the bedroom and woke him up—a big no-no with him. He was angry.

"I told him he had two weeks to get a job or get out, and I walked toward the door, shaking.

"'Who made you the boss?' he yelled.

"'Me,' I said, still scared to death, but I kept walking. He threw the clock and broke a light fixture a few inches from my head. I kept going. He bounded out of bed, grabbed me by the throat and shoved me up against the wall, choking me. I could hear our terrified 2-year-old son shrieking in the other room. I couldn't breathe. The room was starting to go dark.

"I thought: *This could be it. I could die right now. Am I ready to die?*

"The answer came clearly and calmly, without fear: Yes. I was ready to die, if that's what it took to get away from this man. And I understood for the first time that if I didn't leave, I surely would die.

"I didn't die that morning, but it took another two months before I could arrange to leave safely. My son and I have gone through some hard times since then, but at least we never had to worry for our mental and physical safety. Now we live peacefully and quietly in our new home. My son is happy and confident, full of fun, with lots of friends, and so am I. What a difference!

"I want others in the same situation to understand that if you are living with an abuser, you and your children are in danger whether you stay or go. But if you go, at least you have a chance—and a future that could be wonderful.

"Ask for help (as I did), plan carefully, and go. Don't warn your abuser. Don't believe the promises to change. Just go, carefully.

"And God be with you."

Doc, M.D.: "In my waiting room last month, one woman observed a man inappropriately strike and swear at one of his children. This woman reported it to my staff, who related the incident to me. The man's wife was my patient. I asked her about it, and I learned that there has been a pattern of abuse in their home that I would otherwise never have known about.

"I just wanted to thank whoever that was who reported the incident. Because of her courage—her willingness to be what some would consider a busybody—a family will now be getting some much-needed therapy.

"The African saying about needing a whole village to raise a child is repeated often enough lately to be almost a cliché—but it remains true."

Much Loved of St. Paul: "I'm calling about a dream come true:

"When I was a little girl, watching the Disney show on a Sunday night, I once asked my parents if we could ever go to Disneyland. My father laughed into his beer and told me that no one would *ever* waste their money taking me to a place like that—and *he* certainly would never waste his money on me like that.

"This is one of the least unpleasant—yet still awful—memories of my dad.

"Well, three years ago, my sweet husband packed me and our two girls up for a trip to Disney World. I'll never forget my tears of happiness as I sat in a wheelchair and watched Tinkerbell fly out of the castle, and as I watched the fireworks at night.

"I want to say to kids out there: Don't give up on your hopes, if you've got rotten parents. You can grow up, get away from them, and find people who will truly love you and believe in you."

Good Old Anonymous Bob of St. Paul: "Sometimes, we all need a little wake-up call to remind us of which track we should be riding on.

"Mine happened today, when I was rushing to meet someone for lunch . . . and was late (which is not unusual) . . . and I had a bad case of the Monday Go-Wrongs very much on my mind . . . and I went storming into the restaurant at a hundred miles an hour, trying to make up for lost time . . . and in the process of going through the door, I almost (but, fortunately, didn't) trip over a young child—perhaps no more than 3 years old; about a 30-incher—who was walking with a white cane.

"Probably the smallest white cane I've ever seen.

"It so stopped me in my tracks and riveted my attention for that moment—and set me back, if you will, a notch. Reminded me that my rushing was not the most important thing in the orbit of the Earth today—and that any problem I had had previously was certainly nothing compared to a life without sight.

"Sometimes, one finds important reminders in small and unique places."

R.J. of Hammond, Wis.: "Last night—Saturday night—I witnessed one of the most spectacular light shows that the Almighty has ever staged . . . which is just one of the benefits of living far out in the country and having an unbroken expanse of northern prairie sky in one's back yard.

"I've seen brighter Northern Lights, and more colorful ones a couple of times, but *never, ever* as full of motion and energy as they were last night.

"The northernmost, oh, 40 degrees of the horizon was all lit up with that steady light, bright enough to cast a shadow, and the southernmost 40 degrees was dark, but the entire sky in between was where the action was. It was full of constantly flickering, rolling, pulsating, oscillating, stabbing white light.

"I can't even describe it. If you've ever seen flames and shadows flicker and dance—that's the closest thing I can compare it to, but it had a frenetic energy and a speed that even fire doesn't have. It was as if some celestial pyromaniac was in a frenzy and had taken over the sky.

"I watched 'til almost 1 A.M., until my neck got stiff from looking up.

"When you watch something as awesome as that, like big waves rolling in on the shore, endlessly, it puts humanity in entirely a different perspective. It makes one realize how petty our problems are, how truly tiny a speck we are in the universe, and how pathetically small our power really is. No one on Earth could command or orchestrate or even supply the energy for such a magnificent event.

"Just seemed like a comforting affirmation that we really aren't in charge, after all. Kinda made my hair stand on end, though."

The Queen's Mum of Vermillion: "This goes beyond a simple pleasure, into exquisite delight:

"Last Friday, just as the sun was setting, a huge V-formation of tundra swans flew over the house and headed west into the setting sun.

"Last fall, I watched 10 adults and their cygnets on our pond. A large flock flew over, heading east. Two birds wheeled back and settled onto the pond. A short discussion in swan talk ensued, and within minutes, they all just *erupted* out of the water—in hot pursuit of the rest of the flock.

"*Goodspeed,* I thought. *I'll see you in the spring.*

"This has been an emotionally draining time for us, this past winter, and as the sun settled Friday, I knew: It'll rise again tomorrow.

"The seasons pass, and so will adversity. In the meantime, we'll be given strength to endure.

"With the return of the swans, I felt my heart rise in delight."

Laura of Stillwater, at Thanksgiving: "I've been a single parent nearly eight years now, and for some folks like me, the whole *feast* idea of Thanksgiving is a hard thing to swallow, because frankly, we can't afford to have one. We are the ones out here who worry just how we're gonna feed our children 'til the end of the month, let alone a grand feast.

"What I've found to be helpful is to take time aside and find little ways to appreciate what I *do* have.

"One of the most helpful stories I ever heard was about the making of *Mary Poppins.* Walt Disney called in the musicians, the composer, and said he wanted a song to express how people could deal with difficult financial situations and find some sense of cheer when they didn't have any money. The composer told the story of how he sat down at the piano and the words just flew out across the keyboard: 'Feed the birds! Tuppence a bag!'

"Any one of us can take a little piece of bread and find a creature of nature, of God, and share a little crust of bread. I take time out to go down by the river here; the St. Croix River's beautiful here in Stillwater. I like to sit on the rocks and just take a little bit of bread out of my bag that I've bought to take home to feed my son and myself—and just feed the birds.

"It has a sweet irony to it—to think that maybe we can't eat a bird on Thanksgiving, but maybe I can feed one.

"And I get to watch it fly away."